S0-FSP-001

Civilian-Military Relations in Brazil
1889–1898

Civilian-Military Relations in Brazil 1889–1898

By June E. Hahner

University of South Carolina Press
Columbia, South Carolina

Published in Columbia, S.C., by The University of South Carolina Press, 1969
First Edition
Standard Book Number: 87249–146–3
Library of Congress Catalog Card Number: 74–625583
Manufactured in the United States of America
Designed by Damienne Grant

To my mother

Preface

ARMED FORCES HAVE PLAYED a major role in many nations around the globe and have been involved in innumerable changes of government, particularly in the developing countries. Although studies have been made of their behavior while in power or of the means by which they achieved this ascendancy, attention has not been paid to the process by which civilian elements can, at times, peacefully ease the armed forces from direct political control.

In various emerging nations, military officers have brushed aside weak civilian opposition and stepped into positions of preeminence. Civilians have generally been able to displace them only through alliances with disgruntled factions of the armed forces. However, the seemingly inevitable consequence of these ostensive alliances has been the retention of actual power in the hands of the new group of officers, who pay scant attention to civilian interests once victory is achieved. Although military rule may bring certain benefits to the country in question, the civilians are never permitted an opportunity to show their potential.

Brazil is one country where this pattern has not been characteristic. An important external conflict in the 1860's had led to the creation of a large army and a politically minded officer corps. Stimulated by certain civilian political groups attempting to gain military support for their programs, the Brazilian armed forces took control in 1889. Five years later, following a series of military incidents and uprisings, they relinquished the government to civilians, who, free from overt military interference, ruled the country until 1930.

The Brazilian experience has been slighted in the rising number of books in recent years treating various aspects of the political activities of the armed forces in Latin America and elsewhere. Previously, these studies concentrated on European phenomena, and works were produced like Alfred Vagts's *A History of Militarism: Romance and Realities of a Profession,*[1] which still serves as a good introduction to the general problem of the armed forces in politics. But increased interest in other regions of the world and the realization that the armed forces have played a major political role in many non-European countries have led to a number of inclusive, more theoretical studies, such as Samuel E. Finer's *The Man on Horseback: The Role of the Military in Politics.*[2] These in

1. Alfred Vagts, *A History of Militarism: Romance and Realities of a Profession,* Rev. ed. (New York: W. W. Norton & Co., 1937), 1957.

2. Samuel E. Finer, *The Man on Horseback: The Role of the Military in Politics* (New York: Frederick A. Praeger, 1962). See also Samuel P. Huntington, *The Soldier and the State: The Theory and Politics of Civil-Military Relations* (Cambridge, Mass.: The Belknap Press of Harvard University Press, 1964); Morris Janowitz, *The Military in the Political Development of New Nations: An Essay in Comparative Analysis* (Chicago and London: University of Chicago Press, 1964); and Stanislaw Andrzejewski, *Military Organization and Society* (London: Routledge & Kegan Paul, Ltd., 1954).

turn have aroused additional interest and have provided some concepts which might be applied to the armed forces of Latin America, such as the significance of the social origins of the officers.

Since about 1960, historians and social scientists have begun to devote much more attention to the role and activities of the armed forces in Latin America. Previously, these armed forces were generally treated only as peripheral sources of interest or in an unsystematic way. The first major study of military involvement in this region is Edwin Lieuwen's *Arms and Politics in Latin America*,[3] which has had a significant impact on thinking concerning these problems. Lieuwen concentrates on the post-1930 period and follows traditional liberal views as to the irresponsible nature of military activities in Latin America. In the other major inclusive study of the Latin American armed forces, *The Military and Society in Latin America*,[4] John J. Johnson emphasizes their positive activities; he also pays far more attention to Brazil and to some of the ways in which military developments there have differed from those in Spanish America. The ever growing number of works in this general field is thoroughly and ably treated by Lyle N. McAlister in his essay "Recent Research and Writings on the Role of the Military in Latin America."[5]

The tendency has been to concentrate on twentieth-century events. In the case of Brazil, among other countries, this is true in many fields, not just in the realm of military affairs. The significance of the events of the 1889–98 period in Brazilian history has not been realized. A detailed study of one country during such a crucial period may throw much new

3. Edwin Lieuwen, *Arms and Politics in Latin America* (New York: Frederick A. Praeger, 1961).

4. John J. Johnson, *The Military and Society in Latin America* (Stanford: Stanford University Press, 1964).

5. Lyle N. McAlister, "Recent Research and Writings on the Role of the Military in Latin America," *Latin American Research Review*, I (Fall, 1966), 5–36.

light on the relationships between the armed forces and other segments of society.

Despite the frequent use of the term "the military" by many writers in discussing political activities of the officers, there is no such monolithic group. The lack of unity which often exists within "the military" of a particular country is well illustrated by the Brazilian case, especially in the period from 1889 to 1898. Within each branch of the armed forces a number of prestigious leaders commanded rival groupings of fellow officers, and these hostile factions struggled for dominance. For example, one clique tried to restore their leader to power after he had been replaced by another man supported by a temporary coalition of other factions. Politically active senior officers were often disdainful of many of the younger positivist officers produced by the military schools and were offended by their political pretensions. Moreover, the navy felt neglected and abused by the army-dominated government, and the sharp rivalries and conflicts between the two services finally led to a major naval revolt. These divisions and hostilities within the armed forces gave one group of civilians, the *Paulistas,* their opportunity eventually to establish civilian rule.

Another term often used too loosely, especially in older works, is "militarism." This term has commonly been employed to mean the direct intervention of the armed forces in politics or any form of organized violence employed for political ends. However, a more traditional and exacting definition would be that it is "an attitude toward public affairs which conceives war and the preparation for war as the chief instruments of foreign policy and the highest form of public service."[6] Military service would be regarded as ennobling both the person serving the armed forces and the community

6. "Militarism," *Encyclopedia of the Social Sciences,* X, 446.

as a whole, and loyalties to a certain individual or cause would be stressed. Such militarism would be rigidly disciplinarian and hierarchic in its methods and would not encompass the revolts and internal dissensions often found in Latin American armed forces. Moreover, the glorification of war is basically alien to Latin America, a region where few international conflicts have been fought. While manly prowess may be exalted, and violence at times condoned, this is a far cry from the organized, large-scale, centrally motivated process of manslaughter called war. Instead, Latin American armies have tended to direct their attention and energies toward their countries' internal affairs. Like the Brazilian army, they may include officers convinced of the armed forces' special value, patriotism, and responsibility to "save the nation" whenever they believe it needs saving, but this, strictly speaking, is not militarism. In this discussion of the Brazilian experience the term "militarism" will not be used.

Political activities within the Brazilian armed forces were confined to the officer corps and did not extend into the ranks. The common soldiers were separated by an immense social, educational, economic, and even racial gap from the commissioned officers. They were often forcibly recruited from the depths of society, and very few soldiers ever rose out of the harshly treated, poorly paid rank and file into the officer corps. Instead, the troops furnished a rough, malleable mass available for use by the officers in their political maneuvers. The political opinions of the officers and their relations with civilians, not the activities of the troops, were the decisive factors, first under the empire and then during the early years of the republic.

Throughout this book, names will be given in modern Portuguese orthography in the body of the work, but in the footnotes and bibliography authors' names and titles of their works will be cited in the original orthography.

The research on which this book is based was begun in 1963. A grant from the Organization of American States enabled me to spend three months in Brazil conducting preliminary investigations. Late in 1964 I returned to Brazil for a year on a Foreign Area Fellowship Program grant. I wish to tender my gratitude to these organizations for their assistance. My views are, of course, my own.

Of all the Brazilians who aided my investigations, it is to Sr. Odálio Amorim that I would like to express my deepest gratitude, not only for allowing me to consult the Prudente de Morais Papers, which were then in his possession, an overwhelming and unprecedented favor in itself, but also for his kindness and help in suggesting other materials and making many of these available to me. I am most appreciative to Sr. Roberto Piragibe da Fonseca for permitting me to consult the Clodoaldo da Fonseca Papers. I also gratefully acknowledge the assistance given by the staff of the Arquivo Nacional, especially Dr. José Moniz de Aragão, director, D. Maria Luiza Fernandez de Carvalho of the Seção de Documentação Histórica, and José Gabriel Costa Pinto; D. Isabel Morais of the Instituto Histórico e Geográfico Brasileiro; Dr. Américo Jacobina Lacombe, director of the Casa de Rui Barbosa; the late Colonel Walter Santos Meyer, former director of the Biblioteca do Exército; Dr. Herculano Gomes Martheas, director of the Museu Histórico Nacional; Dr. Francisco Marques dos Santos, director of the Museu Imperial in Petrópolis; D. Vera Galluzzi of the archive; Dr. Marcelo Ipanema Morelo, former director of the Arquivo do Estado de Guanabara, Dr. Tragano Quintões, the current director, and Dr. José Luiz Werneck da Silva; D. Constança Wright of the Arquivo Histórico do

Ministério das Relações Exteriores; and Admirals Levi Araujo de Paiva Meira and Levy Scavarda of the Serviço de Documentação Geral da Marinha. I express my appreciation also to Dr. Prudente de Morais Neto, D. Zilda Galhardo de Araujo, D. Eulalia Lahmeyer de Lobo, Dr. José Honório Rodrigues, Dr. Sérgio Buarque de Hollanda, Dr. Daví Carneiro, D. Nícia Villela Luz, Dr. Hélio Vianna, Sr. Olympio de Souza Andrade, Admiral Alfredo de Morais Filho, D. Licidia d'Alincourt Fonseca, and D. Maria de Lourdes Claro de Oliveira.

In this country I want most to thank Professor Richard Graham of the University of Utah for his tireless suggestions and assistance, and I would also like to express my gratitude to Professor Tom E. Davis of Cornell University.

JUNE E. HAHNER

ALBANY, NEW YORK
FEBRUARY, 1969

Contents

Introduction

UNLIKE MOST OF Latin America, Brazil had been without military problems for most of its history until the latter part of the nineteenth century. The Spanish-American countries had often been forced to engage in years of bloody fighting to secure their independence, creating large armies which were not easily dispersed once independence had been achieved. Brazil, on the other hand, had gained independence gradually and peacefully, and this is the most obvious cause of its freedom from military interference in government until the 1860's.

During most of the nineteenth century Brazil lived under a monarchy. In 1808 the Portuguese court arrived in Rio de Janeiro, fleeing Napoleon's armies. Because of the presence of the royal household in Brazil old colonial restrictions were swept away, and a variety of economic and cultural changes followed. Brazil was no longer an exploited colony but a participant in European culture, and her ports were thrown open to the commerce of all friendly nations.

When at the end of the Napoleonic Wars conditions in Europe forced the return of the Portuguese monarch, João VI, the Brazilians feared the loss of all they had gained by the presence of the crown in the New World. And indeed, once the King arrived in Portugal, the Portuguese Parliament tried to reduce Brazil to its former status as an exploited dependency. Many of the native Brazilians were already antagonized by the privileged position occupied by the Portuguese in their local affairs, and they viewed these actions by the Côrtes in Lisbon with increasing alarm. Nationalistic sentiments, which had long existed in Brazil, were fanned into a smoldering fire. Finally the Côrtes ordered Crown Prince Pedro, who had been left as regent in Brazil, to return to Portugal. Elements favoring separation from Portugal supported the Crown Prince in his efforts to maintain Brazilian autonomy. With his refusal to obey the dictates of the Portuguese Côrtes in 1822, the flame of independence at last was able to blaze freely in Brazil, without bloodshed or army participation.

Pedro I ruled as emperor for nine agitated years, until 1831. This ambitious, impetuous Portuguese prince gradually lost the initial popularity which had accompanied his declaration of independence from Portugal. Although he endeavored to rule as a liberal monarch, he was temperamentally an autocrat. Because he appeared to place dynastic considerations above Brazilian ones, and surrounded himself with numerous unpopular and reactionary Portuguese ministers and courtiers, he became further estranged from Brazilians. Tensions between the two elements grew and came to a climax during April of 1831. On April 6 a large crowd demonstrated before the palace in favor of the restoration of a Brazilian ministry, which Pedro I had dismissed for one consisting of unpopular aristocrats. The emperor refused to accede to the wishes of this crowd, and revolution followed. The garrison in the capital joined the movement, and Pedro I was forced to abdicate in favor of his five-year-old son, also named Pedro.

The minority of Pedro II was a time of instability, local mutinies, and reactionary, Republican, and Federalist uprisings. The country was ruled by a series of elected regents during a period of political shocks which threatened the unity of the nation. This experiment with virtual republicanism culminated in a movement to restore the prestige of the central authority by calling on the young emperor to rule, assisted by an advisory council. Although this project was not strictly legal, since the constitution required that the heir remain a minor until the age of eighteen, the people, weary of uncertainty and disorder, were behind it. At the age of fifteen, Pedro II took the oath of office in July of 1840.

By 1850 he was ruling Brazil on his own. The country had entered a period of tranquillity and economic development, and the minor mutinies and military indiscipline of earlier times had disappeared. Commerce expanded, stock companies rapidly increased in number, and coffee became the principal source of national wealth. Until the Paraguayan War (1865–70), the army continued to play a virtually negligible role in the affairs of the nation.

The war with Paraguay greatly increased the political strength of the Brazilian army. Not only did the army grow in size, but its officers acquired a new sense of military spirit and pride. The officers did not, however, unbuckle their swords or relinquish their sense of military honor before entering political chambers. When the imperial government attempted to reduce the army's size following the Paraguayan War, they complained bitterly of abuses and eventually rose against the government. By the late 1880's the once firm foundations of the monarchy had been gradually weakened—it had lost the support of vital groups like the landowners, who had been alienated by the abolition of slavery without compensation, and Republican sentiment had grown in Brazil. The structure was tottering, and only a strong, decisive blow was needed to make it crumble, a blow which the army provided.

The Brazilian armed forces have tended to view themselves as the guardians of the republic they helped establish in 1889. However, while many officers considered themselves ultimately responsible for the decisions of the ruling civilians, whom they frequently thought unequal to the task of directing the nation, they have usually not claimed any right to govern by themselves. Instead of employing direct violence or political take-overs, they have generally preferred using influence and indirect pressure. Some officers have even worked for a nonpolitical army. Only during the initial five years of the First Republic (1889–1930) was the government subject to frequent revolts and open military dominance. But certain civilians then gained control of the governmental structure and in the process helped assure the absence of such direct military interference for decades to come.

The Brazilian experience would suggest that the achievement of civilian government does not depend entirely on the attitudes of the armed forces themselves and on their willingness to desist from political activities. Unless civilian groups generally refrain from attempting to use the armed forces for political gain, it is much more difficult to establish and preserve civilian rule. At times Brazilian civilians favored military participation in the government. When other methods failed, they tried to use the officers to overthrow a regime they opposed. Thus, during the monarchy some Republicans endeavored to gain military support to overthrow the empire;

after the initial shock of the officers' role in establishing a republic had worn off, some monarchists attempted to use them to subvert this republic. In both cases the Brazilian officers were thereby strengthened.

But not all civilians countenanced military participation in politics or attempted to use revolt to achieve their goals. While many civilians objected to the dominant position occupied by the armed forces during this period, only one cohesive, economically powerful group, the landowners from the state of São Paulo, succeeded in forcing the officers out of the government and in gaining predominance for themselves. Unlike the monarchists, who either violently condemned the armed forces for overthrowing the empire in 1889 or attempted to stimulate military plots against the new regime, the *Paulistas* neither antagonized major segments of the armed forces nor supported the main military uprisings which wracked the young republic.

The *Paulistas* needed political stability to ensure the continued economic progress of their home state. The center of the dominant coffee economy, São Paulo was quickly becoming the richest and most powerful area of Brazil. Even before the destruction of the monarchy many *Paulistas* had striven for the creation of a federal republic which would assure them the necessary local autonomy and revenues to further this development. But incessant insurrections against a military government would interfere with steady growth, damage Brazilian credit abroad, and frighten away immigrants needed to work the coffee plantations.

When the navy revolted in September, 1893, the army faction in power was forced to seek civilian aid, especially from the *Paulistas*. Their state was situated between Rio de Janeiro, where the rebellious fleet threatened the seat of the government, and the far southern states, where another major revolution was raging. Under the republic the *Paulistas* had created their own armed force in the form of a state militia, and they were therefore powerful enough to hold the balance between the opposing military factions. They supported the army-dominated central government and in return secured the election of one of their number as the first civilian president of Brazil.

During his term of office civilian rule was consolidated through judicious compromise where necessary, firmness at the right times, and skillful manipulation of divisions within the armed forces. When some officers miscalculated national sentiments and fostered an attempt at assassination, he was able to move swiftly against his most outspoken enemies and then legally and peacefully pass the government to the next president, a fellow *Paulista*. Although subsequent civilian regimes, unlike Brazilian governments during the early part of the nineteenth century, would have to contend with ever present and powerful armies, they would, nevertheless, rule without direct military interference until 1930.

While many civilian groups opposed the officers' control over the government, which they had seized in 1889, only the *Paulistas* were able to displace them. The lack of unity within the armed forces provided the men from São Paulo with the necessary opportunity. Through a policy of judicious cooperation with the faction that held power, these civilians helped ease military elements from power and achieve some semblance of civilian control for themselves and for most of Brazil's later history. The events of that period are not irrelevant to the current situation in Brazil.

CHAPTER I

Rising Military Self-Consciousness under the Empire

DURING THE LAST YEARS of the empire the Brazilian armed forces gained a position of power and influence in the political life of the nation. Often believing themselves maltreated by civilian politicians, and desirous of speaking out on various issues, they clashed with the government in a series of incidents during the 1880's. Some dissident politicians attempted to gain their favor and supported their position in the press. Finally, encouraged by certain Republican adversaries of the monarchy, army officers delivered the decisive blow to this venerable institution and were prepared to step vigorously into the breach left by its sudden demise.

In the century preceding the overthrow of the empire, the army had been steadily increasing in strength. Not until Brazil gained independence early in the nineteenth century did the nation possess an army of any importance. During the colonial period Portugal had been unable to maintain numerous garrisons in its widely scattered dependencies and had relied largely upon a local militia in Brazil. Since independence was achieved without long years of warfare or ensuing chaos, the Brazilians did not have occasion to need a large army.[1]

Under Pedro I, the first ruler of independent Brazil, the small army was at times as unruly as the emperor himself. His heedlessness in matters of military practice contributed to army indiscipline. Hostilities often arose between Portuguese elements and the native Brazilians, the rank and file were frequently disorderly, and the Rio garrison took part in the overthrow of Pedro I.

During the minority of Pedro II, a period of domestic discord and instability, the army contributed to the nation's disorder. Besides participating in numerous barracks mutinies, it often played a part in the reactionary, Republican, or Federalist uprisings which took place.

By the time Pedro II took the oath of office in 1840 and later began ruling on his own, about 1850, these revolts had disappeared. With them vanished the minor mutinies and military indiscipline of earlier times. The country was more prosperous and stable, and, despite occasional international incidents, a large army was not necessary.

The Paraguayan War (1865–70) marked a change in the position of the army within Brazilian society. The war had

1. General aspects of the armed forces during the empire are discussed by: F. J. Oliveira Vianna, *O occaso do império* (São Paulo: Companhia Melhoramentos de São Paulo, [1925]); Christiano Benedicto Ottoni, O advento da *república no Brasil* (Rio de Janeiro: Typ. Perseverança, 1890); Felisbello Firmo de Oliveira Freire, *História constitucional da República dos Estados Unidos do Brasil* Vol. I and III (Rio de Janeiro: Typ. Aldina, 1894–95) Vol. II (Rio de Janeiro: Typ. Moreira Maximino, Chargas & C., 1894); Clarence H. Haring, *Empire in Brazil: A New World Experiment with Monarchy* (Cambridge, Mass.: Harvard University Press, 1958); João Pandiá Calogeras, *A History of Brazil* trans. Percy Alvin Martin (Chapel Hill: University of North Carolina Press, 1939).

grown out of the alliances of Argentine parties with warring factions in Uruguay, the long-standing interests and entanglements of many Brazilians with their neighbors, and the ambitions of the cruel Paraguayan dictator, Francisco Solano López. During the five years of fighting the Brazilian armed forces were constantly enlarged, until the nation possessed a powerful army which the virtually bloodless struggle for independence had not created.

After the war many Brazilian officers were not content to return to the old pattern of a smaller, less conspicuous army. The army felt victimized by the civilian politicians both during and after the war, and became more willing to question orders. According to one sympathetic contemporary observer, the returning victors were "no longer the absolutely passive army" of prewar days. After enduring "all kinds of hardships," they encountered "the ingratitude" of the government. The officers were ready to "debate the acts of overbearing administrations," as they had learned to do in the Plata region.[2]

The time lapse between the end of the war and the commencement in 1879 of a series of incidents between the imperial government and the more politically minded officers is too great to lend complete credence to the contention of some officers and others that the Paraguayan War hispanized the Brazilian army. But the war did create a large army whose officers, idle after the war, had more time to take part in politics. They resented the continual reduction of army size following the conclusion of this conflict, as well as their relatively low salaries and the meager appropriations granted the army. The end of rapid promotions and of the payment of salaries in gold also led to dissatisfaction. As an unyielding monarchist later admitted, this was "a forgotten, badly organized, poorly

2. Demétrio Seixas, *O golpe d'estado de 15 de novembro. (Ao exército e à armada)* (Pôrto Alegre: Typ. da Livraria Americana, 1890), p. 171.

instructed, and poorly paid" army, justly discontented with itself and with everyone else.[3]

One politically minded officer later summarized this view of the army's treatment by the government and the offended dignity of the officers. "After its return from the Paraguayan War," he recalled, "the Brazilian army began to perceive the low regard which the government had for the military institution." Because of the "ill will, inequity, routine procedures, and neglect of the government, owing to the technical ignorance of the ministers and their slight acquaintance with army personnel," the army was being inexorably reduced to a state of decay, "despite the officers' ceaseless protests." Like many other officers, he felt that the civilian politicians did not appreciate their worth and that the war ministers, generally civilians, were not truly aware of the needs of the army.[4] The government had not understood the "important mission" carried out by the army during the war "with a valor and self-denial admired by the entire civilized world."[5]

Even the Duque de Caxias, Luís Alves de Lima e Silva, one of the nation's venerable military leaders, had encountered difficulties with civilian politicians. He was indispensable for the Paraguayan War effort, and his incompatibility with the Prime Minister had led to the downfall of a ministry during the critical days of the war.

Various political groups tried to gain the favor and support

3. Eduardo Paulo da Silva Prado (pseud. Frederico de S.), *Fastos da dictadura militar no Brasil* 3rd ed. ([Lisbon]: n.p., 1890), pp. 5–6.

4. Of the sixty-three war ministers during the reign of Pedro II, twenty-seven were military and thirty-six civilian. However, most all of the officer-ministers held their positions during the early years of his reign. Of the thirty-eight ministers between 1865 and 1889, twenty-nine were civilians and only nine military (See Theodorico Lopes and Gentil Torres, *Ministros da Guerra do Brasil, (1808–1950)*, 4th ed. (Rio de Janeiro: Borsoi, 1950), pp. 12–15.

5. Jacques Ourique, "A revolução de 15 de novembro," *Jornal do Comércio*, January 4, 1890, p. 2.

of the officers. For years the Conservative Party cultivated the popularity of Caxias, while the Liberals seized on other popular officers. At times the party out of power would try to use the army and its grievances as an instrument to combat their opponents' policies and force them out of office. The Republican Party, a small minority, wished to capitalize on military sentiments to advance the progress of its ideas within the nation. At first some Republicans simply supported military complaints against the government, but later a few hoped to use the army to overthrow the empire.

The abolition of Negro slavery, the first important national issue arising after the Paraguayan War, greatly affected the armed forces. Not only was the Military School a focus of abolitionist propaganda, but abolitionist sentiments, fanned by the abolitionists themselves, spread among the officer corps. The abolitionists were pleased by the warm reception given an abolitionist leader from the north at a military school on the outskirts of the capital in 1884; but this reception led to a disciplinary incident, for the school's commander questioned the right of his superiors even to inquire into the matter, and he was therefore removed from command. Later the abolitionists applauded the stand taken by the Club Militar, the political spokesman of the army officers, on October 25, 1887, protesting the government's order to apprehend fugitive Negro slaves. In the name of the club, Marshal Manoel Deodoro da Fonseca,[6] one of the most popular and respected army officers, delivered a petition to the Regent, Princess Isabel, asking that the army not "be in charge of capturing poor Negroes

6. Brazilian names are rarely given *in extenso*, but the selection of a shortened version differs from English or Spanish usage. Each individual generally has a shortened form of his name by which he prefers to be called, and there is no set rule for determining this form. For example, Manoel Deodoro da Fonseca is generally called Deodoro da Fonseca, or simply Deodoro. The Brazilian practice will be used in this book.

fleeing slavery."[7] One contemporary noted that when the soldiers were told to " 'tie up those Negroes, who do not wish to work,' " they answered, " 'not this, for this is not a job for soldiers, but for slave-catchers.' "[8] The abolition question had expanded the political consciousness of the officers, and civilian abolitionists, seeking their support, had helped bring them closer to the political arena.

A series of minor disciplinary incidents during the 1880's, the so-called "military question," became a major focus of political discontent. The officers' desire to speak out, to place their grievances before the public, and to gain a stronger position in the political life of the nation was greatly stimulated by these events, thus generating additional conflicts. In order to weaken the monarchical government, certain Republicans supported the officers during these squabbles, thereby increasing the importance of the disputes and helping to turn the army against the imperial government. Through these incidents military self-awareness was increased and the political power of the officers became more evident. The government was by turns pusillanimous or precipitate in its responses, thus exacerbating the problem.

The concern of the officers for the free right to criticize and discuss governmental matters and to organize themselves politically became evident in 1879. Early that year the naval and war commissions of Parliament proposed a bill reducing the number of troops and eliminating certain positions in both army and navy, in the name of economy. Many officers met to condemn these measures as a death blow to the armed forces and nominated a commission to oppose the measures and take the issue to the press. Not only did an 1859 regulation forbid

7. Antonio Ilha Moreira, *Proclamação e fundação da república* (Rio de Janeiro: Imprensa Nacional, 1947), p. 38.

8. Christiano Benedicto Ottoni, *Autobiographia de C. B. Ottoni* (Rio de Janeiro: Typ. Leuzinger, 1908), p. 346.

officers to deal with service matters in the press, or to criticize their superiors, but another such regulation had been published in September of 1878. Nevertheless, the press debate was allowed to continue, and the proposed bill was eventually abandoned.[9]

During this press controversy a small group of officers in Rio Grande do Sul, the southernmost region of Brazil and a center of troop concentration and agitation, even founded a newspaper which attacked the proposed troop reduction as a first step toward the annihilation of the army. They proclaimed that they, "the officers, lovers of order and entrusted with sustaining the empire," would not hesitate "to be the greatest revolutionaries," if these "false representatives of the people" permitted a drastic "reduction in the size of the armed forces."[10]

This same group of officers also attempted to found a political party to represent their interests. Not only were they disdainful of civilian politicians as "deaf to the complaints of the nation and blind to its needs," but they felt threatened by the "decrease in size of the already small army." Since this army had been "persecuted, ridiculed, and maltreated," and had no national voice defending it against the other social groups, they would form a military political party through the army garrisons of all the provinces "to defend the real interests of the country."[11]

In 1883 the issue of proper relations between the officers and the government again appeared in the open, when a sena-

9. José Maria dos Santos, *Bernardino de Campos e o Partido Republicano Paulista. Subsidios para a história da república* (Rio de Janeiro: José Olympio, 1960), pp. 28–29; Tobias Monteiro, *Pesquisas e depoimentos para a história* (Rio de Janeiro: Francisco Alves & Cia., 1913), pp. 127–28; Seixas, *O golpe d'estado de 15 de novembro*, p. 184.

10. *O Rebate*, June 1, 1879, in Demétrio Seixas, *O golpe d'estado de 15 de novembro*, pp. 166–67.

11. Seixas, *O golpe d'estado de 15 de novembro*, pp. 171–73.

tor proposed creating for officers an insurance fund with obligatory contributions. The officers opposing this measure selected one of their number to present their viewpoint in the press.

In 1886 two major incidents occurred. Once again, it was the right to take grievances to the public and to defend military honor that was at stake. Following his discovery of some seeming irregularities in army administration in his regiment, Colonel Ernesto Augusto da Cunha Matos became involved in a controversy with a civilian deputy of the Chamber. Talking to the press, the officer continued the exchange of insults and also criticized the war minister. The minister disciplined the colonel and had him placed under arrest for forty-eight hours. In response to this action, justified under military regulations, the army officers united in defense of their comrade.

Later the same year another personal clash was generalized into a major conflict. Lieutenant Colonel Antônio de Sena Madureira had submitted articles on military affairs to a newspaper in Rio Grande do Sul. In one of these articles he attacked a senator's speech which accused him of indiscipline. Receiving a reprimand from the war minister, Sena Madureira protested "in the name of the pride and dignity of the military" and condemned the minister's "unique theories" that an officer could not defend his reputation against a senator. "Familiar with the legislation governing the army," he felt he had the right to demand that the minister show him which "article of the disciplinary regulations" prohibited "the officers from defending themselves when their dignity was impugned," for he could never accept such a situation.[12] He was strongly supported by his colleagues in Rio Grande, including the popular and impulsive Deodoro da Fonseca. Feelings con-

12. *A Federação*, September 25, 1886, in Demétrio Seixas, *O golpe d'estado de 15 de novembro*, pp. 179–80.

tinued to run high throughout the army, and a meeting of the officers was called for February, 1887, in Rio de Janeiro, the capital, to discuss the complaints of the army. On February 2, some two hundred army and navy officers voted, without discussion, for Deodoro's motion that they "not consider the conflict between the military officers and the government concluded with honor" until the government fully retreated and removed the "unconstitutional" censures from the officer's record.[13]

In two bitter, protesting letters to the emperor, Deodoro reflected the officers' offended dignity and impatience. For him, "only someone who was not a soldier" and who could "not understand the slightest notion of military pride and dignity" could permit such "an insult to the military!"[14] In this "very serious matter," only someone unaware of the "consequences" could blindly face the coming "storm," if this "injustice" were not rectified.[15]

The ministry, apprehensive and uncertain, had submitted the question of the constitutionality of the regulations to a military council, which naturally supported the officers' position. It held that officers, like all other citizens, possessed the right of freedom of discussion in the press. However, not all the officers were willing to stop at this point. The Viscount of Pelotas, Marshal José Antônio Correia da Câmara, a popular hero of the Paraguayan War, continued to speak of "the displeasure which the army felt with the bungled handling of the affairs of the war ministry."[16] He and Deodoro published

13. *Gazeta de Notícias*, February 3, 1887, p. 1.

14. Manoel Deodoro da Fonseca to Pedro II, Rio de Janeiro, February 3, 1887, in Raymundo Magalhães Júnior, *Deodoro: A espada contra o império* (São Paulo: Companhia Editôra Nacional, 1957), I, 207.

15. Deodoro to Pedro II, [Rio de Janeiro, February 12, 1887], Arquivo do Museu Imperial, Maço 26 D. 956.

16. Viscount of Pelotas to Deodoro, Pôrto Alegre, February 27, 1887, Clodoaldo da Fonseca Papers.

a manifesto demanding the "spontaneous" canceling of the censures. They complained about the "scorn" and "ridicule" showered upon the officers, the "administration's arbitrariness in its repressive acts" of reprimanding Sena Madureira and Cunha Matos, and the offenses to the "dignity of armed citizens"; they refused to accept the subservient and demeaning role of "Janizaries" or mercenaries. Like other officers, Deodoro and Pelotas held as a basic principle that "the right to defend themselves in the press, sanctioned by the penal laws, is a right common to all citizens and that it is not lawful to deprive army officers of this right, without violating the imperial constitution."[17]

Tensions increased, until the government gave way under pressure a few days later. In the oppressive atmosphere of the Senate chamber, the Viscount of Pelotas reminded the government that Pedro I had been overthrown by a revolution and that the government should reconsider its actions, for no one knew what might happen tomorrow. All the garrisons but one had secretly declared full support for Deodoro. After Pelotas' speech, many of the opposition Liberals joined with the Conservatives to seek a peaceful solution for the crisis threatening the very institutions of government, and the Senate voted to "advise" the government to yield.[18]

Following the army's victory in this Sena Madureira inci-

17. Pelotas' and Deodoro's Manifesto "Ao Parlamento e à Nação," in *País*, May 14, 1887, p. 1.

18. Monteiro, *Pesquisas e depoimentos*, pp. 144–61. See also Heitor Lyra, *História da queda do império* (São Paulo: Imprensa Nacional, 1964), I, 92–133; José Maria dos Santos, *Bernardino de Campos*, pp. 34–36; Evaristo de Moraes, *Da monarchia para a república (1870–1889)* (Rio de Janeiro: Ed. Athena, [1937]), pp. 26–85; Freire, *História constitucional*, I, 202–205; Oliveira Vianna, *O occaso do império*, pp. 146–59; Ottoni, *O advento da república*, pp. 84–88; Haring, *Empire in Brazil*, pp. 132–35; Percy Alvin Martin, "Causes of the Collapse of the Brazilian Empire," *Hispanic American Historical Review*, IV (February, 1921), 28–32; Charles Willis Simmons, "The Rise of the Brazilian Military Class, 1870–1890," *Mid-America*, XXXIX (October, 1957), 230–34.

dent in 1887, a group of officers founded the Club Militar to give the army a sounding board and a spokesman for its grievances. In June, 1887, the first meeting of the Club Militar was held, and Deodoro was acclaimed president. One member even suggested the organization of a military slate of candidates for the senatorial campaign in the state of Rio de Janeiro. The officers most closely connected with the founding of this organization were among the most politically active of the last years of the empire and the first years of the republic.[19] Moreover, according to a contemporary civilian, the Club Militar's members were the "most influential officers in the army."[20] As one officer later remarked, the club itself was "created to defend their rights and improve their position."[21] In the coming years it would continue to serve as a focus for the expression of military attitudes and as a center for many officers' political activities.

In 1888 a new incident arose involving the navy, the more aristocratic and hitherto less politically involved of the services. A lieutenant captain, in civilian dress, was arrested for creating a disturbance in the streets of Rio de Janeiro. According to an eyewitness, the officers called the police action "an outrage upon the dignity and rights of the navy," and the officers "held meetings, appointed committees and demanded the dismissal of the chief of police and the punishment of the chief offending persons. . . . conflicts followed between the police and squads of marines on the streets."[22] Confronted by this display of military strength, which was backed by a

19. Magalhães Júnior, *Deodoro*, I, 218–19; Gerardo Majella Bijos, *O Clube Militar e seus presidentes* (Rio de Janeiro: n.p., 1960), p. 8; Lyra, *História da queda do império*, I, 140–53.

20. Ottoni, *Autobiographia de C. B. Ottoni*, p. 345.

21. Ilha Moreira, *Proclamação e fundação da republica*, p. 36.

22. Jarvis to Bayard, March 12, 1888, United States Government Diplomatic Archives, National Archives, Brazil, Despatches, RG 59, Vol. 48.

good proportion of the opposition press, the government once more gave way and dismissed the police official involved. Shortly afterwards, the ministry itself resigned.

Later that same year, the seventh army battalion clashed with the São Paulo police. Arguing that the chief of police had not observed the proper formalities on entering the battalion's quarters, the Club Militar in Rio de Janeiro met and protested. Although the government removed the battalion from São Paulo, it gave in to military pressure and dismissed the police chief.[23]

Throughout this series of incidents comprising the "military question," the officers made clear their belief in their right to express themselves publicly and to participate actively in politics. Reacting violently to hesitant government attempts to curb their political activity, they continued to present their views in public debate and in the press on any matter of interest to them. They felt that the government was insufficiently concerned with their welfare and believed that it was attempting to weaken the army and turn it into a group of passive sustainers of the regime, virtual mercenaries or "Janizaries." At any time they could construe civilian acts as affronts to their honor and, like the Viscount of Pelotas, hold that an officer had the right to defend his honor, law or no law, "above all else."[24] When an officer accused the government of offending his honor, his comrades tended to come to his defense in the name of military solidarity. These desires for virtually unlimited public expression and political participation were not, however, systematically expressed by the often inarticu-

23. *Província de São Paulo,* November 24, 1888, p. 1; November 25, 1888, p. 1; *Rio News,* December 5, 1888, p. 2; December 15, 1888, p. 2; Freire, *História constitucional,* I, 210–11; Magalhães Júnior, *Deodoro,* I, 336; Evaristo de Moraes, *Da monarchia para a república,* p. 87; Ottoni, *O advento da republica,* pp. 88–89.

24. Monteiro, *Pesquisas e depoimentos,* p. 129.

late officers, and they were not shared by many of them, especially those in the navy.

Despite these clashes between officers and the government, the officers as a group were still largely loyal to the emperor. Their indiscipline, extreme sensitivity, and rebelliousness, even when supported by the Republicans, did not indicate a revolutionary aim. They were interested in securing and increasing their privileges, not in setting up a republic or in advocating specific political programs or ideas. Only among the cadets of the Military School, under the influence of Benjamin Constant Botelho de Magalhães, a popular positivist and Republican professor of mathematics, was Republican sentiment strong. Older, more prestigious officers like Deodoro da Fonseca, who was in his sixties, did not have Republican convictions. It was clear that if the general dissatisfaction among the officers were to be of wide significance, senior officers like Deodoro must be persuaded to move against the monarchy. To this task the Republicans now turned.

Republican sentiment in Brazil dates back at least as far as the late eighteenth century to the conspiracy in Minas Gerais known as the *Inconfidência*. However, this republicanism remained largely quiescent until the ministerial crisis of 1868 and the formation in 1870 of a Republican Club, which in that year issued the manifesto regarded as the official beginning of the Republican Party. While many of the changes this party demanded strongly resembled those advocated by the Liberal Party, the one distinctive aim of the Republicans was to abolish the monarchy.

A small minority, the Republicans had no hope of overthrowing the monarchy by themselves, but with armed support from the officers they might succeed in establishing a republic. Shortly after the foundation of the Republican Party, its members engaged in a public discussion of the army's role within the nation. Some correspondents of *A República* felt that one day free nations could dispense with armies, the instruments of tyranny.[25] Others favored an armed citizenry over a permanent army, which was a "burdensome consumer and an instrument of menace." All this would change when these "slavish citizens" were replaced by a "class of citizen-soldiers" under a better form of government.[26] The directors of *A República* concluded, however, that there was no basic incompatibility between a regular army and a republic; they accepted the "undeniable necessity of having a moralizing armed force which would be the faithful interpreter of the people and guarantee its sovereignty."[27] They then called for an improvement in the state of the army, and they acknowledged that officers could express political opinions. This was the start of the Republican effort to support an army which might not be so devoted to the monarchy.

Yet several Republicans from São Paulo, which had the strongest and best organized Republican Party in Brazil, took a dim view of military political pretensions. *Paulistas* like Bernardino de Campos and Américo Brasiliense did not encourage army support. In his speech of February 6, 1888, in the São Paulo legislature, Bernardino de Campos, president of the *Paulista* Republican Party, defined the party's position regarding the "military question." Instead of supporting military demands against the government, he accused the monarchist regime of "cowardice when confronted by the army's demonstrations and the Visconde de Pelotas' and Marshal Deodoro's manifesto."[28] He gave no support to army griev-

25. *A República*, January 19, 1871, p. 3.
26. *A República*, March 18, 1871, pp. 1–2.
27. *A República*, May 6, 1871, p. 1.
28. Speech of Bernardino de Campos, February 6, 1888, São Paulo (state), *Annaes da Assemblea. I Sessão de 1888* (São Paulo: Typ. Correio Paulista, 1888), p. 167.

ances and appeared to be ruling out the possibility of proclaiming the republic through a military uprising.

Some Republicans in Rio de Janeiro, however, continued to woo the officers. During the early days of the "military question" of the 1880's, a Republican newspaper in Rio de Janeiro voiced two recurrent military fears often stimulated by opposition journalists—government ingratitude and the threat of army annihilation. Attacking the "absolute and despotic government" of the empire with all available means, these Republicans viewed the army as a potential ally. They alleged that the government, unable to "benefit by the valiant and courageous army which returned from the Paraguayan War," was "afraid of" the troops, and, to protect the monarchy, "scattered them throughout the vast area of the empire, gradually diminished them, and would finally destroy them."[29]

In Rio Grande do Sul, the scene of the Sena Madureira incident and a center of Republican sentiment, the young Republican leader Júlio Prates de Castilhos vehemently supported the officers in his newspaper. This dour and energetic positivist attacked the government for "attempting to humiliate them and humble the pride of the army, under the pretext of military discipline."[30] By playing on the officers' honor and dignity, he attempted to generalize the "military question" so as to turn their animosity toward a particular ministry into opposition to the empire as a whole. He declared that the Madureira question was not "an unimportant incident" but a "question of military honor, of the dignity of the army, and directly affected the most important moral interests of the nation."[31]

29. *O Republicano,* May 29, 1884, p. 2.

30. *A Federação,* September 27, 1886, in Othello Rosa, *Júlio de Castilhos. I parte. Perfil biográphico. II parte. Escriptos políticos* (Pôrto Alegre: Livraria do Globo, 1928), p. 155.

31. *A Federação,* September 30, 1886, in *ibid.*, p. 164.

One Republican, Aristides Lôbo, saw an opportunity to gain political advantage from the assassination of a journalist by several officers in 1884. During the trial Aristides suggested to Joaquim Saldanha Marinho, leader of the Republican Party, that the Republicans come to the officers' defense, for this could "be a major element of disturbance" and they should "seize control of it."[32]

At times Saldanha Marinho also defended and encouraged the officers' insubordination. In his articles in a Republican journal, he provided them with a theoretical justification for their actions and gave them a general principle of disobedience on which they could base further incidents. Citing various historical precedents and laws, Saldanha Marinho argued that the officers possessed the necessary "judgment for recognizing the legality of orders before executing them." Each of these "Brazilian citizens" had an "incontestable right" when so convinced to tell the war minister he was "outside the law" and exercising "an absolute judgment" he did not possess, and, therefore, to refuse to obey those orders.[33]

Such a doctrine opened the way to armed revolt. The belief that "there is disobedience only when the order is legal" has been used to justify various revolutions all over Latin America and would be used in Brazil during the Naval Revolt of 1893–94. Nevertheless, Saldanha Marinho argued that "failure to obey an illegal order is not a revolutionary act, and instead, a procedure authorized by regular law; and far from subverting law and public safety, it is the most effective means for maintaining them."[34]

While Saldanha Marinho claimed that this defense of the officers by Republicans was based simply on the "sincerity of

32. Aristides Lôbo to Saldanha Marinho, Rio de Janeiro, April 30, 1884, Arquivo do Estado de Guanabara, 41-1-59, Saldanha Marinho Collection, XII, 100.

33. *Revista Federal,* I, No. 6 (October 31, 1886), p. 3.

34. *Ibid.,* p. 2.

their beliefs," and that the military was "not cooperating with any of the parties," he was clearly attempting to win their political sympathies.[35] When some members of the Club Militar proposed Marshal Deodoro da Fonseca for the Senate, Saldanha Marinho asked the Republicans of the province of Rio de Janeiro to support Deodoro's candidacy.[36] And in 1887, during one of the crucial episodes of the "military question," Saldanha Marinho criticized the government for not having "revoked the anarchizing censures" against Lieutenant Colonel Sena Madureira.[37]

Starting about 1887, several *Paulistas,* like the popular Francisco Glicério, began to see the army as a potential ally to be cultivated. Francisco Rangel Pestana, one of the owners of a leading newspaper, the *Província de São Paulo,* once suggested that the Permanent Commission of the *Paulista* Republican Party come to an understanding with army leaders to bring about a revolution, but the commission refused to consider this idea at that time.[38]

In November of 1888, during the incident of the "military question" involving the São Paulo garrison, two local Republican journals, the *Província de São Paulo* and the *Diário Popular,* came to the support of the officers. The *Província de São Paulo* insinuated a still larger role for the officers: "the military have already overthrown the Cotegipe ministry. They can overthrow—who knows what? because, frankly, in our rundown, corrupt country, they are the only ones who know how to behave with true and praiseworthy solidarity."[39]

35. *Revista Federal,* I, No. 8 (October 31, 1886), p. 4; (December 31, 1886), p. 2.

36. João Tomaz da Porciúncula to Saldanha Marinho, Petropólis, July 20, 1887, Arquivo do Estado, 41–1–59, Saldanha Marinho Collection, XII, 84.

37. *Revista Federal,* I, No. 9 (February 5, 1887), p. 2.

38. Edith Sabóia, "Francisco Rangel Pestana. (Notas biográficas por ocasião do centenário do seu nacimento, 1839–1939)," *Revista do Arquivo Municipal* (São Paulo) LXI (September–October, 1939), p. 38.

39. *Província de São Paulo,* November, 24, 1888, p. 1.

A few days later the *Diário Popular* declared that this "new edition of the military question" was also "provoked by the excesses and abuses of the civil authority."[40] The publisher of this journal, Manuel Ferraz de Campos Sales, speaking in the provincial legislature, accused the government of confusing "military discipline with servile submission," and this statement no doubt pleased many officers. Campos Sales also implied that all the government's measures, and its capitulation before the firm attitude of the officers, resulted from the fact that it was "a government constantly terrorized by the fantasma of a republic."[41]

A Republican newspaper in Rio Grande do Sul, the *Denúncia* of Porto Alegre, attempted to gain army support to overthrow the empire. Hailing the officers as "the true, genuine, only ones responsible for the destiny of this country before History," these Republicans declared that the army should no longer relegate "this responsibility to individuals unworthy of such a great honor," but should rather take "upon their shoulders the difficult task." They urged the army to cease being "an obedient machine in order to become a thinking body, with its own will, initiative and aspirations," and to establish a republic "now." The officers were told: "in this part of the world monarchy is a noxious plant, uproot it!" The Republicans of Pôrto Alegre declared that they were counting on the army in the approaching struggle, and with its "mighty effort" added to theirs, that they would create "the great Brazilian republic."[42]

Some Republicans, although aware of the possible consequences of supporting military assertions and demands, were

40. *Diário Popular*, November 27, 1888, p. 1.

41. Speech of Campos Sales, January 15, 1889, São Paulo (state), *Annaes da Assemblea. Segundo anno da 27ª legislatura. Sessões ordinarios e estraordinarias de 1889* (São Paulo: Typ. d'O Federalista, 1889), pp. 6–8.

42. *Denúncia* (Porto Alegre), September 7, 1888, pp. 3–4.

not fearful for the future. Early in 1889 a Republican in Minas Gerais strenuously denied that the Republicans wished to "implant a military dictatorship in the country." However, he maintained that the army was "the only stronghold where patriotism . . . still holds sway, resisting the corruption of the monarchical government." Apparently believing that the republic would be established by some sort of revolutionary uprising, he wanted the Republican Party to consider the necessity of having a military leader as the first president of the republic. To those who feared the officers, this Republican attempted to demonstrate "the impossibility of a military dictatorship in a federal republican regime," even if the army wished it. However, "during the revolutionary phase," only a military leader and an "energetic government" could avoid "the terrible carnage of civil war."[43]

As these Republicans realized, a successful revolt was impossible without the support of influential senior officers like Marshal Deodoro da Fonseca. The small Republican current within the army, centered around Lieutenant Colonel Benjamin Constant, would be helpless unless joined by the larger group of senior officers who were still loyal to the emperor. As Campos Sales, one of the leading *Paulista* Republicans, later recalled, Deodoro was "loved to the point of idolatry in the army," and "no one else exerted such a power of fascination for attracting and directing the armed forces in a movement against the monarchy."[44] While "Benjamin Constant was the idol of the youth," according to one officer, it was "Deodoro who had the military prestige," for the army was far from united in its political beliefs and in its loyalties.[45]

43. Américo Werneck, "A dictadura militar republicana," *A Revolução* (Campanha, Minas Gerais), I, No. 13, (March 31, 1889), pp. 1–2.

44. Manuel Ferraz de Campos Salles, *Da propaganda à presidencia* (São Paulo: Typ. A Editôra, 1908), p. 54.

45. Lauro Muller, in *Jornal do Comércio*, November 16, 1921, p. 4.

Deodoro was no Republican despite his increasing irritation with the politicians. In 1888 he wrote one of his nephews, a pupil at the Military School and a Republican, not to accompany those "fools or crackpots" or "meddle in republican questions," since a "republic in Brazil is impossible, for it will be a real calamity." While it was "bad" with the monarchy, it would be "worse without it," since Brazil was unprepared and uneducated for a republic.[46] Quintino Bocaiúva, a Republican from Rio de Janeiro who had long attempted to generate military hostility toward the imperial government, placed little confidence in Deodoro. Early in 1889, in a letter to a close friend relating the troubles of the Republican movement, he declared that the recent "death of Madureira was a disaster for us, and we cannot rely on Deodoro."[47] Deodoro's lack of Republican sentiments further demonstrates the absence of solidarity among the politically conscious army officers.

Despite Deodoro's uncertainty, actual plans to overthrow the government were being formulated by early November of 1889. Some officers hoped to create a republic, but many others wished simply to overturn the ministry of the Viscount of Ouro Prêto, Afonso Celso de Assis Figueiredo, who had seriously antagonized the army. Ouro Prêto was a strong-willed, impetuous man, and he lacked the flexibility needed to reconcile the army. He broke precedent by appointing officers to the cabinet posts of Minister of War and Minister of Marine. But they were not the most popular officers, and their appointments did not win him any support.

At this point, certain Republicans and opposition journalists attempted to rouse military sentiments to a frenzy. By raising the spectre of a monarchist effort to dissolve or seriously weaken the army, they hoped to turn the officers com-

46. Deodoro to Clodoaldo da Fonseca, Rio de Janeiro, September 30, 1888, and October 16, 1888, Clodoaldo da Fonseca Papers.

47. Quintino Bocaiúva to Gabriel Cruz, Rio de Janeiro, February 19, 1889, Archivo do Museu Histórico Nacional (uncatalogued).

pletely against the government. As the last Rio police chief under the monarchy recalled, the press was "provoking and inciting the discontented elements" among the officers.[48] Their success was vital in bringing about a republic at this time and in placing the officers in control of the new regime.

Rui Barbosa, a dissident Liberal turned Republican and a brilliant journalist, used any available issue as a weapon for attacking the ministry of Ouro Prêto. The *Diário de Notícias*, which Rui took over early in 1889, closely followed military incidents. Like other seekers of military support, Rui charged the government with fostering "unreasoning obedience" in the army and with wishing for "Janizaries," or "slaves in uniform," and "venal praetorians" instead of brave and honorable Brazilians. He continually accused the government of plotting to reduce the size of the army and disperse its units throughout the provinces. And he declared that the patriotic army could not "subscribe to its own extinction."[49]

An avowedly Republican paper, the *Correio do Povo*, also incited the army against the government. Proclaiming the army to be "the most patriotic class in the nation" and defending its members in conflicts with the ministry, this journal decried the government's "express intention to disparage and destroy the armed forces" in order to turn them into "a legion of submissive slaves on which they can depend in every emergency." Praising the officers as the "sole sustainers of our monarchical institutions," this newspaper clearly implied that the army should act to prevent its impending dissolution and to save the nation, with whose future it was charged.[50]

Quintino Bocaiúva, Republican editor of the *País*, had long

48. Report of José Basson de Miranda Osório to Ouro Prêto, Rio de Janeiro, December 15, 1889, Arquivo do Museu Histórico Nacional, P. 28, No. 13.

49. *Diário de Notícias*, October 25, 1889, p. 1; October 27, 1889, p. 1; November 4, 1889, p. 1; November 9, 1889, p. 1.

50. *Correio do Povo*, November 7, 1889, pp. 2–3; November 8, 1889, p. 1; November 9, 1889, p. 1; November 13, 1889, p. 1.

supported the officers. In the weeks preceding the overthrow of the empire, he methodically attempted to build up military feeling and to persuade the army that it must choose immediately between an armed movement or its own dissolution. The smallest action of the imperial government was construed as an "intention to strangle the army through the pressure of persecutions." Like other journalists, Bocaiúva hammered away on a supposed plot to organize "a police army as a counterpoise to the regular army, which represents a national, patriotic institution." He described in detail the imperial government's "plan to disorganize the army" by scattering it "in small contingents throughout the vast area of the empire."[51]

Despite the efforts of these Republicans, the army as a whole was not merely an instrument of civilian ambitions to be used by clever politicians for their own ends. Some opposition leaders had fanned the flames of military discontent, but they had not ignited the fire. The armed forces were no one's docile instrument, but instead, a power of their own.

With the Republicans beating the drums of military pride, however, events did move more swiftly. Additional officers were brought into the military plot against the government. Finally, at a meeting of the Club Militar on November 9, 1889, Benjamin Constant was virtually empowered to organize a revolution against the emperor. Decrying the "government's evil intents" against the officers, he requested "full powers to free the military from a state of affairs incompatible with its honor and dignity." If he were unable to convince the government of its errors in a few days and settle the matter through legal means, he was willing to die in the public plazas for the nation. Other officers urged that Benjamin be given power to

51. *País,* October 28, 1889, p. 1; October 30, 1889, p. 1; November 10, 1889, p. 1.

resolve "once and for all, in the most honorable manner for our class, all the questions arising from the misguided politics of which we were the victims," so that they "soon would breathe the air of a free homeland." Benjamin was entrusted with the task of finding a solution "equally honorable for the army and the nation," and the solution he found, six days later, was the proclamation of the republic.[52]

During the interval, Benjamin Constant met with influential officers like Deodoro da Fonseca and with a few civilian Republicans, including Quintino Bocaiúva and, later, Rui Barbosa. Deodoro, a key man in these calculations, continued to waver between the respect he held for the emperor and his sense of military pride and solidarity. Finally, Benjamin persuaded him to join the Republicans in overturning the monarchy instead of merely substituting one ministry for another. Deodoro was heard to declare that "with the monarchy, salvation is not possible for the nation or the army," since the government was trying "to annihilate the army."[53] Then Benjamin Constant and the others sounded out other army officers and secured their collaboration. While a few naval officers were eventually included in the conspiracy, it was predominantly an army movement.

The location of contingents of the armed forces would contribute to the success of the revolt. The existence of a large army garrison in the capital facilitated individual officers' participation in political disputes in the center of town, only a trolley ride away.[54] Dissident civilians and officers combined

52. Atas of Club Militar, session of November 9, 1889, Arquivo do Club Militar. See also Jacques Ourique, in *Jornal do Comércio,* January 4, 1890, p. 2; and Report of José Basson de Miranda Osório to Ouro Prêto, December 15, 1889, Arquivo do Museu Histórico Nacional, p. 28, No. 13.

53. Jacques Ourique, in *Jornal do Comércio,* January 5, 1890, p. 2. See also José Bevilacqua, in *Gazeta de Notícias,* July 17, 1890, p. 1.

54. In 1888, out of a total of 11,748 men in the army, 1,839 were stationed in Rio de Janeiro; in 1889, with 13,152 men in the army, 1,911 were garrisoned

easily, and opposition propaganda was aimed at the smaller groups. It was not necessary to influence the whole army, just the Rio garrison. The empire lacked general support from the politically functioning minority, and no other segment of the armed forces would contest the events which would occur in the capital in mid-November of 1889.

The actual uprising was precipitated by false rumors spread about the city on November 14 that various regiments were to be dispersed at once throughout the provinces and that a number of influential army leaders, including Deodoro da Fonseca and Benjamin Constant, were to be arrested. Late that evening troops began to move against the government. Then the palace forces mutinied and marched to the war office, where the cabinet had gathered under the direction of the Prime Minister, the Viscount of Ouro Prêto. On the morning of the fifteenth the barracks troops under the command of Marshal Floriano Peixoto, the Adjunct General of the army, who knew of the plan for the uprising, refused to obey Ouro Prêto's orders to attack the rebellious forces and fraternized with them instead. As Ouro Prêto related, Deodoro declared that "he placed himself at the front of the army in order to revenge the very grievous injustices and injuries it had received from the government. . . . Only the army, he asserted, knew how to sacrifice itself for the nation, and, nevertheless, the politicians who up to now had directed the country had maltreated it."[55]

---

in Rio. (Brazil, Ministério da Guerra, *Relatório apresentado à Assemblea Geral Legislativa na terceira sessão da vigesima legislatura pelo ministro e secretario de estado dos negocios da guerra Thomaz José Coelho d'Almeida* (Rio de Janeiro: Imprensa Nacional, 1888), *Anexos*, p. 3; Brazil, Ministério de Guerra, *Relatório apresentado à Assemblea Geral Legislativa na quarta sessão da vigesima legislatura pelo ministro e secretario de estado dos negocios da guerra Thomaz José Coelho d'Almeida* (Rio de Janeiro: Imprensa Nacional, 1889), *Anexos*, p. 12.

55. Visconde de Ouro Prêto, Affonso Celso de Assis Figueiredo, *Advento da dictadura militar no Brasil* (Paris: F. Pichon, 1891), p. 69.

Up to this point, Deodoro and other officers may still have felt that this was just a movement to secure "redress for our injured pride" from a ministry attempting "to discredit the officers."[56] But with the aid of rumors such as one that the emperor was going to call upon a leading statesman from Rio Grande do Sul, Gaspar Silveira Martins—a bitter personal enemy of Deodoro—to head a new ministry, Deodoro was persuaded to accept a change in the form of government. He proclaimed the republic that afternoon.

By the late 1880's the once firm foundations of the monarchy had been gradually weakened. The landowners, long some of the firmest supporters of the monarchy, had become alienated through the abolition of slavery without compensation in 1888. This final settlement of the slavery issue, which had long agitated the country, resulted in a financial loss to the planters and provoked much bitterness and resentment. Some of the landowners left the Conservative Party, which had promulgated the abolition bill, for the Liberal Party, which had originally advocated it. Others now supported the Republicans. The vast majority, however, simply withdrew from politics and from any active support of the emperor. Other groups like the clergy, upset by the conflict between secularism and ultramontanism in the 1870's, were also estranged from the monarchy. The emperor himself, though still respected and esteemed by many, no longer commanded the veneration necessary to uphold the monarchy in Brazil, and few were willing to see a "third Reign." His daughter, the Princess Imperial Isabel, was generally thought to be under clerical influence, and her husband, the Conde d'Eu, was a foreigner and deaf, qualities which did not contribute to his popularity. Strident

56. Speech by General Almeida Barreto, in José Candido Teixeira, *A república brazileira. A última propaganda. Apontamentos para a história, datas gloriosas, factos memoraveis* (Rio de Janeiro: Imprensa Nacional, 1890), pp. 131–32.

Republican propaganda had helped to corrode these already weakened foundations of the monarchy, and the army had delivered the decisive blow.

On November 15, 1889, Pedro II had been resting in Petrópolis, a resort town a few hours ride from the capital. He had hesitated too long, first not believing that the uprising was serious, and then believing that he had sufficient support to put it down easily. He never attempted a reconciliation with Deodoro. The emperor, an old man before his time, had been strangely oblivious to the growing dissatisfaction with the monarchy and to the discontent of the officers. This upright and hard-working ruler was somewhat pedantic, rather than profound, in his intellectual interests, and the breadth of his knowledge was not matched by an equivalent depth. He did not understand or sympathize with many of the changes occurring in Brazil's economic structure and some of the political needs and demands of the country's educated élite. Shortly after the declaration of the republic, the emperor and his family were ordered to leave the country.[57]

Although proclamation of the republic came as a surprise

57. Accounts of the events of November 14 and 15 differ widely. Compare, for example, Oliveira Vianna, *Occaso do império*, pp. 167–206; Freire, *História constitucional*, I, 372–81; Ottoni, *O advento da república*, pp. 97–106; with Magalhães Júnior, *Deodoro*, II, 8–74; Lyra, *História da queda do império*, II, 145–51, 161–382; Ilha Moreira, *Proclamação e fundação da república*, pp. 46–54; and Bocaiúva to D. Tulia Solon, Petrópolis, July 31, 1902, Arquivo do Instituto Histórico e Geográfico Brasileiro, L. 419, D. 28. Two very careful accounts are José Maria dos Santos, *Bernardino de Campos*, pp. 70–84; and Evaristo de Moraes, *Da monarchia para a república*, pp. 133–78, 207–18. For a useful compilation in English see Mary Wilhelmine Williams, *Dom Pedro the Magnanimous: Second Emperor of Brazil* (Chapel Hill: University of North Carolina Press, 1937), pp. 327–43.

Concerning general analyses of the various factors involved in the downfall of the monarchy, the traditional account in English is that by Percy Alvin Martin, "Causes of the Collapse of the Brazilian Empire," *Hispanic American Historical Review*, IV (February, 1921), 4–48. A much more recent analysis is that by George C. A. Boehrer, "The Brazilian Republican Revolution: Old and New Views," *Luso-Brazilian Review*, III (Winter, 1966), 43–57.

to the people of the country, it met with virtually no resistance. The only "casualty" was the slightly wounded naval minister. A few monarchists did try to organize a counterrevolution, but they had no success.[58] As one foreign diplomat described this "most remarkable revolution," which was "entirely unexpected by the government or people," the empire had been overthrown "without riotous proceedings, or interruption to the usual avocations of life."[59] The people had remained "unconcerned, and in the midst of official salutes and celebrations, you could not hear a single firecracker, the inseparable signal of displays of noisy festivity by the people of Rio de Janeiro.[60]

Only a segment of the army, that stationed in Rio de Janeiro, had actually participated in the revolt. The lack of resistance by other army contingents, or even by the supposedly monarchist navy, demonstrates the basic weakness of and lack of support for the monarchy. But even though its supporters had become apathetic, this venerable institution might not have given way then without the officers' blow. Their action gave them a commanding position in the nation's government.

58. See André Rebouças, *Diário e notas autobiográficas* (Rio de Janeiro: José Olympio, 1938), pp. 349–50.

59. Robert Adams to Blaine, November 19, 1889, National Archives, Brazil, Despatches, RG 59, Vol. 49.

60. A. Coêlho Rodrigues, *A república na América do Sul ou um pouco de história e crítica offerecido aos Latino-Americanos* 2d ed. (Einsiedeln, Switzerland: Typ. dos Estabelecimentos Benzinger & Co., 1906), p. 16.

CHAPTER II

The Officers in Control: The Provisional Government

THE PROVISIONAL GOVERNMENT, set up on November 15, 1889, was virtually a military regime. Although some civilian Republicans participated in the government they had helped to establish, they were not able to exercise decisive influence on matters of importance to the officers or prevent them from infringing on civil liberties. After a year of executive rule, provisional President Marshal Deodoro da Fonseca convoked the Constituent Assembly, a predominantly civilian body which soon clashed with him.

From the beginning the provisional government was dominated by the officers. They had carried out the revolution against the monarchy, and their arms were sustaining the republic. A leading Republican described the situation: "For the present, the character of the government is purely military, and should be that way. The deed was theirs, theirs alone, because the collaboration of the civilian element was almost nil. The people were like dumb beasts, astonished, surprised, unaware of what it signified. Many honestly believed they were watching a parade."[1] Another civilian Republican described the fall of the empire as "a military revolution," a "conquest of the army, which had allied itself for this purpose to the civilian element of the Republican Party."[2]

Although the civilian Republicans had played an important part in the preparations for the fall of the monarchy, they were unable to exercise great power under the provisional regime. During the empire very few officers had held governmental positions, administrative or legislative, in the capital or in the provinces, but now the situation was reversed. Marshal Deodoro da Fonseca headed the government and determined major policy. While civilians directed the ministries of finance, justice, foreign affairs, and agriculture, their power was limited to areas beyond the interest of the officers. The important posts of war minister and navy minister were given to military officers, which was contrary to the general practice under the monarchy. As a civilian Republican noted, "power was actually in their hands. A civilian clothed with authority either submitted to the direction delineated by the military milieu in which he lived, or he retired from his office, either voluntarily or by being dismissed."[3] Or, as a foreign observer summarized the matter, it was "a military government, tempered by nepotism."[4]

Throughout the country the officers wielded the crucial power. Perhaps because the Republicans were few in number

1. Aristides Lôbo, letter to *Diário Popular* (São Paulo), November 18, 1889, p. 1.

2. Freire, *História constitucional,* II, 80.

3. *Ibid.,* p. 81.

4. James Fenner Lee to Blaine, December 12, 1890, National Archives, Brazil, Despatches, RG 59, Vol. 50.

and basically unknown to him, Deodoro appointed military men to run many of the states. As Quintino Bocaiúva recalled some years later, "both Marshal Deodoro and Benjamin Constant were almost completely unacquainted with the republicans."[5] Unfamiliar with the give-and-take of politics, many of the officers were unable to deal with political opposition without resorting to infringements on individual liberties. Officers who were not appointed to state positions also attempted to influence the political affairs of the states. As one civilian noted, "the Club Militar appointed its own delegations in the states, where similar bodies with the same orientation were organized, to give expression to the army's stand on the most important political events in the country."[6] In the first few weeks following their revolt against the monarchy, the armed forces solidified their powerful position both in the states and in the central government without encountering any open opposition.

On December 18, 1889, the brooding calm of the initial month of the provisional government was shatttered by a mutiny of some troops in Rio de Janeiro, which led the government to take additional measures emphasizing its military character. A group of approximately eighty soldiers, most of them intoxicated, took advantage of their officers' absence to unfurl the imperial flag and cry "long live the emperor." They then entrenched themselves in their quarters, which were quickly assaulted and taken over by regular army units. The Republican sentiments of many of the officers had not trickled down to the rank and file, who were far removed from political preoccupations and agitation. Minor mutinies and acts of indiscipline on the part of the troops had not been uncommon under the empire and would continue under the republic. But

5. Quintino Bocaiúva to D. Tulia Solon, Petrópolis, July 31, 1902, Arquivo do Instituto Histórico e Geográfico Brasileiro, L. 419, D. 28.

6. Freire, *História constitucional*, II, 81.

the provisional government feared possible conspiracies and counterrevolutions and became alarmed.[7]

Another event contributed to this rising sense of alarm. The leaders of the provisional regime thought Pedro II had accepted a large sum of money, designated for the support of the former imperial family, before departing for Europe, but there was a misunderstanding on this point. When the news arrived that he had rejected the funds, the government became disturbed, fearing that the monarchists would construe his action as a rejection of the republic and a willingness to be used as a center of resistance to the new order.[8]

Drastic measures followed. The emperor and the Viscount of Ouro Prêto were formally banished, some personal enemies of Deodoro were exiled, and imperial property was sold. In addition, a state of siege was proclaimed. The decrees of December 23, 1889, created a military tribunal for the examination and sentencing of civilians accused of conspiring against the government or of any acts of sedition. The *Tribuna Liberal*, the only opposition paper in Rio de Janeiro, was forced to suspend publication because it had published articles critical of "the republican-military movement" which resembled "Spanish *pronunciamientos*."[9] No regime of terror followed the new decrees, but the other journals judged it prudent to remain quiet.

7. Max Leclerc, *Cartas do Brasil*, trans. Sérgio Milliet (São Paulo: Companhia Editôra Nacional, 1942), pp. 23–24; *Rio News*, January 6, 1891, p. 3; José Maria dos Santos, *Bernardino de Campos*, pp. 136–37.

8. Monteiro, *Pesquisas e depoimentos*, pp. 312–24; Leclerc, *Cartas do Brasil*, pp. 28–29; Evaristo de Moraes, *Da monarchia para a república*, pp. 170–78; Freire, *História constitucional*, II, 20–22; Lyra, *História da queda do império*, II, 432–35.

9. *Tribuna Liberal*, December 13, 1889, p. 1; December 15, 1889, p. 2; December 25, 1889, p. 1. See also Leclerc, *Cartas do Brasil*, pp. 27–30, 118; *Rio News*, January 6, 1891, p. 3; Evaristo de Moraes, *Da monarchia para a república*, pp. 193–97; Adams to Blaine, December 28, 1889, National Archives, Brazil, Despatches, RG 59, Vol. 49; Carlos de Laet, "Imprensa," *A década republicana* (Rio de Janeiro: Campanhia Typ. do Brasil, 1899), II, 86–98.

The following March the decrees were reactivated, and some civilians were tried for sedition by military courts. Anyone spreading "false news and alarming reports" was subjected to the penalties of the December 23, 1889, decree. The authors of a poster calling on the people to act against a regime which was handing the nation over to Argentina were tried by a military commission under the terms of this decree.[10]

Freedom of the press continued to be a critical issue between civilians and officers throughout the life of the provisional government. The major press incident that occurred, one which caused numerous civilians to fear for their civil liberties, was the assault on the editorial rooms of the *Tribuna.* This opposition journal had carried biting articles by a Brazilian monarchist residing in Europe and had attacked "the military dictatorship" which held the "unhappy country" under "the inexorable yoke of armed Brazilians."[11] Such criticisms incensed Marshal Deodoro da Fonseca, and his nephews attempted to intimidate the editor. Campos Sales, the Minister of Justice, learned that Deodoro had ordered the paper's suspension and its editor's arrest, and the minister secured a promise that nothing would happen. But on the evening of November 29, 1890, a party of thirty or forty soldiers in civilian dress, led by officers connected with Deodoro's household, raided the *Tribuna's* offices, breaking up fixtures and furniture and wounding several persons, one of whom later died. There was no police opposition to the attack. Deodoro might not have known of the actual plans for the assault, but nevertheless, those responsible for it were never punished.[12]

Civilians were virtually helpless in the face of such inci-

10. *Diário Oficial,* March 30, 1890, p. 1361; José Maria dos Santos, *Bernardino de Campos,* pp. 176–77; *Rio News,* March 31, 1890, pp. 2, 3, 4; April 28, 1890, p. 2.

11. *Tribuna,* September 5, 1890, p. 1; January 10, 1891, p. 1.

12. Campos Salles, *Da propaganda à presidencia,* pp. 54–56; João Dunshee de Abranches Moura, ed., *Actas e actos do governo provisório* (Rio de Janeiro:

dents. Deodoro's cabinet signed a formal tender of resignation to be effective if the criminals were not punished and if better guarantees for personal liberty were not given, but the ministers soon agreed to accept a vague promise of future guarantees. The editors of Rio's leading papers met to declare their intention to use "every effort, . . . even to the collective suspension of their journals," if "punishment" were not imposed and "the want of security" rectified. However, although they did continue to agitate for convictions during the investigations, they never carried out their ultimate threat to stop publication.[13]

The high prestige and importance of members of the armed forces is also evident in an incident involving the principal members of the provisional government. At a military parade and demonstration arranged by Deodoro's friends in January, 1890, Major Inocêncio Serzedelo Corrêa, an officer long personally loyal to Deodoro, "in the name of the people, the army and the navy, acclaimed Marshal Deodoro *generalissimo* of the Brazilian army, Lieutenant Colonel Benjamin Constant, brigadier-general, and Rear-Admiral Wandenkolk, vice-admiral of the navy."[14] The civilian members of the ministry were not neglected; a few months later each received the rank of brigadier-general. For a long time afterward, the press, sometimes in derisive terms, referred to them as "generals."[15]

Many civilian Republicans began to express disappointment with the basically military government they had helped

---

Imprensa Nacional, 1907), pp. 387–88; Laet, "Imprensa," *A década republicana*, II, 108–11; James Fenner Lee to Blaine, December 12, 1890, National Archives, Brazil. Despatches, RG 59, Vol. 50; *Rio News*, December 1, 1890, p. 3; January 13, 1891, p. 3; *Jornal do Comércio*, November 30, 1890, p. 1; *Tribuna*, January 10, 1891, p. 1.

13. *Gazeta de Notícias*, December 3, 1890, p. 1; Dunshee de Abranches, *Actas e actos*, p. 389; Campos Salles, *Da propaganda à presidencia*, pp. 57–58; *Rio News*, January 13, 1891, p. 3; February 10, 1891, pp. 4–5.

14. *Jornal do Comércio*, January 16, 1890, p. 1.

15. Leclerc, *Cartas do Brasil*, pp. 98–99; *Rio News*, January 13, 1891, p. 3; January 27, 1891, p. 5.

establish. Perhaps some were disappointed that the provisional regime had prolonged itself instead of turning the reigns of government over to them. One civilian and longtime Republican viewed the doubling of army size as a "danger for liberty and the federal principle."[16] According to the local press, another believed that the "danger to the republic" consisted not in monarchical reaction but in the "prolongation of the dictatorship," which continued to "exercise absolute sway."[17] Still another called on the "original republicans" to unite and renew the agitation for a republic, which had not yet been established.[18]

Many civilians hoped the Constituent Assembly, called to reestablish the nation on a legal basis through the promulgation of a Republican constitution and the election of the first president and vice-president, would return the nation to civilian control. However, the congressmen were elected under conditions carefully regulated by the government, and this resulted in the selection of government candidates, including many officers, who composed approximately one-fourth of the delegates. The government also published a draft of a constitution, which some at first thought had actually been promulgated. Therefore, the Constituent Assembly began its labors in November, 1890, without great public prestige, for it was generally assumed that it would not be independent or able to criticize the acts of the provisional regime.[19]

Despite the circumscribed role which the government

16. Ottoni, *O advento da república*, p. 124.

17. *Rio News*, January 20, 1891, p. 4.

18. Speech of Martinho Prado, in Constituent Congress, session of January 17, 1891, Brazil, *Constituinte. Annaes do Congresso Nacional* (Rio de Janeiro: Imprensa Nacional, 1891), II, 341–49.

19. *Rio News*, May 19, 1890, p. 3; June 23, 1890, p. 2; June 30, 1890, p. 3; August 11, 1890, p. 2; September 15, 1890, p. 2; September 22, 1890, p. 2; February 3, 1891, p. 3; Freire, *História constitucional*, III, 3, 293; José Maria dos Santos, *Bernardino de Campos*, pp. 195–96.

seemed to have envisioned for the Constituent Assembly, not all of its members remained quiescent. An oppositionist current soon appeared, and it continued to grow and resist the military forces in the government. In fact, the clashes and sharp discussions began with Deodoro's opening message, supposedly delivering the "destinies of the nation" into the hands of Congress. The opposition also closely questioned the government on the virtual dismissal of the first ministry and strongly opposed the new, more conservative one.

Freedom of the press remained a vital issue in civilian-military relationships in Congress. Various congressmen recited stories of the wrecking of opposition journals by groups of soldiers and of threats to editors throughout the country. After the *Tribuna* incident, a motion was presented that "the Constituent Congress hopes and expects that the government of the republic will not rest until the authors of the assault are discovered."[20] Despite bitter opposition by military men in the assembly, the motion was adopted. However, Congress resumed its other tasks without pressing the question any farther. As one reporter noted, officers of the local garrison "declared that the troops were in a state of readiness, eager to teach the congressmen a lesson if they dared vote a motion reproving the attack against the monarchist paper."[21]

The armed forces occupied a strong position within the country, and Congress knew it. In the provinces as well as in the capital, they maintained the stability of the administration. As one civilian congressman described the situation, Deodoro "enjoyed indisputable prestige among the nation's armed forces. This assured him the greatest probabilities of

20. Session of February 2, 1891, Brazil, *Constituinte. Annaes do Congresso Nacional*, III, 2–12.

21. João Dunshee de Abranches Moura, ed., *O golpe de estado. Atas e atos do governo Lucena* (Rio de Janeiro: Oficinas Gráficas do Jornal do Brasil, 1954), p. 47.

emerging victorious in any emergency conflict between him and Congress."[22]

Within the Club Militar the officers discussed provisions of the projected constitution which might affect their interests. Long before Congress met, they had nominated "a commission to collaborate with the provisional government on the part of the projected constitution affecting the legitimate interests of armed forces."[23] Upset by articles proposing officers' disenfranchisement in senate and presidential elections and their ineligibility for elected office, the club members appointed commissions to combat these provisions.[24]

In the face of such military pressure, it is not surprising that the congressmen quietly acquiesced to the officers' desires. As one civilian congressman recalled, "the lack of liberty of the civilian element in Congress during all the discussions affecting the officers was highly discernible. . . . no subject which closely concerned military matters was openly debated," even though contrary opinions existed.[25] Only on less important issues did the officer-congressmen bother to speak out, as when one denounced as "anti-military and unjust" a proposed amendment giving the federal government the power to remove commanders of military districts on the request of state governors.[26]

The final act of the Constituent Assembly was to elect a president and a vice-president. Again civilian opposition elements clashed with the officers, and again the desires of the armed forces prevailed. To many Brazilians, Marshal Deodoro

22. Freire, *História constitucional,* II, 3.

23. Atas of Club Militar, Ordinary Session, May 10, 1890, Arquivo do Club Militar.

24. Atas of Club Militar, Sessions of General Assembly, November 5, 1890; November 8, 1890; Arquivo do Club Militar.

25. Freire, *História constitucional,* III, vi–vii.

26. Speech of Serzedelo Corrêa, February 16, 1891, *Constituinte. Annaes do Congresso Nacional,* III, 189.

da Fonseca seemed the natural candidate for the presidency, and the army strongly supported him. However, the opposition forces believed that Deodoro had already shown his inability to govern well and that the country should have a civilian ruler. Many supported the candidacy of Prudente José de Morais Barros, the president of the Constituent Assembly. A veteran of the Republican "propaganda," this austere and determined representative of the powerful state of São Paulo was firmly committed to civilian rule.

Although he maintained that he had not actively sought the nomination, Prudente refused to withdraw his name.[27] Some *Paulistas* doubted his success, but they worked hard for his election. He was also supported by many "historic" Republicans and by dissident leaders like Demétrio Ribeiro of Rio Grande do Sul, who feared that Deodoro's election would consolidate the power of his enemies in his home state.

The divisions within the armed forces now began to appear. There were a few military men among those working for Prudente's election. Instead of presenting a united front in defense of their colleague Deodoro, they were supporting a civilian, who, ironically, would later use the internal divisions within the army to advance civilian control. Not only were some naval elements becoming more discontented with an army-dominated government and with Deodoro, but Deodoro was even unable to command the loyalties of all the army fac-

27. Compare the account of Prudente's candidacy given by Campos Sales in *Da propaganda à presidencia* (pp. 68–70), which depicts Prudente as refusing to withdraw his candidacy and the *Paulistas* as voting for him to avoid, "forever, the responsibility of Prudente de Morais' defeat" (*ibid.*, p. 71), with Prudente's account in a letter to Antônio Mercado, Cambuquira, May 28, 1902, (Copy enclosed in letter of Antônio Mercado to Prudente de Morais Filho, São Paulo, March 1, 1908, Prudente de Morais Papers). According to Prudente, he had cited reasons of ill health, the need for the opposition to "cast blank ballots" instead of having its own candidate, and the *Paulistas*' "promise to vote for Deodoro," but Campos Sales and others accepted his candidacy despite his contrary arguments.

tions. These dissident elements had originally promoted the candidacy of Marshal Floriano Peixoto, but when his election appeared impossible, they switched to Prudente and backed Floriano for vice-president. Prudente's civilian supporters accepted this maneuver to secure part of the military vote.[28]

Deodoro and most of the officers reacted with hostility to the opposition posed by the candidacy of Prudente. As provisional president, Deodoro had greeted the demands of Congress as personal slights, and he viewed this civilian candidacy as an additional insult and an unpardonable affront. Rumors began to circulate as to measures the army might take if Deodoro were not elected. Police and troop movements were increased, and some officers opposed to Deodoro's candidacy were transferred to posts outside of Rio.

Even without orders from Deodoro, many officers were prepared to move against Congress if he were not elected. In the Club Militar and elsewhere officers continually discussed the election. The few who opposed Deodoro were far outweighed, in strength and in numbers, by his supporters. One officer declared that if Congress did not elect Deodoro he would dissolve Congress and "go to the public square with my comrades and acclaim him with bullets."[29] Some, it is true, sympathized with a Rio Grande do Sul cavalry manifesto protesting an army circular which had called for direct military intervention to secure Deodoro's triumph, but they were opposed by a

28. Campos Salles, *Da propaganda à presidencia*, pp. 62–65; Dunshee de Abranches, *Atas e atos do governo Lucena*, pp. 65–66; José Maria dos Santos, *Bernardino de Campos*, pp. 227–28; Freire, *História constitucional*, II, 300–302; *Rio News*, March 3, 1891, p. 3; James Fenner Lee to Blaine, December 12, 1890, National Archives, Brazil, Despatches, RG 59, Vol. 50; Custódio José de Mello, *O governo provisório e a revolução de 1893* (São Paulo: Companhia Editôra Nacional, 1938), I, 46–47.

29. *Oficio* of Colonel Antônio Carlos de Silva Piragibe, Rio de Janeiro, November 10, 1890, read in Club Militar, session of February 18, 1891, Atas of Club Militar.

number of infantry and artillery officers with strong regimental support.[30]

It was obvious that such direct intervention would not be necessary; the threat alone was sufficient. The congressmen knew that Prudente's backers had inadequate armed support to insure his retention of the presidency even if he were elected. As a reporter later recalled, "the eve of the congressional session was agitated and gloomy. . . . The most terrifying rumors circulated. And the general conviction was that revolution would spread from the barracks to the streets if Marshal Deodoro's candidacy did not emerge victorious from the congressional vote." The same reporter spent the night in a local artillery barracks and observed that "everything had been prepared to begin firing. . . . The congressional palace would have been razed if Deodoro had not emerged victorious from the balloting."[31]

Marshal Deodoro da Fonseca was elected the first constitutional president of the Republic of Brazil on February 25, 1891. The vote was 129 for Deodoro and 97 for Prudente de Morais. Many civilians had refused to be intimidated by Deodoro's military supporters, and various dissident officers had also cast their votes for Prudente. The election of the vice-president was held separately, and Floriano Peixoto won by a large margin: 153 votes to 57 for his nearest rival, Admiral Eduardo Wandenkolk.[32] Besides gaining the votes of those civilians who wanted to elect Prudente on the same ticket, Floriano also received support from army elements who preferred him to the admiral. Deodoro's lack of real popularity

30. Atas of Club Militar, sessions of September 13, 1890; November 8, 1890; February 18, 1891; February 23, 1893; *Tribuna*, September 9, 1890, p. 1; September 10, 1890, p. 1; *Rio News*, November 10, 1890, p. 2.

31. Dunshee de Abranches, *Atas e atos do governo Lucena*, pp. 67–72.

32. *Diário do Congresso Nacional República dos Estados Unidos do Brazil*, II, No. 40 (February 26, 1891), p. 555.

among the congressmen was evidenced by the silent reception he received on inauguration day, in contrast to the enthusiastic reception which Floriano was given.[33]

The establishment of the republic on a constitutional basis through the promulgation of the constitution and the presidential election did not greatly alter the situation within the nation. Since the Constituent Assembly was legally transformed into the first Congress without new elections, the conflict between this basically civilian body and Marshal Deodoro da Fonseca would continue. The armed forces would maintain their important role in the government during the next few years, but the hostilities and jealousies within the armed forces, which were demonstrated in the February elections, would continue and increase.

33. José Joaquim de Medeiros e Albuquerque, *Minha vida. Memórias* 2d ed. (Rio de Janeiro: Calvino Filho, 1933), I, 202–203.

CHAPTER III

The Disunited Armed Forces

DURING THE EARLY YEARS of the republic, divisions within the Brazilian armed forces led to one military incident after another. In addition to hostilities between various factions within the army, the traditional rivalry and jealousy between the army and the navy was exacerbated. The result was, first, political activity on the part of naval officers, and then the Naval Revolt of 1893–94, a movement which can best be understood in the light of this rivalry, rather than as a monarchist undertaking. Some civilians participated in several of the armed movements. Eventually, one group of civilians removed the officers from direct control over the government by taking advantage of the divisions within the armed forces and supporting a military regime against its military opponents.

Less than a year after his election as first constitutional president, Marshal Deodoro da Fonseca was forced out of office by a group of officers. While his fall was due partially to his unconstitutional dissolution of the hostile, basically civilian Congress on November 3, 1891, it stemmed in larger measure from the dissatisfaction of certain military factions, especially the naval officers. Without their antagonism, Deodoro's opposition could never have overthrown him, for the civilians were powerless and unable to act.

The old antagonisms between Deodoro and the Congress were not erased by the change from a provisional to a legally elected regime. Vehement comments and personal attacks were exchanged freely between Deodoro's supporters in Congress, particularly his officer-relatives, and his detractors. Civilian congressmen cried out against the usurpation of power by military state governors and accused Deodoro of violating the constitution and intervening in the states. His delay in presenting budget estimates to the Chamber of Deputies caused further indignation, as did expenditures of public funds, often on the army and navy, without specific appropriations.

Deodoro was unable to adjust to the give-and-take of political life. One of seven brothers who had followed their father in choosing a military career, he had spent his whole life in the army. Through personal bravery and steadfastness he had become extremely popular within the army, especially in the days before he exercised political power. Although he was not, as some depicted him, just an overgrown child with a majestic white beard, Deodoro lacked political sophistication or astuteness. When he attempted to command congressmen like raw recruits, he encountered opposition and hostility. His choice of subordinates and his generosity with positions led to even greater discontent. As one of his brothers later recalled, Deodoro was "generous, magnanimous and good, credulous and trusting in everyone whose character he supposed equal to his."[1]

1. João Severiano da Fonseca to Clodoaldo da Fonseca, Rio de Janeiro, August 16, 1893, Clodoaldo da Fonseca Papers.

Interpreting the actions of the refractory Congress as personal insults, Deodoro reacted by dissolving it on November 3, 1891. As in other times of crisis, martial law was declared in Rio de Janeiro and restrictions were placed on the press; the supposed danger of monarchist reaction was used to justify these measures. In his manifesto to the nation, Deodoro charged that from the very beginning the Constituent Assembly had recast the constitution he had given it, attempting to transfer "exorbitant powers" to the legislative branch. "Thoroughly imbued with hatred and passion," Congress had passed factious laws, displayed "an itching for unconstitutional legislation," and demonstrated its "thirst for self-aggrandizement." Moreover, the congressmen had attacked him, the very man who had "established the republic without bloodshed" and had been "chosen by fate, or by Providence, for the realization of a work of grandeur and sacrifice!"[2]

Groups opposed to Deodoro soon began to coalesce. Armed resistance to Deodoro began with the rising of two garrisons in Rio Grande do Sul, but the decisive action was centered in Rio de Janeiro. Various military factions merged into a body so strong that resistance by Deodoro's supporters was clearly incapable of success and, therefore, not attempted. Effective dissent centered in the navy. The ambitious Admiral Custódio José de Melo, an opponent of Deodoro since the provisional government, secured the allegiance of most of the ships in the Rio harbor, but this was not sufficient. One important and influential admiral, Luís Felipe Saldanha da Gama, opposed the armed movement against the government as an illegal act. Some other officers were either personally loyal to Deodoro or concerned with the destructive effects a revolt would have on military discipline. Since Admiral Melo lacked army support, he held constant conferences with Marshal Floriano

2. Deodoro manifesto, *Diário Oficial,* November 5, 1891, pp. 4563–67.

Peixoto and General José Simeão, who had opposed Deodoro's election. Their support proved decisive. Soon the cavalry and the artillery were behind the movement, and Deodoro was left with little more than the infantry corps.[3]

One of the leading figures in this movement, working quietly and virtually unobserved, was Marshal Floriano Peixoto, vice-president of the republic. In all his political maneuvering Floriano demonstrated an ability to move cautiously and capably, never acting till success was assured. Unlike many of his contemporaries, he always held his tongue and never informed anyone of all his plans. Some Brazilians have attributed such traits to a supposed mixed ancestry, saying that he was a *caboclo* from the north. Floriano might not have had any Indian ancestors, but he did generally present an inscrutable face to the various clamoring political factions, allowing several to believe that he sympathized with them. Although he lacked the flamboyance, personal style, or attractive personality of some leading officers, Floriano was a competent soldier and a keen judge of men, and he was able to build up a loyal group of followers. As vice-president under Deodoro, he spent much of his time away from the capital and for the most part kept out of congressional squabbles, long maintaining the confidence of various opposing elements.

In a confidential letter to Prudente de Morais, the leading *Paulista* opponent of Deodoro, in April, 1891, Floriano expressed his opposition to "the reactionary politics of the present government," for "everything goes badly and each day is

3. José Carlos de Carvalho, *O livro da minha vida. Na guerra, na paz e nas revoluções (1847–1910)* (Rio de Janeiro: Typ. do Jornal do Comérico, de Rodrigues & C., 1912), pp. 100–19; Serzedello Corrêa, *Uma figura da república. Páginas do passado* 2d ed. (Rio de Janeiro: Freitas Bastos, 1959), pp. 44–46; Custódio José de Mello, *O governo e a revolução de 1893* (São Paulo: Companhia Editôra Nacional, 1938), I, 18, 37–39, 56–62; *Gazeta de Notícias*, November 25, 1891, p. 1; Noronha Santos, *A revolução de 1891 e suas consequências*. Vol. II of *Floriano. Memórias e documentos*. (Rio de Janeiro: Serviço Gráfico do Ministério da Educação, 1939), pp. 79, 87.

worse." Floriano seemed to sympathize with the *Paulistas,* who felt persecuted by the Deodoro government, and he acknowledged that their "great state, like others, is a captive of the ill will" of those in power. But he urged them "always to resist within the legal limits," for "provoke us as they will, we will let them be the ones to depart from legality," as was to occur on November 3, 1891.[4]

Deodoro's friends, like the conservative Baron of Lucena, his chief minister and a personal friend since the days of the empire, believed that Floriano was loyal to the regime. In his conversations with Floriano, Lucena received assurances of loyalty and denials of participation in plots against Deodoro, although Floriano steadily refused to take any measures which might avoid the clash.[5] Deodoro and Lucena, relying on Floriano's promised support, miscalculated the military strength of their own forces and that of their opponents.

In mid-November news of the uprising in Rio Grande do Sul reached Rio de Janeiro, and the workers on the central railroad, stirred up by a dissident naval officer, went on strike. Then Deodoro attempted to arrest various opponents of his regime, including Admiral Custódio de Melo, Admiral Eduardo Wandenkolk, and General José Simeão. This action triggered the revolt. Melo avoided arrest and took control of the naval vessels in the Rio harbor. The other military opposition elements signified their adherence, and Deodoro, weakened by illness and left with only the army infantry, handed the government over to Floriano.[6] While Deodoro spoke of his "desire not to allow civil war to break out," and Floriano

4. Floriano to Prudente, Barbacena, April 9, 1891, Prudente de Morais Papers.

5. Lucena to Cesario Alvim, Rio de Janeiro, November 1, 1891, in Monteiro, *Pesquisas e depoimentos,* pp. 333–43.

6. Mello, *O governo provisório,* I, 90–92; *Gazeta de Notícias,* November 24, 1891, p. 1; *Rio News,* November 24, 1891, p. 3; José Carlos de Carvalho, *O livro da minha vida,* pp. 107, 120–36; Monteiro, *Pesquisas e depoimentos,* pp. 359–66.

praised Deodoro's "abnegation and patriotism" for "resigning his power in order to prevent war between brothers," it was Deodoro's realization of the impossibility of successful resistance that actually brought about his resignation.[7]

Deodoro's overthrow was due primarily to naval efforts, not to the civilian opposition forces, and many army elements were displeased with this show of naval power. The local press noted that the "navy has carried off the honors this time, and that the army is sulking."[8] Less than two weeks later a large number of naval officers felt obliged to issue a manifesto denouncing "enemies of the nation" for spreading "absolutely false, alarming rumors" about the danger of a monarchist restoration, for these rumors were circulated "in order to discredit the revolution" which "the Brazilian Navy" had "made." While the naval officers maintained that "the greater part of our glorious army is in complete agreement with us," the manifesto was evidence that many army officers were not.[9] As Admiral Melo later recalled, a "great part of the army" was unhappy with the overthrow of their "idol."[10] Even foreign diplomats could note the "constant jealousies and strife between the army and navy."[11]

Military force continued to be employed in politics. The officers controlling the central government used loyal military men against dissident state governors, both officers and civilians. Shortly after Floriano assumed office, a series of military

7. Deodoro, Renunciation message, November 23, 1891, Arquivo Nacional, Cod. 675; Message of Vice-President Floriano Peixoto, *Diário Oficial,* November 24, 1891, p. 2450.

8. *Rio News,* November 24, 1891, p. 4.

9. *Jornal do Comércio,* December 6, 1891, p. 2.

10. Mello, *O governo provisório,* I, 125; See also Augusto Carlos de Souza e Silva, *O almirante Saldanha e a revolta da armada. Reminiscencias de um revoltoso* (Rio de Janeiro: José Olympio, [1936]), p. 103.

11. Conger to Blaine, January 18, 1892, National Archives, Brazil, Despatches, RG 59, Vol. 52.

movements deposed the state governors who had supported Deodoro's coup d'état of November 3. Instead of being widely based popular movements, as Floriano's followers claimed, these were prime examples of the use of armed force in political affairs. Often a special military representative was sent to the state capital, the governor was overthrown, and an officer assumed the governorship. In Ceará, in the northeast, to take one example, a variety of military elements participated in the maneuvers leading to the deposition of the governor, General José Clarindo de Queiroz. The pupils of the military school in Fortaleza, the state capital, were hostile to the eleventh infantry battalion as well as to the state police. General Joaquim Mendes Ourique Jacques was sent to this state and gave his support to the military school, telegraphing Floriano to urge that the eleventh battalion be ordered away from the capital. Floriano approved, supporting the "mettlesome military school," and soon a minor civil war broke out between the state police and the cadets, who marched on the governor's palace, forcing the surrender of General Clarindo. Afterwards, Clarindo claimed that the federal government had promoted "anarchy" in all the states, "deflecting the armed forces from their rightful role in order to implant despotism in the whole country and shed the blood of the people."[12]

Similar events occurred in all the other states, with the exception of Pará, whose officer-governor had denounced Deodoro's coup. Officers were sent to various states to help induce governors to resign. Floriano's special military envoy to Espírito Santo, Lieutenant Colonel Inocêncio Serzedelo Corrêa,

12. Manifesto to nation of General Clarindo, March 18, 1892, in Carvalho, *O livro da minha vida*, pp. 485–93. See also Noronha Santos, *A revolução de 1891*, pp. 171–77; General Joaquim Mendes Ourique Jacques to war minister, Forteleza, February 15, 1892, and Floriano to Commander of 11th infantry in Forteleza, February 15, 1892, in Noronha Santos, *A revolução de 1891*, p. 247; telegram of Segismundo Mouza P., Igido Viana Luz, and Gonçalvez da Rocha to Floriano, Ceará, November 27, 1891, Arquivo Nacional, Cx 1206.

told the state governor that the "Federal Government had no confidence in governors" who had supported Deodoro's coup; the governor soon resigned.[13] In a long letter to Floriano, the former governor of Paraná related how the seventeenth battalion had deposed him and proclaimed its commander governor of that state.[14] As the former governor of Amazonas lamented, these movements overthrowing "state governors were never promoted by the people, but were counseled and decided upon by the federal government."[15]

Floriano had not hesitated to employ the armed forces in state politics, despite civilian objections. Some civilians cooperated with the officers against their political enemies, for there would always be civilians willing to use military dissensions or military force against those in power. One such civilian was Aristides César Spinola Zama of Bahia, long a vehement opponent of military rule, or at least of Marshal Deodoro da Fonseca.[16]

Military elements opposing the central government also resorted to the threat or use of force. The first movement against Floriano was a revolt of imprisoned soldiers at the Santa Cruz fort in Rio de Janeiro on January 19, 1892, which was quickly and easily put down. The soldiers' leader had issued an ultimatum demanding the return of Deodoro to

13. Serzedelo to Lieutenant Colonel Manuel Prescíliano de Oliveira Valadão, Vitória, December 8, 1891, Arquivo Nacional, Cx 1206. See also Colonel Gouvea to Floriano, Vitória, November 24, 1891, Arquivo Nacional, Cx 1206.

14. Genoso Marques dos Santos to Floriano, Curitiba, December 1, 1891, Arquivo Nacional, Cx 1206. See also Legislative Assembly of Paraná to Floriano, November 29, 1891, Arquivo Nacional, Cx 1206.

15. Carvalho, *O livro da minha vida*, pp. 480–81.

16. Aristides César Spinola Zama to Floriano, Bahia, February 2, 1892; March 9, 1892; April 4, 1892; April 17, 1892; Arquivo Nacional, Cx 1198. See also José Gonçalves da Silva to Rui Barbosa, Bahia, November 23, 1891; Arthur César Rios to Rui Barbosa, Bahia, November 23, 1891; Arthur César Rios to Rui Barbosa, Bahia, November 24, 1891; Argollo to Farilla, Bahia, November 24, 1891; November 25, 1891; Arquivo Nacional Cx 1206.

power; later he claimed to have obeyed the "chiefs of his party," naming Admiral Saldanha da Gama and General José Almeida Barreto, who denied that they had had any part in the revolt.[17]

Early in April of the same year, a more far-reaching conspiracy in favor of Deodoro ended in failure. A group of officers, combined with a few civilians, attempted to form a coalition of military elements strong enough to overthrow Floriano. The Baron of Lucena held several conferences with dissident military men, often partisans of Deodoro or deposed state governors, who were eager to move against Floriano. These officers disposed of some cavalry and infantry and expected assistance from the Rio police, but they lacked sufficient naval support and did not control enough forces for immediate success. On the day set for the revolt, April 1, 1892, nothing happened.[18]

Thirteen generals and admirals involved in this poorly planned conspiracy had prepared a manifesto urging Floriano to resign. On April 6 this manifesto appeared in the local press, demanding presidential elections and blaming the "current disorganization in the states" on the "undue intervention of the armed forces in deposing state governors."[19] Floriano reacted swiftly to this challenge to his power and his govern-

17. José Almeida Barreto, in *País,* January 22, 1892, p. 3; Saldanha da Gama to Rear Admiral Coêlho Neto, Mogy das Cruzes, São Paulo, January 23, 1892, in Honorato Candido Ferreira Caldas (pseud. Kleber), *A legalidade de 23 de novembro. Coordenação didactica de tres elementos syntheticos: Secção militar d'O Combate, documentos historicos, Congresso Nacional comprehendido de novembro de 1891 a setembro de 1892* (Rio de Janeiro: n.p., 1892), pp. 174–75; *Gazeta de Notícias,* January 20, 1892, p. 1; January 21, 1892, p. 2; *Diário do Congresso Nacional. República dos Estados Unidos do Brasil,* June 21, 1892, pp. 360–62.

18. Carvalho, *O livro da minha vida,* pp. 171–80; Dunshee de Abranches, *Actas e actos do governo Lucena,* pp. 133–39; articles of F. G., in *O Dia,* April 10, 1901, p. 1; April 11, 1901, p. 1; April 12, 1901, p. 1; April 13, 1901, p. 1.

19. *Gazeta de Notícias,* April 6, 1892, p. 1.

ment by retiring the thirteen senior officers, some of whom continued to protest this treatment.[20]

The pro-Deodoro variety of opposition to Floriano came to an unsuccessful climax on April 10, 1892. A demonstration in honor of Deodoro was followed by an attempt to depose Floriano. Again Floriano reacted vigorously and swiftly, showing that he possessed the will and the power to suppress such uprisings. Charging that "such commotions disturbing the public order made any regular government impossible and would inevitably lead to general anarchy" and "the horrors of *caudillismo,*" he declared a state of siege and arrested a number of the demonstrators and other opponents of his regime.[21] Many of them were exiled for several months to remote military stations on the Amazon, where one described life as a "continual, painful scourge, due to the plague of mosquitos of all sizes and of ferocious impulses."[22]

In no other state did federal intervention, the deposing of governors, and factional strife lead to such serious consequences as in Rio Grande do Sul, Brazil's southernmost state. The fierce political life in this distinctive region of Brazil has often taken a violent turn, and a bitter civil conflict was shaping up by 1891. Political animosities had been growing among the different factions since the overthrow of Governor Júlio Prates de Castilhos in November, 1891, after the ouster of Deodoro da Fonseca from the presidency. First one group and then another controlled the state government. By mid-1892 the struggle had resolved itself into a conflict between the partisans of Júlio de Castilhos, a positivist and fervent Republican, and those of Gaspar da Silveira Martins, who had been a leading figure under the monarchy.

20. *Diário do Comércio,* April 8, 1892, p. 1; *Combate,* May 15, 1892, p. 1.
21. *Diário Oficial,* April 13, 1891, p. 1577.
22. Carvalho, *O livro da minha vida,* p. 213.

Despite numerous protestations of neutrality, Floriano came to support Castilhos. Floriano and Castilhos were not on the best of terms—Castilhos had voiced approval of Deodoro's coup d'état of November 3, 1891, had sympathized with the thirteen generals and admirals in their forced retirement, and had criticized Floriano publicly—but Castilhos was a Republican. As a young man he had fiercely attacked the monarchy, and this energetic, dogmatic, and humorless Republican would never permit a return to the old institutions. In contrast, Silveira Martins favored a parliamentary form of government, and his enemies continually accused him of monarchist and separatist tendencies. As Floriano telegraphed one officer in Rio Grande, he was "convinced that only republicans could save the Republic," and he would aid them.[23] The army should not support every government which might attain power. Floriano advised the army commander in Rio Grande that "of the series of governments which has occurred in this state, you should lend support to the one which best reveals republican opinions and upholds the consecrated principles of the federal constitution."[24] Then he notified Castilhos' nominee for governor of his full support and removed one of Castilhos' opponents from the command of a nearby garrison.

After a few minor incidents, Castilhos' armed opponents surrendered. Many of the partisans of Silveira Martins and his party, known as the *Federalists,* went into hiding or sought refuge in Uruguay and continued their plotting from just across the border. During 1892 hatreds and passions continued to blaze throughout the countryside. As one officer described

23. Floriano to Major Caetano de Faria, Rio de Janeiro, May 10, 1892, Prudente de Morais Papers.

24. Floriano to General Bernardo Vasques, Rio de Janeiro, June 17, 1892, Prudente de Morais Papers.

the scene, "this state suffers from a plethora of patriotism."[25] Instead of attempting to conciliate their enemies, Castilhos' partisans engaged in acts of violence against them which only increased their resistance. A military emissary of Floriano in Rio Grande wrote that the Marshal could have no idea "of the horrors which have been perpetrated; the number of murders is extremely high, since everywhere men, women, and children have their throats cut as if they were sheep; pillaging is far too developed, so that there are no guarantees, either individual, or material."[26]

In February, 1893, bands of *Federalist* exiles invaded Rio Grande do Sul from Uruguay, and bloody and savage fighting began. The Castilhos government was unable to drive out the *Federalists*, and the long, bitter struggle continued. The federal government forces in Rio Grande, which were largely officered and recruited locally, split, and some aided Castilhos while others aided the *Federalists*.

In such a chaotic situation the aims of the various combatants were not always clear. Júlio de Castilhos seemed to be struggling principally to maintain himself in power, and no one doubted his Republican sentiments, although many denied his democratic ones. His supporters continued to assert that the object of the *Federalist* revolt was to restore the monarchy. However, some of Silveira Martins' allies, like Demétrio Ribeiro, were staunch Republicans and approved the positivist-inclined government of Rio Grande but did not support Castilhos. While Floriano's army supporters in Rio de Janeiro might claim that the "pseudo-Federalists" had "unfurled the flag of restoration," the actual government commanders in the

25. General Antônio José Maria Pego Júnior to Floriano, Pôrto Alegre, October 18, 1892, Arquivo Nacional, Cx 1197.

26. General João Telles to Floriano, Bagé, November 2, 1892, in Wenceslau Escobar, *Apontamentos para a história da revolução de 1893* (Pôrto Alegre: Officinas Gráphicas do Globo, 1920), p. 130.

field did not speak of monarchism; instead, they tended simply to praise their soldiers for their "patriotic tenaciousness" and "perseverance" and stress that a quick victory would enable them to return to their "homes," words which sounded much the same as those of the insurgent leaders.[27] The leading *Federalist* commanders categorically denied as "a monstrous slander" the charge that their "object" was "the restoration of the monarchy," for they were fighting to "liberate Rio Grande from tyranny" and "end the regime of persecutions" and "unheard-of violences."[28] Perhaps a few *Federalists* hoped for a return to the empire, but the vast majority were struggling for the overthrow of the Castilhos government, which had turned them out of office, for vengeance, and for more local autonomy.

Another charge lodged against the *Federalists* was that of separatism. The *gaúcho* state of Rio Grande do Sul, situated in the far south of Brazil and exposed to strong influences from the neighboring Platine republics, had long been the center of a profound local feeling and had maintained itself as an independent state from 1835 to 1845. A few *Federalists* published interviews in Platine newspapers looking forward to the separation of Rio Grande from Brazil and its eventual union with Uruguay.[29] This would undoubtedly please the Uruguayans and perhaps induce them to furnish more aid to the

27. Valadão to Lauro Sodré, Rio de Janeiro, March 1, 1893, Prudente de Morais Papers; General Francisco Lima to "Soldados da divisão do Norte," December 5, 1893, Arquivo do Instituto Histórico e Geográfico Brasileiro, L. 296, D. 14959; General Rodrigues, Order of the Day, January 16, 1894, Arquivo do Instituto Histórico e Geográfico Brasileiro, L. 296, D. 14976.

28. Manifesto of principal Federalist chiefs to the nation, Santanna do Livramento, March 15, 1893, in Raul Villa-Lobos (pseud. Epaminondas Villalba), *A revolução federalista no Rio Grande do Sul (Documentos e commentarios)* (Rio de Janeiro: Laemmert & Co., 1897), pp. 3–5.

29. *Rio News*, March 21, 1893, p. 4; July 26, 1893, p. 5; Daví Carneiro, *O Paraná e a revolução federalista* (São Paulo: Atena Editôra, [1944?]), pp. 57–69; Mello, *O governo provisório*, I, 305–309.

revolutionaries. One of the *Federalist* leaders spoke of proclaiming "the independence of the state of Paraná and the two neighboring southern states," Santa Catarina and Rio Grande do Sul, should São Paulo not join them against Floriano.[30] To what extent this view was held is uncertain. In any case, the range of opinions among the *Federalists* rendered successful cooperation difficult, as was the case in other revolts against a determined and energetic Floriano Peixoto.

While the *Federalist* rebellion was still raging in the south, hostilities involving other segments of the armed forces culminated in the Naval Revolt of 1893–94. The Rio Grande conflict helped precipitate this revolt, the most dangerous military uprising against the Floriano regime, for the Rio Grande crisis stimulated additional opposition to the Marshal and provided opportunities for dissident military elements to demonstrate their hostility. An auditing agency of the treasury opposed the many extraordinary and unauthorized expenditures arising from the conflict in the south. When the finance minister, an army officer, protested Floriano's efforts to weaken this agency, he was forced to resign and later was imprisoned during the Naval Revolt.[31] Admiral Custódio José de Melo resigned as naval minister and publicly attacked Floriano's harsh policy in Rio Grande as a danger and "a perennial source of evils for the republic."[32] Shortly afterward, the Club Naval chose him as president.[33] Eduardo Wandenkolk, another

30. Gumercindo Saraiva, Order of the Day, April 7, 1894, in Villa-Lobos, *A revolução federalista no Rio Grande do Sul*, p. 254.

31. Serzedello Corrêa to Floriano, Rio de Janeiro, April 27, 1893, Arquivo Nacional, Cx 1198; Serzedello Corrêa, *Uma figura da república*, pp. 31–34, 52–54; "Estudo sobre os fundamentos da constituicionalidade do acto de 17 de dezembro de 1892 que creau o Tribunal de Contas. Critica do regulamento consequente d'este acto sub o ponto da vista da constituição," April, 1893, Arquivo Nacional, Cx 1197; Felisbello Firmo de Oliveira Freire, *História da revolta de 6 de setembro de 1893* (Rio de Janeiro: Cunha & Irmãos, 1896), pp. 31–38.

32. *Jornal do Comércio*, April 30, 1893, p. 2.

33. *Rio News*, May 23, 1893, p. 5.

admiral long involved in political activities, but headstrong and lacking in political discernment, left for Montevideo in April, 1893, and then joined the *Federalists,* taking possession of a coastal steamer and unsuccessfully attacking the city of Rio Grande.[34]

Well aware of the hostile attitudes of a large portion of the navy, Floriano ordered a number of ships and officers away from Rio de Janeiro and reorganized and strengthened the Rio army garrison. But on the night of September 5, naval officers took possession of all the vessels in the Rio harbor and called on Floriano to resign.[35]

Frictions long left smoldering erupted in flames. During these first years of the republic the traditional rivalries and contentions between the army and navy had been intensified. No longer was the navy favored and less politically minded, as under the empire. Like some army officers, naval men voiced opinions on nonmilitary matters and took part in political movements against the government. They thought Floriano Peixoto was favoring the army in appointments and appropriations, and attempting to subordinate the navy. Somewhat like various army officers before November 15, 1889, the naval officers now felt that their service had been neglected and ill-treated and their honor damaged.

In an appeal to their "comrades" on board a government cruiser, rebel officers in Buenos Aires concentrated on naval grievances. While they claimed to be fighting a government hostile to liberty, their message was a call to arms in the name

34. Wandenkolk to Rui Barbosa, on board *Júpiter,* July 20, 1893, Arquivo da Casa de Rui Barbosa, Pasta Eduardo Wandenkolk; *Jornal do Comércio,* April 14, 1893, p. 4; "Proclamation of Wandenkolk," in Villa-Lobos, *A revolução federalista no Rio Grande do Sul,* pp. 108–109.

35. Souza e Silva, *O almirante Saldanha e a revolta da armada,* pp. 167–72; Arthur Silveira da Motta Jaceguay, *Organização naval. Artigos publicados na Revista Brazileira e Jornal do Commercio em 1896* (Rio de Janeiro: Typ. Leuzinger, 1896), p. 52; *Jornal do Comércio,* September 7, 1893, p. 1; *Jornal do Brasil,* April 29, 1895, p. 1.

of naval solidarity, the "traditions of our class," and the "honor" of the navy. Since the "squadron is almost totally with the revolutionary movement," all officers should join their comrades against a "dictatorship" which impugned their honor, questioned their loyalty, and humiliated them.[36]

While the leader of this revolt, Admiral Custódio de Melo, declared that he was fighting "to restore the sway of law, of order and of peace," he was far more upset by Floriano's treatment of the navy.[37] He later admitted that, because of the "partiality of the Marshal in the distribution of justice between the officers of the two services" and the "clear intention to debase the navy," the naval officers "saw, in the executive power, an enemy" and "had no other means but to seize their arms" in order to "obtain justice."[38] Melo was convinced of the justification for revolution, for "according to history, all means are lawful for extinguishing a tyranny." Since the Brazilian armed forces were obliged by the constitution to sustain the laws and institutions of the nation, Melo considered them obliged to act whenever, in their opinion, a government was behaving illegally.[39]

Custódio de Melo had long demonstrated his interest in political affairs, as well as an overriding ambition for political power. Ever since the declaration of the republic, this self-important and verbose admiral had devoted most of his energies to the kind of activities that led to his participation in the Naval Revolt.

The events of the naval insurrection finally forced even those who had refused to accept the idea of the "just" revolu-

36. Proclamation of Brazilian officers in Buenos Aires to the officers and crew of the *Tiradentes*, October, 1893, in Honorato Candido Ferreira Caldas, *A deshonra da república* 2d ed. (Rio de Janeiro: Imprensa Montenegro, 1895), pp. 140–45.

37. Manifesto of Admiral Mello, *Jornal do Comércio*, September 8, 1893, p. 1.

38. Mello, *O governo provisório*, II, 269.

39. *Ibid.*, pp. 78, 292–95, 314–49.

tion to join the rebellion. Admiral Luís Felipe Saldanha da Gama, an able and respected officer who believed in obedience and duty, had always eschewed politics and—although a monarchist by sympathy—had supported the Republican governments against all of the various armed movements, including the overthrow of Marshal Deodoro da Fonseca. Of an aristocratic bearing and background, Saldanha da Gama refused to stoop to political maneuvering. While disturbed by the "grievous situation of our poor Brazil" and the "wretched and mournful state of affairs," he remained apart from political struggles, although, as he wrote, "solicited by *all sides*" and experiencing "difficulties in maintaining my role of upright and honorable officer."[40] A "gentleman" according to many of his contemporaries, he cared for the navy and its traditions rather than for political power, and he disdained many of those scrambling for power. As head of the Naval School, this proud and dedicated admiral emphasized discipline and efficiency in classwork and stressed physical education as well as instruction in the social graces.

When the Naval Revolt broke out, Saldanha da Gama, director of this strategically located school, declared his neutrality. Earlier he had refused the leadership of the rebellion, and he had not been informed of further plans. If he had either joined the insurgents or supported the government, the conflict might not have remained a relative stalemate so long.

Melo originally believed that the presence of the rebel fleet in the Bay of Guanabara, threatening the defenseless city of Rio de Janeiro, would force Floriano to surrender. As Saldanha da Gama was heard to remark the morning the revolt broke out, Melo thought that this was "the 23rd of Novem-

40. Saldanha to First Lieutenant João de Miranda Ribeiro, Rio de Janeiro, March 21, 1893; Saldanha to cousin Joca (copy), Rio de Janeiro, April 23, 1893, Arquivo do Serviço Geral da Marinha, Box 70, Ministério da Marinha.

ber (1891) again and that he was "very soon going to dine in Itamarati," the presidential palace. But he was "deceived," for "Floriano is tough, he does not surrender like that."[41] Moreover, Melo had not expected the foreign squadron in the harbor to hinder the bombardment of the city. During the prolonged struggle, both sides were generally limited to exchanges of fire, marked, according to one observer, by "remarkably bad gunnery."[42]

Saldanha's fervent desire to maintain the Naval School apart from political struggles for the sake of the future of the navy prompted his neutrality in the Naval Revolt. Less than a year before, he had confided to a friend his hope for sufficient "time to achieve the proper influence on these new generations of officers," and during school vacation he confessed himself "wild for classes to begin, since that way I will be able to keep the *boys* more removed from the corrupting atmosphere which envelops this capital."[43] Therefore, after the outbreak of the Naval Revolt, he wrote the naval minister that his neutrality was designed to "shield the school and its pupils from the effects and consequences of the revolt, for these pupils are at this moment the only hope of the navy and the nation." "The best way to achieve this purpose" he said, "is to keep these

41. Souza e Silva, *O almirante Saldanha e a revolta da armada,* p. 126.

42. Thompson to Gresham, October 13, 1893, National Archives, Brazil, Despatches, RG 59, Vol. 55.

43. Saldanha to First Lieutenant of the Army João de Miranda Ribeiro, Rio de Janeiro, December 15, 1892, and March 21, 1893, Arquivo do Serviço Geral da Marinha, Box 70; See also Souza e Silva, *O almirante Saldanha e a revolta da armada,* pp. 15–19, 28–42, 79–98, 120; Augusto Carlos de Souza e Silva, *O almirante Saldanha. Commandante em chefe na revolta da armada. Reminiscencias de um revoltoso* (Rio de Janeiro: Editôra A Noite, 1940), p. 9; *Notas de um revoltoso. (Diario de bordo). Documentos authenticos publicados pelo "Commercio de S. Paulo"* (Rio de Janeiro: Typ. Moraes, 1895), p. 135; João Dunshee de Abranches, *A revolta da armada e a revolução rio grandense. Correspondencia entre Saldanha da Gama e Silveira Martins* (Rio de Janeiro: M. Abranches, 1914), I, 9; Dunshee de Abranches, *Atas e atos do governo Lucena,* pp. 126–30; Carvalho, *O livro da minha vida,* pp. 114, 136, 172.

pupils quartered together under my personal supervision until the final conclusion of the conflict."[44]

As the revolt progressed, Saldanha da Gama's position grew less tenable. An impasse did occur after his declaration of neutrality, as he had foreseen, but his efforts to conciliate the two deadlocked groups and end the naval outbreak were unsuccessful. As one insurgent recalled, "during the whole time Admiral Melo was in the bay, the majority of the naval cadets were enthusiastic for our cause, and only Saldanha's iron discipline prevented them from joining the fleet."[45] The naval rebels continually attempted to persuade him, and Floriano's government put pressure on him to decide, while at the same time turning elsewhere for the aid necessary to crush the rebellion. Saldanha's "neutrality" became insupportable, and those under his command propelled him toward the insurgents. Finally, although he had never believed in the right of the armed forces to rebel against the government, he joined his comrades in their efforts to unseat Floriano.[46]

Saldanha's adherence to the revolt brought to the insurgents a number of men and young cadets whom they greatly needed. One of the problems constantly facing the naval rebels had been that of a limited fighting force, which prevented successful operations on land and even hindered sea maneuvers.

But Saldanha also brought his monarchist sympathies, which alienated many civilians and officers. In his manifesto deploring revolts, he blamed the terrible existing conditions

44. Saldanha to Naval Minister, *Jornal do Comércio*, September 26, 1893, p. 1.

45. *Notas de um revoltoso*, p. 109.

46. Souza e Silva, *O almirante Saldanha. Commandante em chefe na revolta da armada*, pp. 13–14, 27–38; Souza e Silva, *O almirante Saldanha e a revolta da armada*, pp. 113–18, 149, 179–80; *Notas de um revoltoso*, pp. 32–33, 109–13; Freire, *História da revolta*, pp. 232–39; Raul Villa-Lobos (pseud. Epaminondas Villalba), *A revolta da armada de 6 de setembro de 1893* (Rio de Janeiro: Laemmert & C., 1897), pp. 368–69.

and "militarism" on the "military sedition" of November 15, 1889, of which the "present government" was "nothing but a continuation." Therefore, Saldanha proposed that the nation be allowed to choose freely the form of government under which it wished to develop.[47]

This call for a plebiscite was construed as a desire to restore a fallen regime which had few sympathizers in the nation or in the navy. A few rebel officers abandoned their posts, and others attempted to explain away the manifesto. The government and its supporters redoubled their efforts to discredit the revolt as a monarchist movement. For example, one pro-Floriano paper referred to Saldanha as "the lackey of dictatorships" and condemned his "self-seeking and unpatriotic machinations" to restore "ancient, musty, and odious dynasties."[48] A new, somewhat insecure regime with a questionable legal status saw enemies everywhere, and, as in the Rio Grande conflict, claimed to be defending the republic against its monarchist opponents.

Although Melo and other naval officers continually denied any desire to restore the fallen regime, they could not completely free themselves from the monarchist taint. They did accept some money from monarchist sources, but the rumors of large contributions were greatly exaggerated and the naval rebels were often very short on funds.[49]

47. Saldanha manifesto, Ilha das Cobras, December 7, 1893, in Dunshee de Abranches, *A revolta da armada e a revolução*, I, 11–12.

48. *País*, December 15, 1893, p. 1.

49. See *Notas de um revoltoso*, pp. 135–39, 146–50; Mello, *O governo provisório*, II, 78, 314–19; Souza e Silva, *O almirante Saldanha e a revolta da armada*, pp. 302–305; Freire, *História constitucional*, III, 6–8; Dunshee de Abranches, *A revolta da armada*, I, 29–30, 68–69; II, 25–29; Saldanha to Carlos Landares, Montevideo, October 9, 1894, Arquivo do Serviço Geral de Marinha, Box 70; Conde de Leopoldina to Rui Barbosa, Lisbon, December 17, 1893; January 8, 1894; February 7, 1894; Arquivo da Casa de Rui Barbosa, Pasta Conde de Leopoldina.

The naval insurgents also lost potential civilian support through their failure to set up a civilian regime to replace that of Floriano, as some claimed they desired. Melo did attempt to institute a provisional government with the *Federalist* insurgents, but without success. These were two distinct movements, each composed of a number of disparate elements; both movements had great difficulties in suppressing internal conflicts, and neither could cooperate with members of another rebellion.

Not long after the outbreak of the Naval Revolt, Admiral Custódio de Melo began his efforts to form a provisional government with the *Federalist* insurgents. He had agreed with Silveira Martins, the *Federalist* leader, that the regime would include the *Federalists* and the local authorities in Santa Catarina, who were thought to be favorable to the revolutionary movements.[50] Late in September, 1893, Melo sent a naval officer who had been a participant in the Republican movement of November 15, 1889, Captain Frederico Guilherme Lorena, to Santa Catarina to make contact with the civilian and military revolutionaries from Rio Grande and to form a government. But the provisional regime he established in Santa Catarina on October 14, 1893, was composed solely of three naval officers. When Silveira Martins insisted that the regime be reorganized without "positivism and militarism," Melo wrote Captain Lorena to "reconstitute the provisional government," since they were "placed in the dire necessity of being an ally of the revolutionaries of Rio Grande."[51] But Lorena

50. Villa-Lobos, *A revolução federalista no Rio Grande do Sul,* xci–xcviii, 141–81; *Notas de um revoltoso,* p. 166; Melo to Lorena, Rio de Janeiro, October 10, 1893, in Villa-Lobos, *A revolução federalista,* pp. 147–49.

51. Gaspar da Silveira Martins to Custódio José de Melo, Montevideo, November 1, 1893, in Villa-Lobos, *A revolução federalista,* pp. 181–83; Melo to Captain Lorena, Rio de Janeiro, November, 1893, in Villa-Lobos, *A revolução federalista,* pp. 182–84.

angrily refused, holding Silveira Martins to be as bad as "Floriano and his troupe."[52]

Hoping to improve matters, Melo left for Santa Catarina. The *Federalist* forces had recently invaded that state, and early in December the various leaders met in Desterro, the seat of the provisional government. Bitter words were exchanged during the tumultuous meetings between Melo, the other naval officers, and representatives of the Rio Grande revolutionaries. Unable to achieve any satisfactory cooperation with Lorena or with the representatives of Silveira Martins, Melo decided to cruise along the coast and did not return to Rio de Janeiro. One of the naval members of the provisional government joined the *Federalists,* and one of Melo's chief subordinates left for Rio to serve under Saldanha.[53]

The Naval Revolt was a military undertaking, and, as one of the insurgents admitted, "the civilian contribution to the revolt in Rio was insignificant."[54] Only a handful of civilians believed the naval officer's claims that they were fighting against tyranny and for civilian control. Civilians could see that a military revolt was not the best way to end military rule. If this naval insurrection had succeeded, the probabilities of the rebels' handing the government over to civilians were slight, and future revolts by discontented and jealous military elements would be encouraged. The civilians could not come to power through alliances with insurgent military factions. Although some civilians remained relatively aloof from this

52. Lorena to Melo, Desterro, November 26, 1893, in Villa-Lobos, *A revolução federalista,* pp. 186–88. See also Lieutenant J. Machado to Melo, Desterro, October 17, 1893, Arquivo Nacional, Cx 1209.

53. *Notas de um revoltoso,* pp. 166–69; Villa-Lobos, *A revolução federalista,* xcix–cv, 187, 256; Saldanha da Gama to Carlos Landeres, Montevideo, November 21, 1894, Arquivo do Serviço Geral da Marinha, Box 70; Demétrio Ribeiro to Melo, Buenos Aires, November 16, 1893, Arquivo Nacional, Cx 1209.

54. Souza e Silva, *O almirante Saldanha. Commandante em chefe na revolta da armada,* p. 123.

conflict, which they viewed as a struggle for supremacy between two military groups, others aided Floriano and through their desperately needed support helped return the country to civilian rule.

When the revolt broke out, Floriano reacted quickly, calling in army and police forces and mobilizing the national guard. He arrested opponents, placed controls on communications and the press, and put pressure on Congress to declare martial law. Since the insurgents controlled all the naval vessels in the country, Floriano set to work acquiring a new fleet. After unsuccessfully attempting to purchase United States ships in the Rio harbor, he contracted for vessels, at high cost, in the United States and Europe.[55]

In addition to the presence of a hostile fleet in the harbor of Rio de Janeiro and the revolution in the southern states, another uprising was threatening in the north, in Pernambuco. The commander of the local military district there complained that, "frankly speaking, indiscipline has reached the highest degree" and that "some officers of this garrison" were involved in a separation attempt of the whole northern part of the country.[56] But the governor of Pernambuco, who was loyal to Floriano, his comrade in arms, took measures against those who were "daily insulting and slandering the federal government," and nothing serious developed.[57]

After more than six months of resistance to the government of Marshal Floriano Peixoto, the Naval Revolt collapsed. The

55. Thompson to Gresham, October 2, 1893, National Archives, Brazil, Despatches, RG 59, Vol. 55; For ship negotiations in the United States, see correspondence and reports, Arquivo Nacional, Cx 1198, and reports of Minister Salvador de Mendonça, Arquivo Histórico do Ministério das Relações Exteriores, Missões Diplomaticas Brasileiras, 233/4/11, Washington, Oficios, 1893–96.

56. J. Vicente Leite de Castro to Floriano, Recife, November 7, 1893, Arquivo Nacional, Cx 1198.

57. Alexander Barbosa Lima to Floriano, Pernambuco, October 27, 1893, Arquivo Nacional, Cx 1198.

insurgents received little support outside the navy, the army remained basically loyal to Floriano, and some civilians also aided the government. The assistance given Floriano by these civilians, particularly those from the powerful state of São Paulo, proved devastating. Moreover, the insurgents themselves were far from united. The *Federalists* from Rio Grande do Sul refused to cooperate, and the leaders within the navy were always at odds. Admirals Melo and Wandenkolk had long opposed each other as well as Floriano, and Wandenkolk refused to give his "approval to the Naval Revolt" since Melo headed it.[58] Melo and Saldanha, both sensitive men with quick tempers, also found cooperation difficult.

Another factor in the failure of the insurrection was the intervention of foreign ships in the harbor of Rio de Janeiro. Under pressure from them the rebels had agreed not to shell the defenseless city, and the government had promised to do nothing to provoke such a bombardment. However, Floriano fortified the city and had time to build up his own fleet. When Saldanha was in charge of operations in the bay, he attempted a more vigorous policy, and relations between the insurgents and the foreign ships, especially the American ones, grew worse. Saldanha tried to "prevent merchandise passing into the customhouse" to deprive the government of needed revenue.[59] But this ran counter to the aims of the United States foreign policy of promoting commercial expansion in the agitated and depression-ridden 1890's. Brazil had signed a reciprocal trade agreement with the United States, and the Cleveland government felt that under Floriano, rather than

58. Eduardo Wandenkolk to Marshal Eneás Galvão, Fortaleza de Santa Cruz, September 7, 1893, in Ouro Prêto "Armada Nacional," *A década republicana*, V, 93.

59. Statement of British Consulate General, Rio de Janeiro, December 12, 1893, National Archives, U.S. Legation, Brazil, RG 84, Communications with Naval Officers and Others.

under the insurgents, Brazil would remain open as a market for American goods.[60] In January, 1894, the commander of the American squadron in the harbor denied Saldanha the right to establish a blockade and warned him that molesting of American vessels would not be permitted. On January 29, Saldanha was forced to pull back his ships, following a show of force and determination by the powerful American squadron. The way was then open for normal commercial activity in the harbor of Rio de Janeiro.[61] The importance of this intervention was recognized by Floriano's friends, who held demonstrations in honor of American solidarity and later would even erect a statue to Monroe, celebrate the fourth of July, and serenade the American ambassador.[62]

After a final vain and bloody attempt to capture the arsenal

60. See Walter LaFeber, *The New Empire: An Interpretation of American Expansion, 1860–1898* (Ithaca: Cornell University Press, 1963).

During this period Great Britain was viewed as one of the chief roadblocks to the Latin American markets needed by the United States, and the British seemed willing to accept Saldanha's blockade. However, American intervention was not the main cause of the collapse of this revolt.

61. Many Brazilians have tended to believe that American policy was governed by a fear of monarchism in the hemisphere and by a belief that the insurgent movement was dominated by monarchists. For differing Brazilian interpretations of the American action, see Joaquim Nabuco, *A intervenção estrangeira durante a revolta* (Rio de Janeiro: Freitas Bastos & Cia., 1932); Freire, *História da revolta de 6 de setembro de 1893*, pp. 308–28; Sérgio Corrêa da Costa, *A diplomacia do marechal. Intervenção estrangeira na revolta da armada* (Rio de Janeiro: Ed. Zélio Valverde, 1945), pp. 71–73, 191–205.

Some of the naval insurgents were well aware of the economic motivation behind the American action, as was, for example, the anonymous author of *Notas de um revoltoso,* (pp. 173–74). In an interview in an American newspaper, Saldanha da Gama denounced American "interference in Brazilian affairs" and declared that "whatever commercial advantages the United States won by the outcome of the affair at Rio" would "only be temporary." (New York *Herald,* May 6, 1894, p. 10). Compare this cognizance of American motives with LaFeber, *The New Empire,* p. 211. In September of 1894 the reciprocity treaty was abrogated by the Floriano government.

62. Thompson to Gresham, November 10, 1893, June 17, 1894; July 12, 1894; November 21, 1894; National Archives, U.S. Legation, Brazil, RG 59, Vols. 55–57; *País,* November 17, 1894, p. 2; Caldas, *A deshonra da república,* pp. 204–207; New York *Herald,* May 6, 1894, p. 10.

at Niterói, directly across the bay from the city of Rio de Janeiro, the rebels lost all hope of success. Their supply of food and arms dwindled, and no aid arrived from Melo in the south. Finally, on March 13, 1894, they surrendered and sought refuge on the Portuguese ships in the harbor. Later Saldanha, along with some of the other rebel officers, joined the *Federalists* in Rio Grande do Sul, where he died in battle in June, 1895, two months before that long struggle drew to a close. Melo sought exile abroad. While many factors, including foreign intervention, had played a part in the defeat of this naval attempt to unseat Floriano, the support the Marshal received from crucial civilian sectors, especially the *Paulistas,* and the lack of effective cooperation among those opposing the government proved decisive.

This was the last and most serious of the military revolts against the Floriano regime. No longer would any military group see a possibility of success in challenging him, and major military rebellions against the government would be discouraged for years to come. While some civilians were involved in a few of the incidents, the uprisings stemmed from military rivalries as well as from attitudes and beliefs found in the officer corps. Some civilians would be able to profit from these military divergencies, and the Naval Revolt would provide them with the opportunity to end the years of direct military rule which followed the proclamation of the republic in 1889.

CHAPTER IV

Political Attitudes of the Officers

THE CONTINUED PARTICIPATION of both army and navy officers in the military revolts and incidents of the early years of the republic reflected a widespread view that such activities lay within their rightful sphere of action. Since the days of the "military question" under the empire, officers had refused to condone any doctrine of "passive obedience." Furthermore, many felt that the civilian politicians were unequal to the task of governing the nation and considered that the army, because of its proclamation of the republic, must exercise a special responsibility for the destiny of the republic. Positivist thought, which influenced many of the younger officers, also helped to encourage their political activities. On the other hand, a number of older officers looked down on their younger, philosophizing colleagues and on their political activities, although they themselves were involved in such affairs.

Still others opposed military participation in politics altogether but were unable to impose these views on the officer corps as a whole, especially while the government remained in military hands. In their political beliefs, as in their political activities, the Brazilian armed forces were far from united.

Some officers were coming to believe that the armed forces must play the part of arbitrator, a role somewhat similar to that once exercised by the emperor with his moderating power.[1] They would stand above party and group strife and ensure the proper decisions for the defense of the constitution, the rights of the nation, and the republic. Many felt that the army was entrusted with a special historic mission, which had led it to declare a republic and consequently assume the responsibility for the direction of that republic. Discussions on various political issues, such as those in the Club Militar, were justified by the reminder "that the military has become responsible for everything which has occurred in our country since the 15th of November" of 1889.[2] The officers' political manifestoes usually included a reference to the role of the "members of the military estate" as "the sustainers of the Federal Republic."[3] As one officer insisted, "the historic mission of embodying the summation of national aspirations was reserved to the armed forces."[4] He believed that the army's "mission is not to govern nor to direct the Nation. But it is certain that it will

1. For a modern exposition of the role of the army as a moderating force, see Gilberto Freyre, *Ordem e progresso. Processo de desintegração das sociedades patriarcal e semipatriarcal no Brasil sob o regime de trabalho livre. Aspectos de um quase meio seculo de transição do trabalho excravo para o trabalho livre, e da monarquia para a república* (Rio de Janeiro: José Olympio, 1959), I, 50.

2. Atas of Club Militar, Session of General Assembly, October 11, 1890.

3. Lieutenant Colonel Hermes Rodrigues da Fonseca and Captain Clodoaldo da Fonseca, "À nação," Rio de Janeiro, February 18, 1892, in *País*, February 19, 1892, p. 3.

4. Lauro Sodré, open letter to the Republican electorate of Pará, August 15, 1890, in *Crenças e opiniões* (Belém: Typ. do Diário Official, 1896), p. 259.

always influence its destinies . . . to maintain the work of November 15th, which it had so powerfully helped to create. . . . In the crises which can still place the life of the new regime in jeopardy, . . . the army will have to act as a necessary factor for the salvation of the Republic."[5]

Violent opposition to the doctrine of "passive obedience" had characterized the "military question" of the 1880's and had extended into the republic. For example, one motion of the Club Militar attacked any "despotism attempting to reduce the soldier to an unthinking instrument, a servile and automatic machine, through the principle of passive obedience."[6] Benjamin Constant Botelho de Magalhães, a principal figure in the establishment of the republic and the first war minister in the provisional government, reflected military opposition to the concept of passive obedience and stressed the military role in ensuring the progress of the nation and the republic. For him, the soldier should never be "a servile and malleable instrument through passive and unthinking obedience." Rather, he should be "the embodiment of the national honor and an important co-operator toward progress" and "the intelligent and well-intentioned support of republican institutions."[7]

Officers participating in military movements ranging from minor manifestations to the Naval Revolt justified their behavior by the need to "save the nation" and the republic and the duty not to remain passive servants of the government. As one former officer proudly noted when he buckled on his sword and set out to participate in the November 23, 1891,

5. Lauro Sodré, *A proclamação da república* (Rio de Janeiro: Serviço Gráfico do Ministerio da Educação, 1939), p. 44.

6. Atas of Club Militar, Session of General Assembly, November 5, 1890.

7. Brazil, Ministério da Guerra, *Relatorio apresentado ao presidente da República dos Estados Unidos do Brazil pelo general de brigada Benjamin Constant de Botelho Magalhães* (Rio de Janeiro: Imprensa Nacional, 1890), p. 33.

movement against Marshal Deodoro da Fonseca, he was acting "to defend the integrity of the national soil and to guarantee the nation's institutions which govern us: it is a commitment of honor and, from the moment that we do not know how to satisfy or fulfill it, we shall cease to be officers and become vile mercenaries whose guiding principle is 'to serve, indifferently, whoever pays the highest wages.' "[8] The possession of such a right of intervention, and the recognition by civilians of its existence, meant that a mere threat was sufficient.

Many officers seem to have thought little of the civilian politicians who were accustomed to ruling the nation. On the eve of the overthrow of the monarchy, in one of the "blood pacts" of loyalty drawn up by groups of Benjamin Constant's youthful followers, a number of students of the Military School railed against the "holders of law degrees monopolizing the nation's government."[9] Under the republic the officers in government continued to speak disdainfully of the *casacas* (literally, full dress or frock coats), and their inability to rule the country properly. Deodoro was also impatient with civilians, and, not long before his overthrow in November, 1891, one reporter noted that "his bad mood, on this occasion, was manifested especially against the *casacas*, as the civilians were habitually termed in military circles."[10] In presenting reasons for accepting his resignation, one naval minister under Floriano could think of no stronger way to describe the insufficiency of his power than to say that "the minister is no better than a mere signer of decrees, and can be even a *casaca*."[11]

8. José Carlos de Carvalho, *O livro da minha vida*, p. 143.

9. *Ata da Sessão do Club Militar de 9 de novembro de 1889. Coleção de pactos de sangue e mensagens, recebidos por Benjamin Constant* (Rio de Janeiro: Gab. Fotocartográfico do Ministério da Guerra, 1939; unpaged).

10. Dunshee de Abranches, *Atas e atos do governo Lucena*, p. 62.

11. Coelho Neto to Floriano, Rio de Janeiro, June 1, 1894, Arquivo Nacional, Cx 1209.

On one occasion Benjamin Constant pointed out the officers' sense of mission and consciousness of exercising a protective role within the nation, as well as expressing the feeling that the people did not properly appreciate them. During a speech intended to calm the various elements of the provisional regime and to deny rumors that a dictatorship was to be proclaimed, Benjamin virtually accused the nation of injustice and ingratitude for not having placed absolute confidence in the deserving soldiers. As the local press reported, he "accused the people of common ambition and ingratitude, not recognizing the good which had been done it, and attempting to bite the hand which protected it." He reiterated the fact that the army had always shielded and defended political liberties throughout Brazilian history.[12]

Even officers opposing the government demonstrated hostility toward civilian politicians. One vehement adversary of Marshal Floriano Peixoto, General Honorato Caldas, attacked the basically civilian Congress for having obsequiously lent itself to Floriano's "machiavellian," unpatriotic machinations and declared that history would term this body "a congress of unscrupulous henchmen, of incompetents; an anonymity."[13] Another of Floriano's officer-opponents, Jacques Ourique, condemned the Congress as being "composed in large part of execrable and docile instruments of the most unbridled ambitions and interests."[14] He referred to the civilian management of the *País*, a pro-Floriano newspaper, as "thieving *casacas*."[15] Although he considered himself a Republican, he expressed contempt for both monarchical and Republican statesmen. The monarchists, in their blindness, had served the

12. *País*, February 17, 1890, p. 1.
13. Honorato Caldas, *A deshonra da república*, pp. 54–56.
14. Jacques Ourique, *O drama do Paraná. Episódios da tyrannia do marechal Floriano Peixoto* (Buenos Aires: n.p., 1894), p. 12.
15. *Ibid.*, p. 19.

monarchy, not the nation; and the Republicans, mere job seekers, had shown themselves "incapable and inept for the methodical, scientific, and practical organization of a free country and a republic created in accord with the grandiose conception of South American liberty."[16]

One of the strongest intellectual influences affecting the political behavior of the officers, particularly the younger ones, was positivism. Benjamin Constant, "the idol of the youth," according to one of his devoted pupils,[17] had greatly contributed to the spread of positivist and Republican ideas while professor of mathematics at the Military School. For some twenty years he had taught in military schools in Rio de Janeiro and had served as a channel for the diffusion of positivist thought, which became the dominant philosophy in the Military School.[18]

Those who considered themselves positivists did not hold to a uniform set of beliefs. Two different schools of positivism found many adherents in Brazil. Miguel Lemos and Raimundo Teixeira Mendes, the leaders of the Brazilian Positivist Apostolate, followed Pierre Lafitte and orthodox Comtian ideas on social and religious matters and on the organization of society, laying great stress on the preponderance of the

16. Jacques Ourique, "A revolução de 6 de setembro," *Correio da Tarde*, January 3, 1896, p. 1.

17. Lauro Muller, "Conferencia commemorativa do 15 de november," *Jornal do Comércio*, November 16, 1921, p. 3.

18. The main military academy, founded in 1810 by João VI, had long included courses of civil engineering, and the separation between the civil and military studies was only begun in 1858 and completed in 1874, when the Central School became the Polytechnic School and the Military School a separate institution, thus divorcing the two groups and possibly contributing to a feeling of military alienation and group pride.

The Escola Militar in Rio de Janeiro was the most important though not the sole army academy in Brazil training the young officers. The one in Pôrto Alegre, a similar degree-granting institution for most of this period, was also strongly positivistic in orientation. In addition, there were several preparatory schools, schools of practice, and a school for sergeants. Later a war college was created for superior officers.

family and on the importance of individual liberties. In political terms, August Comte, the founder of positivism, conceived of Western civilization as having entered the transitional period between the metaphysical and the positive eras of history. The French Revolution had put an end to monarchy as a legitimate form of government, and Comte advocated a temporary Republican dictatorship to succeed it and to bring about order and progress, incorporating the proletariat into modern society. In this proposed republic, power would be concentrated in the hands of one man who would be virtually unchecked, even by a legislature devoted exclusively to budgetary matters, but full civil liberties would be respected.

The other type of positivism current in Brazil in the latter part of the nineteenth century was a more heretical variety, that of Emile Littré. This was the positivism of Benjamin Constant, under whose auspices positivist moral and political ideas penetrated the military academies. Benjamin and others of this school rejected the religious aspects of positivism and concentrated more on the method of positivism and on some of its political and moral aspects. This type of positivism was never transformed into a sect, with its own cult and forms of worship, as was the Brazilian Positivist Apostolate.

Many of the young officers subscribed to neither of the two schools of positivism existent in Brazil. Their ideas were often nebulous and only partially positivist. They had not studied Comte as deeply or as carefully as the erudite gentlemen of the Positivist Apostolate. The young officers frequently selected the authoritarian connotations of this doctrine and interpreted to their own liking the positivist concept of a republican dictatorship, which according to orthodox theory would not be under military control. They did not fully accept the positivism of August Comte or that of Benjamin Constant. Orthodox positivism stressed evolution, not revolution, but Benjamin and his students had been the most enthusiastic Republicans advocating the overthrow of the empire through military force, and many continued to be involved in political demonstrations and revolts. The ideas of the French positivists were often poorly assimilated, and the result was sometimes a half-baked positivism, full of undigested lumps of thought.

Positivist influence on the new republican government stemmed from the general intellectual climate and spirit engendered by the varieties of positivist thought in Brazil rather than from the efforts of any organized positivist movement or group. The Positivist Apostolate was not able to influence events as it wished. Shortly after the proclamation of the republic, Miguel Lemos and Teixeira Mendes attempted a rapprochement with Benjamin Constant, who had broken with them several years earlier. No doubt they hoped to increase their influence over the young republic through its war minister and take advantage of this excellent opportunity to put their ideas into practice. They presented Benjamin with a model for a constitution to transform the provisional Republican government into a positivist Republican dictatorship, with basically all of the power being exercised by one man, who would be limited only by a legislature with purely budgetary powers.[19] They also urged this form of government direct-

19. Miguel Lemos and Raimundo Teixeira Mendes, *Bazes de uma constituição ditatorial federativa para a república brazileira* (Rio de Janeiro; Na Séde do Apostolado Pozitivista do Brazil, 1890). Note especially Title IV on the dictator and Title VII on the budgetary assembly. See also Raimundo Teixeira Mendes, *Exame do Projecto da Constituição apresentado pelo Governo Provisorio e Indicação das correcções indispensaveis para harmonisar sufficientemente tal projecto com as exigencias capitaes da situação brazileira* (Rio de Janeiro: Na Séde do Apostolado Pozitivista do Brazil, 1890); Miguel Lemos, *Constitução sem Constituinte* (Rio de Janeiro: Tip. Central de Evaristo Costa, 1890); Miguel Lemos and Raimundo Teixeira Mendes, *Representação enviado ao Congresso Nacional propondo modificação no projecto do Constituição apresentado pelo Governo e contendo como annexo o opusculo "Razões*

ly on the provisional Republican regime and the Constituent Assembly, but to no avail. The Constitution of 1891 overwhelmingly reflected its federalist, liberal origins and exhibited virtually no positivist influence.

The first few years of the republic, nevertheless, were the period of greatest positivist strength in Brazil, in the government as well as among the officers and in many intellectual circles. A number of positivists held government positions; they helped to effect long-sought reforms, such as the separation of church and state, and attempted to enact some labor laws. But the positivists were not the only ones who desired these reforms.

Perhaps the greatest purely positivist victory was the adoption of a national flag with the positivist motto, "Order and Progress." The flag engendered strong feelings on all sides and remained a particularly touchy matter for the positivist inclined officers. Any possible attempt to change it led to protests against such a "highly criminal" project by "our political charlatans" who would "profane the memory" of Benjamin Constant, the "Founder of the Brazilian Republic."[20]

---

contra a lei de grande naturalisação" (Rio de Janeiro: Na Séde do Apostolado Pozitivista do Brazil, 1890). They also promoted books dealing with the republican dictatorship, such as Jorge Lagarrigue's *A ditadura republicana segundo Augusto Comte* trans. J. Mariano de Oliveira (Rio de Janeiro: Apostolado Pozitivista do Brazil, 1897).

20. Students of Escola Superior da Guerra, September 16, 1892, in *Jornal do Comércio*, September 18, 1892, p. 5; see also Mello, *O governo provisório*, II, 11–23; *Rio News*, September 6, 1892, p. 5.

Of the studies on positivism in Brazil, João Cruz Costa, *O positivismo na república. Notas sobre a história do positivismo do Brasil* (São Paulo: Companhia Editôria Nacional, 1956), provides a good introduction, especially to Brazilian positivism in its later phases, while Ivan Lins, *História do positivismo no Brasil* (São Paulo: Companhia Editôra Nacional, 1964), is a more detailed study. Also useful are João Cruz Costa, *Contribuição a história das idéias no Brasil (O desenvolvimento da filosofia no Brasil e a evolução histórica nacional)* (Rio de Janeiro: José Olympio, 1956) and João Camillo de Oliveira Torres, *O positivismo no Brasil,* 2d ed. (Petrópolis: Editôra Vozes, Ltda., 1957).

Of the voluminous writings of the positivist leaders on the various reforms,

On December 11, 1889, in the presence of Benjamin Constant, at a meeting in honor of Demétrio Ribeiro, a positivist from Rio Grande do Sul newly appointed Minister of Agriculture in the provisional government, several young officers and positivists gave speeches demonstrating their advocacy of a "republican dictatorship." Lieutenant Captain Nelson de Almeida, the "representative of the fleet," expressed "most ardent hopes" for "the installation of a definitive government which would concentrate all power in the hands of a single man," instead of the existing provisional regime, which, he granted, "had shown itself capable of safeguarding the order and progress of the nation." He concluded that to have "a stable, happy, and prosperous republic, it is necessary that the government be dictatorial and not parliamentary." Then Augusto Tasso Fragoso spoke, declaring that he was representing the "Brazilian army, which had taken upon itself the task of regenerating our country"; he also praised the "doctrine of this new philosophy."[21]

Many of these beliefs are summarized in a statement by a former student of Benjamin Constant. This young officer declared that the army had a glorious mission to perform, and that the army was "largely a product of the military schools, where they [the officers] were taught and absorbed the most

---

the following are of interest: Miguel Lemos, *A separação da igreja do estado. Os dias santificados* (Rio de Janeiro: Tip. Central de Evaristo Costa, March, 1890); Miguel Lemos, *A secularização dos cemiterios* (Rio de Janeiro: Tip. Central de Evaristo Costa, March, 1890); Miguel Lemos, *O calendario positivista* (Rio de Janeiro: Apostolado Pozitivista do Brasil, February, 1890); Miguel Lemos, *A liberdade de profissões i o regulamento para o serviço domestico (*Rio de Janeiro: Tip. Central de Evaristo Costa Apostolado, February, 1890); Raymundo Teixeira Mendes, *A bandeira nacional. Representação enviada ao Congresso Nacional propondo modificações* (Rio de Janeiro: Central do Apostolado Pozitivista do Brasil, 1890); Raymundo Teixeira Mendes, *A commemoração civica de Benjamin Constant e a liberdade religiosa* (Rio de Janeiro: Na Séde Central do Apostolado Pozitivista do Brasil, September, 1892).

21. *Diário Oficial,* December 14, 1889, p. 3.

salutary philosophical principles and the most advanced theories in all departments of positivist knowledge."[22]

Benjamin and his pupils tended to believe in the right and duty of the army to guard Brazil's destiny, and this presupposed their participation in the political process, at least in times of crisis. Some understood the positivist concept of a "republican dictatorship" to be that of strong one-man rule, preferably exercised by a military man. The vague positivist beliefs of a large number of officers who passed through the military schools were chiefly important in propelling them toward a desire for "progress," a belief in a republic, and a dislike of many of the practices of previous civilian governments. Many officers already had an awareness of the importance of the armed forces and a desire to act; the philosophy of Comte furnished them with an additional element of cohesion and purpose.

A number of officers complained that the military schools were emphasizing theoretical studies to the detriment of professional training. For some years after the death of Benjamin Constant in 1891, the intellectual emphasis of the military academies continued to be positivist. One army officer, who favored the creation of a general staff system and the professionalization of the army so that it would become a small, disciplined, well-trained, and fully equipped military organization, criticized "the large number of military schools which we possess unnecessarily, and where today the religion of humanity is still taught, with a scandalous omission of proper military instruction and the discipline of the army."[23] Jacques Ourique, an army officer long immersed in politics, attacked Benjamin Constant for giving such power in the early days

22. Lauro Sodré, open letter to the Republican electorate of Pará, August 15, 1890, in *Crenças o opiniões*, p. 262.

23. Captain Gabriel Salgado, in *Cidade do Rio*, September 24, 1897, p. 1.

of the republic "to the young positivists of the military schools and the army" and for "innocently confiding in the patriotism and thinking ability of the youth he educated in the discipline of an incipient sect whose doctrines are still subject to scientific controversy."[24]

Several of the older officers felt that this excessively theoretical education was impairing the fighting ability of the army and casting a shadow over its future. According to Jacques Ourique, during the last twenty years the military schools had been transformed from "establishments making good soldiers into factories producing cliques of degree holders, more apt at their unwholesome altruistic mysticism, constructing abstract conceptions of platonic republics, than for the rude task of commanding battalions."[25] Admiral Custódio de Melo criticized the instruction in the Naval School, from which "the students depart full of theory, but almost devoid of practice, for the instruction there of the proper military sciences is very incomplete."[26] Even one of Deodoro's officer-brothers feared for the future of an army composed in large part of "boys, coming from the schools, but without judgment and poorly trained."[27]

The younger officers had often entered the Military School more in search of an education than because of a fascination for the profession of arms, and the education they received was in keeping with this desire. It was immaterial to them whether or not this served the aims of the army.

The political discontent of these younger officers is perhaps

24. Jacques Ourique, in *Correio da Tarde,* January 15, 1896, p. 1.

25. *Ibid.,* December 31, 1895, p. 1.

26. Brazil, Ministério da Marinha, *Relatorio apresentado ao vice-presidente da República dos Estados Unidos do Brasil pelo contra-admirante Custódio José de Mello, ministro de estado dos negocios da marinha* (Rio de Janeiro: Imprensa Nacional, 1892), p. 8.

27. Pedro Paulino da Fonseca to Clodoaldo da Fonseca, Maceió, September 8, 1890, Clodoaldo da Fonseca Papers.

related to their low social origins and to the desire to improve their status which led them to enter the Military School. According to this argument, they were poor, ambitious boys who had chosen a military career in order to obtain a free education.[28]

Various officers and civilians of the period held views similar to this. Teixeira Mendes, in his biography of Benjamin Constant, stressed the fact that the Military School was an accessible avenue of education for poor boys. Ximeno Villeroy, one of Benjamin's pupils, recalled that Benjamin, "like so many others, sought out the army to be able to study, in order to clear a path for himself in the world."[29] Another of Benjamin's pupils, Vicente Licínio Cardoso, also described the military School as a haven for "poor boys," and as a home for the Republican spirit, unlike the navy."[30] His daughter later de-

28. Among the contemporary writers who are inclined to such a view is Cruz Costa, who holds that "boys of poor origin," that is, the petit bourgeoisie, not the lower class, sought the Military School "to acquire an education there which their small family resources could not provide" (João Cruz Costa, *Contribuição à história*, p. 364). San Tiago Dantas has stressed "the identification of the army with the middle class"; from this new class, whose sympathies the agrarian monarchy was unable to win, the army chose its officers (Francisco Clementino de San Tiago Dantas, *Dois momentos de Rui Barbosa* [Rio de Janeiro: Casa de Rui Barbosa, 1949], pp. 17–19). Gilberto Freyre has also emphasized the democratic origins of the army officers and describes the army as a social ladder for many mulattoes, in contrast to the white, aristocratic navy (Freyre, *Ordem e progresso*, I, 46; Freyre, *The Mansions and Shanties* [*Sobrados e mucambos*], trans. *Harriet de Onís* [New York: Alfred A. Knopf, 1963], pp. 368–69). An army officer, Nelson Werneck Sodré, is another who postulates a middle-class origin for education-minded army officers (Nelson Werneck Sodré, *Formação histórica do Brasil* [São Paulo: Editôra Brasiliense, 1962], pp. 270–74). A second officer, Francisco de Paula Cidade, held that the majority of the Military School pupils of that period were "youths of modest circumstances, who sought out the army to be able to study" (Francisco de Paula Cidade, "O exército em 1889. Resumo histórico," in *A república brazileira*, p. 250).

29. August Ximeno de Villeroy, *Benjamin Constant e a política republicana* (Rio de Janeiro, 1928), p. 2.

30. Vicente Licínio Cardoso, "Benjamin Constant," in *À margem da história da república (Ideaes, crenças, e affirmações)* (Rio de Janeiro: Edição do Annuario do Brasil, [1924]), p. 296.

scribed his own entrance into the Military School as "the only way of acquiring the instruction he craved."[31] According to a civilian observer of the period, the army officer corps contained many "poor boys" of middle-class origins, and often of mixed races, who had sought out the Military School less from love of a military career than from a desire to distinguish and improve themselves. They were more receptive to political change than the naval officers, who were more aristocratic in social origins and education.[32]

Some contemporaries were in partial disagreement about the social origins of the army officers. Joaquim Saldanha Marinho, the head of the Republican Party under the empire, when defending a number of pupils of the Military School who were being punished by the imperial government for political activities, referred to the cadets as "representatives of the first families of the empire."[33] An officer who had entered the Military School in Rio de Janeiro in the mid-1880's recalled that "at this time, no selection was made for admission to the school . . . influence (*pistolão*) resolved everything."[34]

The lack of biographical data on all but a few of the higher ranking officers makes it difficult to substantiate contentions as to the existence and nature of close ties between the army and the rising middle class.

The available information seems to indicate that there was no strong middle-class consciousness in the army, since there was a general lack of such consciousness throughout the nation. The middle class lacked decisive political strength as

31. Leontina Licínio Cardoso, *Licínio Cardoso, seu pensamento, sua obra, sua vida* (Rio de Janeiro: Ed. Zélio Valverde, 1944), pp. 42, 45–50.

32. Freire, *História constitucional da república*, II, 219–20.

33. Joaquim Saldanha Marinho, *Revista Federal*, I, No. 9 (February 5, 1887), p. 2.

34. Hastimphilo de Moura, *Da primeira à segunda república* (Rio de Janeiro: Irmãos Pongetti, 1936), p. 29.

well as social and ideological cohesion.[35] Certainly the army officer corps as a whole could not have represented the middle class or taken any position reflecting coherent middle-class views since neither the army nor the middle class was unified.

While the younger officers were not as powerful a factor as some writers believed, they did antagonize other groups of officers, and this added to the turmoil of the period. Their activities, beliefs, and training aroused the hostilities of quite a few politically active senior officers. Many of the older army officers had not gone through the military schools, nor had they passed through the hands of Benjamin Constant and other positivist-inclined professors. Like Jacques Ourique, they might glory in "the real man, courageous and firm in the clear and plain conviction of his duty as a soldier and a citizen,"and scorn "that positivist load of degree-holders" and those "pretentious and vain semi-ignoramuses."[36] The differences in educational background and interests between the two groups did tend to promote friction and hostility.[37]

Many of the high-ranking officers who scorned their younger positivist-educated colleagues were themselves deeply involved in the political movements of the period. Since the days of the "military question," and perhaps partially due to those developments under the empire, officers like Jacques Ourique had participated in movements against the government. He criticized the political activities of Benjamin's students, but he himself had taken part with Deodoro da Fonseca in the overthrow of the empire. Perhaps a personal loyalty, such as he bore toward Deodoro, was another factor governing his politi-

35. See Nícia Villela Luz, "O papel das classes médias brasileiras no movimento republicano," *Revista de História*, No. 57 (January–March, 1964), pp. 13–27.

36. Jacques Ourique, *Correio da Tarde*, December 31, 1895, p. 1.

37. See Francisco de Paula Cidade, "O exército em 1889. Resumo histórico," in *A república brazileira*, pp. 249–51.

cal activities. Honorato Caldas, a veteran of the "military question," also continued to be preoccupied with governmental affairs. When the Club Militar expelled the thirteen generals and admirals who had signed the 1892 manifesto urging Floriano to hold a presidential election, he leaped to their defense and accused the young officers in the Club Militar of being "the disciples chastising the masters," for they felt that "for majors and captains it is lawful to interpret the constitution, but not for generals!"[38]

Both these officers were enemies of Marshal Floriano Peixoto and therefore could justify military revolts while at the same time attacking his regime as a military despotism. For them, military movements against the government were valid whenever they personally opposed the government. Caldas attacked the Marshal in a series of newspaper articles in 1892 as the "tyrant" who behaved like the terrible dictators Rosas of Argentina and López of Paraguay, and who seduced his country like a "Brazilian Napoleon."[39] And Caldas defended the Naval Revolt and the *Federalist* revolution. While he accused Floriano of running a "government of the sword," Caldas himself was inclined to use the same weapon when attacking Floriano's regime. Jacques Ourique, a vehement supporter of officers' rights during the empire and the provisional Republican regime, spoke out against the growth in size of the armed forces and their budgets only while Floriano occupied the presidency. He attacked Floriano as a "miserable and cruel idiot," as an "eternal falsifier, eternal liar," and as "wretchedly insane."[40] Before the outbreak of the Naval Revolt, he accused the Marshal of having "ineptly and criminally prepared all the possible elements for a conflagration."[41] He

38. Caldas, *A legalidade de 23 de novembro,* p. 47.
39. *Combate,* May 10, 1892, p. 1; June 1, 1892, p. 1.
40. Jacques Ourique, *O drama do Paraná,* pp. 16–17.
41. Quoted in Caldas, *A legalidade de 23 de novembro,* p. 247.

joined the revolt, a purely military insurrection, which he justified as a "revolt of liberty against the tyranny of Marshal Floriano Peixoto," and he participated in the final phase of the *Federalist* revolt.[42]

The most concrete and well-defined attitude of the officers was their conviction of their right to participate vigorously in government, speaking out freely on all issues, and to increase the size and importance of the armed forces. Ever since the days of the "military question," officers had demanded the right to publish their opinions in the press on virtually any subject, including government policies. The Club Militar, for example, continued to maintain a press commission. Although Deodoro, and especially Floriano, had a few officers arrested or censured for publicly disagreeing with their policies, the officers did not remain silent. Any incident or act could, and usually did, elicit a spate of military charges and countercharges in the press.

At the same time, the officers were intolerant of any published comments critical of them or their politics. While such an attitude was never clearly enunciated, it became evident from their actions. Ever since the days of the provisional government and the attack on the *Tribuna* in November, 1890, various officers had moved against opposition newspapers and editors, both in the capital and in the states. In times of crisis, the officer-dominated government imposed severe restrictions on the press and telegraph system. Even foreign newspapers complained that there was "rigid censorship of all messages" and that it was "difficult to get accurate news of the war in Rio Grande do Sul."[43]

During the Naval Revolt the press suffered even more. Various newspapers in the capital and throughout the country sus-

42. Jacques Ourique, *O drama do Paraná*, p. 6.
43. New York *Herald*, July 13, 1893, p. 3; August 8, 1893, p. 7.

pended publication and some offices were wrecked. After mid-September of 1893, most of the Rio de Janeiro journals gave little daily news, let alone news of rebel activities, and a number were closed by the police.[44] The *Jornal do Comércio*, a leading newspaper, declared that its "silence had been forced," for it had been obliged to bow to *force majeure* after being warned three times by the chief of police.[45] Its editor remained absent from Rio, despite the efforts of a government spokesman to assure him "that there was not the slightest reason" for his departure and to urge him to "support the government" in such a "grave and anguished moment for the country."[46] In October the government imposed overt press censorship, forbidding any publications which would "instigate foreign aggression or could increase internal commotion and excite disturbances."[47]

The government also exerted great pressure on the foreign press in Brazil. Although *L'Echo du Brésil* had never attacked the regime, it was suppressed and its editor expelled. An older foreign journal, the *Rio News*, continued giving daily accounts of events of the revolt, but its editor complained of harassments and threats. Early in December, 1893, this vigorous defender of a free press was suspended, not to reappear until the civilian administration of Prudente de Morais, long after the termination of the naval insurrection.[48] As long as the

44. Carlos de Laet, "Imprensa," *A década republicana*, II, 136–80; *Rio News*, September 14, 1893, pp. 4–7; September 27, 1893, pp. 3–5; November 28, 1893, p. 5; December 5, 1893, p. 4; Captain Andrade Vandette to Floriano, Araranagua, July 7, 1893, Arquivo Nacional, Cx 1194; Conger to Gresham, April 3, 1893, National Archives, RG 59, Vol. 54.

45. *Jornal do Cómercio*, September 23, 1893, p. 1.

46. Ferreira da Costa to José Carlos Rodrigues, n.p., September 16, 1893, Seção de Manuscritos da Biblioteca Nacional, I–3, 2, 34.

47. *Diário Oficial*, October 14, 1893, p. 4365.

48. *Rio News*, October 17, 1893, pp. 3, 5; October 24, 1893, p. 4; October 31, 1893, p. 3; November 7, 1893, p. 4; November 14, 1893, p. 3; November 21, 1893, p. 3; November 28, 1893, p. 5; December 5, 1893, pp. 3, 5; January 2, 1895, p. 3.

officers controlled the government, the press remained insecure, for the officers wished to express their own opinions fully without granting an equal right to their critics.

In Congress, as in the press, the officers made known their demands for strengthening the position of the armed forces. This insistence on increasing the size and budget of the armed services formed their most clearly defined and widespread political demand. A large number of officers were congressmen and helped to secure ever larger appropriations for the growing armed forces. According to one civilian Republican observer, the officer-congressmen were "officers of renown in military circles, but who until November 15, 1889, never were involved in political struggles or in the direction of public affairs." They were responsible for the "deplorable scenes which occurred in Congress, where the right of unlimited insubordination is shamelessly practiced," and where "the most violent discourses have been made by young impassioned officers."[49] In their emotional speeches, they attacked any proposals to decrease or limit the size of the armed forces or the funds expended on them. And they effectively used such arguments as the threat of danger from Argentina, which never materialized.

Many officers received extra promotions, and salaries were increased. In the promotions, as in the forced retirements taking place at the same time, attention was given to the political loyalties of the respective officers, a fact which led to bitter feelings and opposition in some quarters.[50] The officers had generally been poorly paid under the empire, and many strongly desired to remedy this situation under the new regime. The salaries of the officers improved considerably, some

49. Américo Werneck, *Erros e vicios da organisação republicana* (Petrópolis: Typ. do Correio de Petrópolis, 1893), p. 70.

50. Freire, *História constitucional da república*, II, 210–13.

by 40 or 50 percent within a few months of the overthrow of the monarchy, and more "fringe benefits" were provided. The troops' salaries were also increased.

At the same time, the armed forces were enlarged. The decrease in army strength after the Paraguayan War had been one of the officers' complaints under the empire. From a high of approximately 23,000 at the end of the war, the army had been reduced to 15,000 by 1880, and then oscillated between 11,000 and 13,000 for a number of years. In 1889 the army was actually 13,512 strong, compared to the 11,748 of the previous year.[51] But once the republic was established, the army expanded rapidly. A month after the initiation of the new regime, the number of cavalry, artillery, and infantry corps were raised; two more artillery units were added to the current eight, and six more infantry battalions to the thirty already existent. Soon the land force legally included more than 24,000 men and actually contained some 20,000. With the Naval Revolt, a number of additional units were created. To meet these increases, the war department budget rose continually, and "extraordinary" credits were frequent.[52]

51. Brazil, Ministério da Guerra, *Relatorio apresentado à Assemblea Geral Legislativa na quarta sessão da vigesima legislatura pelo ministro e secretario de estado dos negocios da guerra Thomaz José Coelho d'Almeida* (Rio de Janeiro: Imprensa Nacional, 1889), *Anexos*, p. 12; Brazil, Ministério da Guerra, *Relatorio apresentado à Assemblea Geral Legislativa na terceira sessão da vigesima legislatura pelo ministro e secretario de estado dos negocios da guerra Thomaz José Coelho d'Almeida* (Rio de Janeiro: Imprensa Nacional, 1888), *Anexos*, p. 3.

52. João Batista Magalhães, *A evolução militar do Brasil* (*Anotações para a história*) (Rio de Janeiro: Biblioteca do Exécito, 1958), pp. 312–19; Charles S. Jerram, *Armies of the World* (New York: New Amsterdam Book Company, 1900), p. 30; Lopes and Torres, *Ministros da guerra do Brasil*, p. 30; Gustavo Barroso, *História militar do Brasil* (São Paulo: Companhia Editôra Nacional, 1935), p. 83; Roberto Macedo, *A administração de Floriano*. Vol. V of *Floriano. Memórias e documentos* (Rio de Janeiro: Serviço Gráfico do Ministério da Educação, 1939), p. 246; Amador Pereira Gomes Nogueira Cobra, *Brios de gente armada (Páginas republicanas na história do Brazil)* (São Paulo: Beccari, Jannini & Cia., [1924?]), p. 180.

An important aspiration of the officers, which became evident through their actions, was their desire to occupy many government positions which had previously been considered civilian posts. The number of such military officeholders was large and growing, whereas under the empire there had been few. Officers held civilian posts in the diplomatic and consular corps, on the staff of the vice-president, in the city government, public schools, Polytechnic School, telegraph system, railroads, fire department, prisons, city health commission, sanitary inspection departments, port inspection office, cattle importation agency, and slaughterhouses. In the states this situation was repeated. In 1893, eleven of the twenty state governors were officers on active duty; these were the governors of Alagoas, Amazonas, Ceará, Maranhão, Pará, Paraíba, Pernambuco, Piauí, Santa Catarina, Sergipe, and Goiás.[53] The officers were also entitled to hold more than one civil position at a time. For example, some of the army officers on active duty who were legislators were also state governors. Moreover, they received salaries from all their different positions, including those as commissioned officers.

Some officers disagreed with the views of their politically minded colleagues and made strenuous attempts to separate the officer corps from the political scene. While they were unsuccessful during the Floriano regime, their efforts would be of crucial importance once civilians achieved control and attempted to secure a nonpolitical or weakened army which would pose no threat to civilian predominance.

In 1893, when the army was becoming increasingly involved in the *Federalist* revolution and the tensions leading to the Naval Revolt were mounting, some officers saw the danger to the armed forces. Under the inspiration of a young officer,

53. *Jornal do Comércio,* June 25, 1893, p. 1. See also Freire, *História da revolta,* p. 75.

Lieutenant Conrado Muller de Campos, an officers' meeting was held in Pôrto Alegre. "For the purpose of reestablishing peace, tranquillity, and confidence between the members of the armed forces and civil society," these officers "resolved definitely to abandon politics and concentrate exclusively on constitutional purposes."[54] However, not only was this proposal generally rejected, but Muller soon felt obliged to resign from the army as he did not receive his next promotion.[55]

Within the Club Militar, one current of opinion tended to oppose direct involvement in political affairs, or, more specifically, the use of the armed forces by various political factions. Early in 1893 the president of the club advocated "the study of purely military questions, absolutely excluding politics."[56] A circular was published calling on the officers throughout the country to abstain from politics "for the salvation not only of the armed forces but of the country." This circular also attacked "the hypocrisy and lack of patriotism of those politicians" who "attempted to exploit the officers with bribery and blandishments" and who demonstrated an "intention, more or less remote, to dissolve the army"; these politicians "had brought political and anarchic manifestations even inside the barracks, as in Rio Grande do Sul." The club members stressed the need for the army to "reacquire its solidarity" so that it could "complete its incomparable work of the foundation of the republic" and Brazil could progress.[57] Thus, even in an apparent call for abstention from politics, these members of the Club Militar echoed a belief in the role of the armed forces as special guardians of the destiny of the republic they had pro-

54. Francolino Camêu and Arthur Vieira Peixoto, *Floriano Peixoto. Vida e governo* (Rio de Janeiro: Officinas Gráficas da A Norte, 1925), p. 162.

55. José Maria dos Santos, *A política geral do Brasil* (São Paulo: J. Magalhães, 1930), pp. 289–90.

56. Atas of Club Militar, Session of the General Assembly, March 5, 1893.

57. *Jornal do Comércio,* June 16, 1893, p. 1.

claimed, and they were expressing disdain for many civilian politicians who might be attempting to gain their favor. While they were not calling on the army to be apolitical, they were cognizant of the danger of involvement in the Rio Grande do Sul conflict and did not want to be used by the politicians.

Some officers saw the contradiction between this expressed desire to end military intervention in politics and the actual activities and attitudes of the Club Militar. One such officer called the club to account for this circular, which was "conceived in terms not at all accurate for its objective." He attacked the belief that since "the army and navy had the supreme responsibility for the institution of the republic, they must intervene in politics to consolidate their work. Sophism, pure sophism. The military can only properly fulfill its special mission . . . if it remains completely removed from political struggles." Therefore, he advocated the revocation of the constitutional provisions which gave the officers the right to be elected. The French officers did not possess such a right, and the Brazilians, "who in everything seek to imitate France," should also follow her wisdom on this important matter.[58]

Another officer attempted to translate these sentiments into legislation, but military desires to retain the officers' right to hold elective offices concurrently proved too strong. In June of 1893, General Frederico Solon Ribeiro presented a project in the Chamber of Deputies regulating the compatibility of officers for political posts. As he explained to the press, his project was designed to bring about the "dissociation of the armed forces from political movements." He found it necessary to combat opinions "that the dignity and prestige of the military are severely wounded by this project," or that it was "arbitrary" or "visibly badly intentioned." Instead, he defended it

58. Lieutenant Colonel Roberto Trompowski, letter to president of Club Militar, *Jornal do Comércio*, March 14, 1893, p. 1.

as "the realization of a most noble aspiration of the military" and as the "straight road of duty." Furthermore, he pointed out that his motion had not originated in Congress but "in the very midst of the military clubs," and that he, the deputy presenting it, not only belonged "to the honorable faction of the armed forces which inspired it," but, before presenting it, had "taken into account the enlightened judgment of many companions in arms." His project, "besides ennobling the army and navy," would free them from the "demoralizing perspective of *pronunciamientos*."[59] While Solon received some statements from groups of officers in favor of this measure, it was widely attacked by the officer-congressmen, one of whom called it "a usurpation, a crime." Congress gave up the project without further discussion after a hostile demonstration by the students of the Military School.[60]

The time had not yet come when desires to prevent political involvement by the officers could become a reality. The military governments were unwilling to interfere with the political activities of their officer-supporters and unable to control those of their officer-opponents. While the officers demonstrated a noticeable lack of unity in their political ideas and activities, most of them seemed to share certain vague beliefs justifying their participation in politics. Many were convinced that the armed forces had a special role to play in the republic they had helped establish and for whose destiny they were therefore responsible. In the exercise of this "moderating power," they could go as far as actual revolution when they felt that this was the only way to "save the nation." They continued to react violently to the principle of "passive obedience," with which they felt the imperial government had attempted

59. *Jornal do Comércio*, June 25, 1893, p. 1.

60. See Werneck, *Erros e vicios*, pp. 81–85; *Rio News*, September 6, 1892, p. 4; June 20, 1893, p. 4; July 4, 1893, p. 4.

to submerge them, and they looked down upon civilian politicians under the republic. When opinions such as these were added to their personal rivalries and hostilities, they led to the seemingly interminable revolts and political demonstrations of the first few years of the republic. While many civilians might object to such military activities and the attitudes behind them, they were for the most part powerless to prevent these political outbursts.

CHAPTER V

Monarchists and Officers

THE MONARCHISTS were the most vehemently antimilitary segment of the articulate civilian population during the first years of the republic. Since they refused to admit that the monarchy had lacked broad appeal, they were forced to view the political activities of the officers as the sole cause of its downfall. Under the Deodoro and Floriano regimes, many monarchists took a strong public position against military involvement in politics, although some attempted to influence military elements and condoned revolts against the government. Even some former imperial statesmen who were willing to serve the republic still criticized its military nature. The case of civilians who were genuinely stirred by infringements upon their civil liberties was weakened if they were also latent monarchists. Instead of helping to remove the officers from power, their denunciations only strengthened the military men by arousing fears of a monarchist threat to the republic. Eventually, the hard-core monarchists came to the conclusion that only military action could restore the crown, and thus they withdrew their support from those concerned with defending civilian rule.

In newspaper article after article, in Brazil and in Europe, and in countless manifestoes, the monarchists denounced militarized conditions under the republic and recalled the freedom and liberty they had enjoyed under the monarchy. Afonso Celso de Assis Figueiredo (the son of the Viscount of Ouro Prêto, Afonso Celso de Assis Figueiredo, Pedro II's last Prime Minister), spoke angrily of "the overthrowal of governors, the destruction of presses, mass imprisonments, banishments, punishments, executions."[1] For such men, the republic had brought "dictatorship, anarchy, massacres, corruption, degradation, discredit, and finally, imminent bankruptcy."[2] Under the Republican regime, wrote Eduardo Paulo da Silva Prado, one of the most eloquent and vehement of the monarchists, the "armed power of soldiers and sailors" did not have any other limit "beyond that of their will."[3]

This "regime of militarism" came about when, "on November 15th, an insurrection of troops quartered in this capital caused the fall of the monarchy."[4] Since that time, when "the republican government imposed itself on the Brazilian nation by force," it "had maintained itself through compulsion."[5] For monarchists like former minister Tito Franco de Almeida,

1. Affonso Celso de Assis Figueiredo, *Contradictas monarchicas* (Rio de Janeiro: Livraria Moderna, 1896), p. 33.

2. Pedro de Barros, *Cartas monarchistas* (Rio de Janeiro: Ed. Domingos de Magalhães, 1895), p. 7.

3. Prado, *Fastos da dictadura militar no Brasil*, p. 28.

4. Alfredo Paiva, *Questões politicas e sociaes* (Juiz de Fora: Typ. A Vapor de Leite Ribeiro & C., 1891), pp. 12, 23.

5. Affonso Celso de Assis Figueiredo, *Aos monarchistas* (Rio de Janeiro: Livraria Moderna, 1895), p. 31.

"the republic was established by the sword, not simply with its aid, and the sword was consecrated and enshrined—a *fundamental institution of the republic*—by the Constitution of 1891."[6] This constitution "transformed the military forces into a *sovereign*" and made the "power of militarism" the "first power of the republic."[7] For Tito Franco, it was the "coming of the republic which hurled Brazil into the arms of militarism."[8]

Such "militarism" was even more appalling because it showed Brazil to be just another Latin American dictatorship. For Eduardo Prado, ever concerned with Europe and European opinions, the republic had originated in the deplorable Spanish American phenomenon of a *pronunciamiento,* a shameful state of affairs from which he thought the monarchy had saved Brazil. He cringed to think that the world was comparing his beloved nation to one like Peru; such military actions were uncivilized and in Europe could occur only in Spain or in the barbarous Balkans.[9]

Joaquim Nabuco, a member of a distinguished family from Pernambuco who early in life had committed himself to liberal causes, especially the abolitionist movement, expressed similar sentiments. For a decade after the fall of the empire, Nabuco refused to hold public office, remaining loyal to the monarchy, which had helped free Brazil's Negro slaves. Nabuco declared that Brazil would now follow the "painful road along which Latin America trudges in destitution."[10] For him the word *republic* was "discredited before the entire world

6. Tito Franco de Almeida, open letter to *A Patria Paraense,* July 13, 1894 in *Monarchia e monarchistas* (Pará: Typ. de Tavares Cardoso & C., 1895), p. 326.

7. *Ibid.,* pp. 327–28.

8. Tito Franco to *Gazeta da Tarde,* November 17, 1892, *ibid.,* p. 87.

9. Prado, *Fastos da dictadura militar no Brasil,* pp. 69–72, 165–67, 198, 263–64, 360.

10. Joaquim Nabuco, *Reposta as mensagens do Recife e Nazareth,* 2d ed. (Rio de Janeiro: Typ. Leuzinger & Filho, 1890), p. 15.

when accompanied by the qualifying adjective—*South American.*"[11]

For these men, there was no truth in a current Republican belief that the Americas were the home of republics and that Brazil must also be a republic. Eduardo Prado characterized the idea of inter-American fraternity as a "lie" and an "insanity," and mocked the "South American nations" who "wish to be rich and prosperous like the United States" and who thought that they would "achieve this by copying articles of the American constitution."[12] Like Prado, Joaquim Nabuco felt that different conditions within Brazil and the United States necessitated different types of government, and that the United States did not categorically oppose monarchies; for the Americans, "militarism stands far below constitutional monarchy on the hierarchy of governments."[13]

Besides lamenting the general encroachment on civil liberties, the monarchists feared that their opinions would be denied expression. Joaquim Nabuco believed that "the republic does not tolerate the slightest degree of liberty of opinion. It knows that everyone opposes it and it does not have the courage to face the perils of liberty."[14] On the eve of his departure for Europe, Nabuco wrote a fellow monarchist that "the return of the monarchy is not the prerequisite for my return; it

11. Joaquim Nabuco, *Agradecimento aos pernambucanos,* 2d ed. (London: Abraham Kingdom & Newnham, 1891), p. 4; See also Nabuco to Afonso Pena, Paquetá, July 24, 1890, in Joaquim Nabuco, *Cartas à amigos* ed. Carolina Nabuco. Vol. XIII of *Obras Completas de Joaquim Nabuco* (São Paulo: Instituto Progresso Editorial, 1949), I, 185–87.

12. Eduardo Paulo da Silva Prado, *A illusão americana,* 2d ed. (Paris: Armand Colin Cie., 1895), pp. 7–8, 211.

13. Joaquim Nabuco, *Porque continuo a ser monarchista. Carta ao Diário do Commercio* (London: Abraham Kingdom & Newnham, 1890), p. 19; See also Joaquim Nabuco, *Balmaceda. A intervencão estrangeira durante a revolta de 1893. (São Paulo*: Instituto Progresso Editorial, 1949), pp. 104, 133–35, 137–43; Nabuco, *Agradecimento aos pernambucanos,* p. 14.

14. Joaquim Nabuco to Barão do Rio Branco, Lisbon, January 17, 1892, in Nabuco, *Cartas à amigos,* I, 210.

would be enough if they would recognize our opinion as that of political belligerents, instead of treating us as pirates. Belligerents? What am I saying! It would be sufficient if they would grant us the spiritual liberty of our spiritual creation."[15] Eduardo Prado attacked those who construed the constitutional prohibition against congressional projects to change the form of government as a blanket denial of liberty of discussion.[16]

While some monarchists publicly proclaimed their inability to accept the new regime or serve it, others, like the Baron of Rio Branco, José Maria da Silva Paranhos, continued to be active in government during the republic. The Baron of Rio Branco, son of the Viscount of Rio Branco, who had been a noted statesman during the reign of Pedro II, was beginning a long, distinguished career in Brazil's diplomatic service and government. A month after the fall of the empire, he agreed with Rui Barbosa, a prominent writer and jurist who had participated in the immediate events leading to the establishment of the republic and who was then a member of Deodoro da Fonseca's cabinet, that "the question today . . . is no longer between monarchy and republic, but between republic and anarchy," and he stayed at his diplomatic post in Europe.[17] However, the Baron of Rio Branco remained basically disenchanted with the republic. In 1889, shortly before the overthrow of the monarchy, fearing "the state of indiscipline of a part of the army," he had sent various French military books to Prime Minister Ouro Prêto, "asking him to have them translated and distributed in the army and military schools, so

15. Joaquim Nabuco to Carlos de Laet, Rio de Janeiro, December 29, 1891, Arquivo do Museu Imperial, Carlos Laet 29.12.891.

16. See Eduardo Paulo da Silva Prado, *Annullação das liberdades políticas. Commentario ao 4º art. 90 da constituição da república* (São Paulo: Livraria Civilização, 1897).

17. Rio Branco to Rui Barbosa, Liverpool, December 28, 1889, Arquivo da Casa de Rui Barbosa, Pasta Barão do Rio Branco.

that our officers would learn that one of the prime duties of the officer is respect and submission to civil authority."[18] After the declaration of the republic, he felt that "no one could foresee" when they would again have a "representative government and the liberties we enjoyed" under the empire; "only after many years will we be able to have officers who are not concerned with politics."[19]

While Rio Branco continued to serve the republic, he did so in posts far distant from Brazil, and he remained in close contact with many friends who actively opposed the new regime. He made a number of suggestions which were used in Eduardo Prado's articles attacking the republic. In these comments, Rio Branco acidly criticized the position of the armed services in government, the Club Militar, and the activities of officers like Benjamin Constant, who had implanted "the spirit of indiscipline in the students of the military school." He held up the example of the French army, which did not "think about elections and politics."[20] And, as Joaquim Nabuco wrote him, these articles "caused a definitely favorable impression for our cause."[21]

Some monarchists like Afonso Celso called on their fellows to organize and prepare for the return of the monarchy, which they felt was inevitable.[22] Deluding themselves about the current state of opinion in the nation, they could say that "today, as never before, the empire controls powerful elements of popular opinion."[23] Joaquim Nabuco wrote his friends that "the

18. Rio Branco to Conde d'Eu, Paris, March 6, 1890, Arquivo do Museu Imperial, M. 206, Doc. 9397.

19. Rio Branco to Barão Homem de Melo, Liverpool, December 17, 1889, Museu Daví Carneiro, Curitiba.

20. Arquivo do Instituto Histórico e Geográfico Brasileiro, L. 432, D. 27, 28.

21. Joaquim Nabuco to Rio Branco, London, April 18, 1890, Arquivo Histórico do Ministério das Relações Exteriories, Rio Branco Collection, Maço 74, Pasta 1 A.

22. Affonso Celso, *Aos monarchistas*, pp. 7–35.

23. *Ibid.*, p. 8.

people continue to be monarchists," and that "the republic is completely discredited, rotten and ready to collapse, to the general satisfaction" of everyone.[24]

Many seemed to subscribe to the view that the worse things went in Brazil, the better the chances were for a restoration of the monarchy. They would gather together to recall the past and condemn the present, to conspire, and to exchange rumors. They could not realize, unlike statesmen actively participating in political life, that restoration was not possible. As Rui Barbosa affirmed, "the crown . . . cannot return."[25] The monarchists' continued refusal to accept the new regime could only arouse Republican fears of conspiracies and danger to the republic and help maintain turbulent conditions, thus strengthening the position of the officers in government.

While some monarchists like Afonso Celso declared, "woe to the monarchy that returns by way of the barracks or the bridges of war vessels," others hoped to use armed force to restore the old regime.[26] One monarchist later recalled that immediately after the fall of the empire, some had "believed that since the republic had been made by a *coup-de-main*, restoration could be brought about the same way," but their attempts failed and they then "kept absolutely quiet."[27] While many monarchists had been publishing vehement attacks on military participation in government and deploring military uprisings ever since November 15, 1889, some supported the Naval Revolt because it was a movement against a detested government.

Eduardo Prado's *A illusão americana*, published during the

24. Nabuco to Barão de Penedo, London, May 11, 1891, in Nabuco, *Cartas à amigos*, I, 204; Nabuco to Rio Branco October 18, 1891, in Nabuco, *Cartas à amigos*, I, 206.

25. Rui Barbosa, *Cartas de Inglaterra* (São Paulo: Livraria Academica, 1929), p. 131.

26. Affonso Celso, *Contradictas monarchistas*, p. 70.

27. Carlos de Laet to Luís de Orleans Bragança, Rio de Janeiro, October 3, 1900, (draft), Arquivo do Museu Imperial, Carlos Laet 3.10.908.

Naval Revolt and immediately confiscated by the government, was far more than an attack on the Monroe Doctrine and an argument against close relations with the United States. Prado denounced the Republican government as a military regime which denied civil liberties, and he indicated strong support for the Naval Revolt. Describing the situation during the American Civil War, he launched into a discussion advocating recognition of the belligerency of revolutionaries, for revolution was a right. He thus implied that the naval insurgents had the right to oppose the Floriano regime he so detested and that they should be recognized as belligerents. Forced to flee to Europe, Eduardo Prado agreed to be their plenipotentiary to the European nations to help seek recognition of their belligerent status, and he assisted in channeling some funds to the hard-pressed insurgents.[28]

Joaquim Nabuco's publications after the revolt and his correspondence during it also indicate strong sympathy with the naval insurgents. In 1895 he wrote a series of articles for the *Jornal do Comércio* on the 1891 civil war in Chile. At the time, many of Deodoro's opponents in Congress viewed the army-supported President Balmaceda of Chile as a dictator and warmly espoused the cause of the Congressional Party and the Chilean navy. Nabuco was most sympathetic to those struggling against Balmaceda's "tyranny." Like Eduardo Prado, he linked military despotism to the Republican form of government and believed that the "Paraguayan tyranny" had been revived in Brazil "at the points of the same bayonnets and lances which had overthrown it."[29] He drew a sharp distinction between navies and armies and expressed his disdain for

28. Saldanha da Gama to Gaspar da Silveira Martins, Montevideo, September 18, 1894, in Dunshee de Abranches, *A revolta da armada e a revolução*, II, 26–27; Saldanha to Silveira Martins, Montevideo, September 25, 1894, *ibid.*, pp. 33–35; Saldanha to Silveira Martins, Montevideo, October 1, 1894, *ibid.*, pp. 63–64, 67–68.

29. Nabuco, *Balmaceda. A intervenção estrangeira*, p. 139.

all governments controlled by armies. For him, an army revolution, no matter how liberal its original intentions, must assume an authoritarian character, but there could never be a naval despotism.

In a series of newspaper articles criticizing foreign intervention in the Naval Revolt, Nabuco attacked Floriano and sympathized with the insurgents. He contended that Floriano had increased indiscipline in the army and the "danger of militarism" in Brazil. Showing contempt for the civilian Congress, Floriano had used the army to govern the nation and depose state governors. Nabuco contrasted the Marshal's cruel and tyrannical behavior with the generosity and humane actions of the insurgent leader Admiral Saldanha da Gama, an opponent of army militarism and the "most noble model" to which Brazil could then point.[30]

Nabuco continually lamented Floriano's treatment of the navy. In his published articles on the Naval Revolt, he accused Floriano of wishing to "annihilate the rebel squadron, sink the ships," eliminate those opposing him, and prevent all future rivalries between the two services by "making the navy a dependency of the army."[31] Such sympathy for the navy was carried even further in his personal correspondence. To his friends Nabuco complained of the terrible condition of the navy's ships after the revolt; they were not even allowed to control their own arms. He declared that Floriano was acting as if "he wished to put an end to the navy, incorporating it into the army through complicated arts which only he understands."[32]

Besides publicly defending the navy—and, indirectly, the re-

30. *Ibid.*, pp. 267–69, 274–75.

31. *Ibid.*, p. 267.

32. Nabuco to Hilário de Gouvêa, Rio de Janeiro, May 10, 1894, in Nabuco, *Cartas à amigos*, I, 233; Nabuco to André Rebouças, Rio de Janeiro, November, 13, 1894, *ibid.*, pp. 251–52.

bellion—after the termination of the Naval Revolt, Joaquim Nabuco expressed private opinions during the revolt which seem very favorable to the insurgents. His personal attacks on the Floriano regime had been rising in intensity; shortly before the outbreak of the Naval Revolt he wrote that "the crystallization of the republic into a military despotism of the worst order continues. . . . We should expect a national servility exceeding that of Paraguay under López, in a political society more corrupt than that of Argentina."[33] A month before the end of the rebellion, Nabuco believed that the outcome was in doubt and felt that time could "still alter the character of the movement and the nature of the final result."[34] He seemed to be hoping for a naval victory, possibly of a monarchist variety. Several days before the insurgents surrendered, Nabuco mentioned the possibility of success if they took São Paulo and got enough money to buy more ships. Perhaps he was not hinting that such funds should be given to the rebels, but he maintained the conviction that the "revolution will never lose control of the sea," and that "whoever retains mastery of the sea will end up winning. Since Themistocles this is the true policy." However, as a precaution against the seizure of private correspondence which occurred frequently at this time, Nabuco hastened to add that all this was just a "theoretical conviction."[35]

In public, Nabuco denied that there was any threat of a monarchical reaction either in the Naval Revolt or in the *Federalist* revolt of Rio Grande do Sul. But, in a letter to a friend, whom Nabuco asked to "please destroy the political part of this letter," he discussed the advantages of a monarchist solu-

33. Nabuco to André Rebouças, Rio de Janeiro, August 22, 1893, in Nabuco, *Cartas à amigos*, I, 222.

34. Nabuco to Hilário de Gouvêa, Rio de Janeiro, February 14, 1894, *ibid.*, p. 224.

35. Nabuco to Hilário de Gouvêa, Petrópolis, March 10, 1894, *ibid.*, p. 228.

tion to the Rio Grande conflict. He felt that "the free government today desired by Rio Grande sooner or later will take the monarchical form if militarism succumbs in the duel in which it is engaged with the people of Rio Grande."[36]

By favoring or appearing to favor an armed movement like the naval rebellion, the monarchists weakened their already unsteady position. Even if this revolution had succeeded, no restoration would have taken place, while a truly civilian regime would also have been unlikely. Through their activities and denunciations, the monarchists helped persuade civilian Republicans to support Floriano in order to defend the republic and prevent a successful military uprising.

Later, when a civilian government had been elected, some monarchists appeared to believe that the monarchy would not return with a popular movement, that it could be restored only through force. The failure of major revolutions like the Naval Revolt had not convinced them of the impracticality of this method of changing governments, and some monarchists persisted in efforts to play upon the divisions within the armed forces. They had become more desperate and willing to risk such ventures, for, under the civilian presidents, the republic was becoming more firmly established and a peaceful return to the monarchy was becoming even more unlikely. Like some other civilians, who turned to the officers for help when they failed to secure their ends through normal political channels, some monarchists hoped to obtain the assistance of part of the armed forces.[37]

36. Nabuco to Barão de Penedo, Rio de Janeiro, August 9, 1894, *ibid.*, pp. 238–41.

37. Their attitudes were given clearest expression after the date that marks the end of this study, but, as a reflection of the dilemma faced by civilian groups, they deserve mention. A major source of monarchist views is the multivolumed denunciation of the republic written at the turn of the century by a group of leading Brazilian monarchists led by the Visconde de Ouro Prêto, *A década republicana*, 8 vols. (Rio de Janeiro: Companhia Typ. do Brazil, 1899–

The monarchists' vehement opposition to the political activities of the officers in the early years of the republic had no positive effect and could not remove them from power; neither could the later attempts of some monarchists to use the army for their own ends. Like other groups, the monarchists had attempted to profit from divisions within the armed forces, but without success. They did not maneuver skillfully and peacefully, and they lacked a strong power base. Their tattered banner attracted few officers, but it frightened many civilians and officers into taking severe countermeasures.

1901). The author of the section on the army was General Cunha Mattos, one of the most politically outspoken officers under the empire in the days of the "military question," who charged that the government was attempting to eliminate the army, which was "divided, humiliated—almost in dissolution" ("Exército," *A década republicana*, IV, 9). In his section on the navy, Ouro Prêto accused the republic of destroying this body on which the imperial government had lavished special care, and he lamented that frequently the officers, a "class so profoundly wounded" by the government, "had remained passive and had not bestirred themselves; they submitted" ("Armada nacional," *A década republicana*, V, 10, 173).

Other indications of monarchist efforts to secure military assistance for restoration are found in the letters of the pretender Luís de Orleans Bragança, who considered the armed forces "the natural support of the throne," and who held that "a good army is the indispensable complement of the prosperity of a country" (Luís de Orleans Bragança to Candido Guimarães, Nezsider, November 16, 1906, *Revista do Instituto Histórico e Geográfico Brasileiro*, Vol. 240 (July–September, 1958), pp. 345–46; Luís de Orleans Bragança to Carlos de Laet, Nice, March 20, 1908, Arquivo do Museu Imperial, 20.3.908 L.B.Cl.). He was well aware that only through an armed revolt could the monarchy return, for he recognized that "the people will not be the ones to bring about the monarchy. We need the assistance of the officers, or at least of some officers"; once they had almost succeeded, but they lacked "a man of action. Another time we will be more fortunate," for "a handful of resolute men would be enough to wrench our country from the hands of the adventurers who exploit it." (Luís de Orleans Bragança to Carlos de Laet, Sein Inferieure, August 12, 1913, Arquivo do Museu Imperial, 12.8.913 L.B. c DML).

CHAPTER VI

Civilian Opposition to Military Rule

MANY CIVILIANS WHO WERE NOT MONARCHISTS also opposed military activities. A wide variety of civilian groups, including disillusioned old Republicans, zealous defenders of civil liberties, and quarrelsome parliamentarians in Congress, objected to the strong position of the officers within the Brazilian political structure but could not find a workable method of dislodging them.

Civilians were disturbed by many of the officers' attitudes and activities and by their participation in both federal and state government. Much of this civilian anxiety and opposition centered about civil liberties, which were often endangered by various officers and by the military government. Ever since the declaration of the republic, civil liberties had been a key issue in the conflicts between civilians and officers. Civilians objected strenuously to the officers' self-assumed right of revolution and their frequent disregard for legality and constitutionality. While the civilian opponents of military rule were united in their defense of civil liberties and constitutional government, they could not agree on the exact role the armed forces should play. Some went so far as to question the need for a professional army. Others accepted the existence of the armed forces but hoped to professionalize and depoliticize them. And some concentrated on attempts to limit the military budget, as this would help stabilize the economy as well as weaken the armed forces.

The civilians who opposed military rule were faced with the grave problem of how to expel the officers from government without resorting to revolution. If they solicited military aid in ousting the officers controlling the government, their apparent allies might become their new masters, as had occurred after November 15, 1889. Under the empire, some Republicans had encouraged military action against a regime they opposed, and they had learned their lesson. When the navy revolted against the government of Marshal Floriano Peixoto in September of 1893, very few civilians demonstrated any sympathy for the insurgents. Even some who had countenanced minor military demonstrations against the officer-dominated government supported Floriano in opposing this major revolt. Only a few of the most vehement personal enemies of the Marshal or of the Republican regime were in favor of this military movement against the government. Most civilians realized that revolt was not the way to end military rule.

The archtypical defender of civil liberties against military incursions was Rui Barbosa, a political liberal from Bahia who was inspired by English thought and precedent. A small man with an imposing head filled with encyclopedic and almost pedantic knowledge, this eloquent orator and prolific writer, then and now considered one of Brazil's greatest jurists, devoted his considerable talents to the cause of constitutional liberties, both in the press and in the courts. While he had supported the demands of the officers under the monarchy, he vigorously opposed their political activities under the republic, especially after his departure from Deodoro's first cabinet, where he had served as finance minister and had supervised the drafting of the Constitution of 1891. One of the most persistent critics of Floriano Peixoto, Rui never ceased to protest infringements on civil rights.

Under the republic, Rui wrote newspaper articles denouncing the use of armed force by the government against constitutional institutions and civil liberties. Like other civilians, he felt that the freedom of expression was one of the most fundamental rights menaced by the officers, for "the press, more and more, does not represent just an individual liberty; it is a right of the political order."[1] He also protested particular instances of military violence, the military governments in the states, and the deposing of governors through force.

Recognizing that an army was a "necessary danger," Rui proposed that the worst aspects of "militarism" might be avoided if the government were to station the army largely on the frontier, far from urban political struggles.[2] In November of 1889, he had vehemently accused the imperial government of plotting such a move, but in 1893, the politicized army was basically loyal to a government he opposed. Rui did not believe "politics could be demilitarized while the nation's government was in the hands of an armed dictator."[3]

Rui also sought redress in the courts for those he considered oppressed by the government. When Floriano retired the thirteen generals and admirals in April of 1892, Rui questioned

1. *Jornal do Brasil,* August 15, 1893, p. 1.

2. *Jornal do Brasil,* June 16, 1893, p. 1.

3. *Jornal do Brasil,* June 17, 1893, p. 1. See also Rui Barbosa, *Campanhas jornalistics. República (1893–1899)* Vol. VIII of *Obras seletas* (Rio de Janeiro: Casa de Rui Barbosa, 1956), pp. 27–76.

the constitutionality of this action and carried the case to the Supreme Court. Rui also sought writs of *habeas corpus* for the civilians arrested that same month. The next year he defended the civilians who had been forced to accompany Admiral Eduardo Wandenkolk when the Admiral seized the *Jupiter* and attempted to aid the *Federalist* insurgents, and Rui also sought a writ of *habeas corpus* for Wandenkolk and two other retired officers.[4]

Rui Barbosa felt constrained to flee Brazil soon after the outbreak of the Naval Revolt, although he continued to deny having taken the "slightest part, direct or indircet, in the revolutionary movement."[5] And he persisted in attacking Floriano, "the czar of Rio de Janeiro," in the Argentine press.[6] As special correspondent for the New York *Herald*, Rui constantly defended the naval insurgents against charges of monarchism and portrayed their activities in the most optimistic light.[7] He declared that if Floriano "triumphed Brazil would fall under a dictatorship like that of Rosas" of Argentina.[8] The *Herald* repeatedly referred to Rui as Admiral Custódio de Melo's "au-

4. Barbosa, *Cartas de Inglaterra*, pp. 58–66; Eduardo Wandenkolk to Rui Barbosa, Fortaleza de Santa Cruz, July 29, 1893; August 3, 1893; August 10, 1893; August 12, 1893; August 15, 1893; August 24, 1893; August 31, 1893; Arquivo da Casa de Rui Barbosa, Pasta Eduardo Wandenkolk; Luis Viana Filho, *A vida de Rui Barbosa*, 6th ed. (São Paulo: Companhia Editôra Nacional, 1941), pp. 164–76.

5. Rui Barbosa to first secretary of the Brazilian Senate, Rio de Janeiro, September 12, 1893, Casa de Rui Barbosa, Pasta Senado Federal. See also Rui to director of *La Nación*, Buenos Aires, September 19, 1893, in Murilo Ribeiro Lopes, ed. *Rui Barbosa e a marinha* (Rio de Janeiro: Casa de Rui Barbosa, 1953), pp. 76–86; Rui Barbosa, *Rui Barbosa e o exército*. (*Conferência as classes armadas*) (Rio de Janeiro: Casa de Rui Barbosa, 1949), pp. 132–42.

6. Rui Barbosa to director of *La Nación*, Buenos Aires, December 2, 1893, Arquivo da Casa de Rui Barbosa, Pasta Revolução da Armada.

7. D. Woolfe to Rui, Valparaiso, October 26, 1893, Arquivo da Casa de Rui Barbosa, Pasta Henry D. Woolfe; Rui to Woolfe, Buenos Aires, November 3, 1893; November 4, 1893; November 5, 1893; November 18, 1893; December 13, 1893; February 12, 1894; March 13, 1894; March 16, 1894; Arquivo da Casa de Rui Barbosa, Pasta New York *Herald*.

8. Rui Barbosa to New York *Herald*, Buenos Aires, October 30, 1893, Arquivo da Casa de Rui Barbosa, Pasta New York *Herald*.

thorized spokesman in revolutionary matters," or as "Melo's mouth-piece on land."[9]

While Rui refused Admiral Melo's offer of "the position of representative of the revolution (of the Provisional Government) in Europe," he still attempted to aid the insurgents.[10] Melo expressed his "contentment with the services" to "our revolution," and even declared that Rui's "communications to a newspaper of the importance of the New York *Herald* are worth a squadron!"[11] Throughout the revolt Rui remained in constant contact with a former imperial statesman who was supplying the insurgents with needed funds and munitions. In one cablegram to him Rui declared: "Occasion decisive. Victory depends above all on immediate aid. Through telegraph here buy rifles, coal for Santa Catarina. Have courage for this sacrifice. Victorious revolution will compensate you generously. Confide."[12]

After the collapse of the revolution, Rui remained abroad and continued to oppose Floriano and support the exiled former insurgents. He defended them against their detractors in the Lisbon press, but the Portuguese government did not

9. See New York *Herald,* November 19, 1893, p. 4; December 14, 1893, p. 6; December 15, 1893, p. 6; February 11, 1894, p. 7.

10. Melo to Rui, Rio de Janeiro, November 16, 1893. See also Melo to Frederico de Lorena, Rio de Janeiro, November 19, 1893; Melo to Rui, Rio de Janeiro, November 21, 1893; Arquivo da Casa de Rui Barbosa, Pasta Custódio José de Melo.

11. Melo to Rui, Rio de Janeiro, October 10, 1893; November 16, 1893; Arquivo da Casa de Rui Barbosa, Pasta Custódio José de Melo.

12. Rui Barbosa to Leopoldina, Buenos Aires, December 16, 1893, Arquivo da Casa de Rui Barbosa, Pasta Conde de Leopoldina. See also Leopoldina to Rui Barbosa, Lisbon, December 17, 1893; December 22, 1893; London, January 5, 1894; Lisbon, January 8, 1894; February 7, 1894; February 13, 1894; February 27, 1894; March 8, 1894; March 17, 1894; Paris, July 1, 1894; Rui Barbosa to Leopoldina, Buenos Aires, February 17, 1894; March 7, 1894; March 9, 1894; March 16, 1894; Leopoldina to Baron Danvers, London, December 16, 1893; December 30, 1893; Pasta Conde de Leopoldina; Rui Barbosa to Danvers, Buenos Aires, December 15, 1893, Pasta Barão de Danvers.

encourage such activities, and Rui soon felt obliged to leave for London.[13]

The articles he wrote from London are among his most bitter attacks on the Floriano regime. In his venomous denunciations of dictatorships in Latin America he indirectly compared Floriano to the worst of the South American dictators, Gaspar Francia of Paraguay and Juan Manuel de Rosas of Argentina, declaring that "Francia and Rosas are just two figural incarnations, analogous to others."[14] For Rui, the arbitrariness, the imprisonments, and the secret police of Rosas' Argentina had been repeated in Brazil. Rui did not return to Brazil until 1895, after a civilian had taken office as president.

Rui Barbosa was deeply concerned with civil liberties and due process, which he found violated by the political activities of the Brazilian officers. By his constant outcries, he may have alerted others to the danger, but he found no way to remove the officers from the political sphere. His vehement attacks on the Floriano government and his support for the naval insurgents did nothing to bring an end to the danger of military uprisings.

Another civilian apprehensive over military participation in politics was Américo Werneck, a Republican residing in Minas Gerais. Like Rui, he had foreseen no military danger to civil liberties in the days of the monarchy.[15] But he had learned that the army could be a menace, and that the theoretically federal regime provided no safeguard against military

13. Rui Barbosa, *Mocidade e exílio. Cartas* ed. Américo Jacobina Lacombe (São Paulo: Companhia Editôra Nacional, 1934), pp. 213–38; Barbosa, *Cartas de Inglaterra*, pp. 77–80; Luis Viana Filho, *A vida de Rui Barbosa*, p. 185; Dunshee de Abranches, *A revolta da armada*, I, 93–104; Rui Barbosa to *País*, December 14, 1901; Barbosa, *Rui Barbosa e o exército*, pp. 161–63; Murilo Ribeiro Lopes, ed., *Rui Barbosa e a marinha*, pp. 157–77.

14. Barbosa, *Cartas de Inglaterra*, p. 383.

15. See Werneck, "A dictadura militar republicana," *A Revolução*, (Campanha), I, No. 13 (March 31, 1889), pp. 1–2.

dominance in government. In the initial stage of the republic he had favored rule by a military leader in order to prevent civil disorders. But no serious opposition to the republic appeared during the provisional government, and Werneck opposed Deodoro's election in 1891 as "a degrading victory of military *caudillismo*."[16]

An admirer of Rui's journalistic campaigns in favor of "civil government," Américo Werneck also criticized the infringements on civil liberties, military intervention in the states, and the political activities of the Club Militar.[17] Without engaging in personal attacks, he offered a thoroughgoing criticism of the evils resulting from military predominance in government. He thought "militarism the worst enemy of the republic, signifying the intervention by the officers in the mechanism of government, beyond their sphere of capacity."[18] The officers had acquired many special privileges, and Werneck strongly felt that they "should not have more rights than the magistrates and other citizens." Instead, they should be "disciplined and orderly."[19] According to him, the army had been "abusing its intervention in the social movement, involving itself in partisan emotions, fomenting civil discords, occupying positions foreign to its temperament and training, usurping rights, violating the discipline indispensable to a military organization, corrupting the mission of government, and making our adversaries unjustly assert that it proclaimed the republic for its exclusive enjoyment."[20] Werneck pointed out that "the states controlled by civilians prosper in peace," but in those governed by officers a "bloody struggle begins at

16. Américo Werneck, *O Brazil: Seu presente e seu futuro* (Petrópolis: Typ. da Gazeta de Petrópolis, 1892), p. 17.

17. Werneck, *Erros e vicios*, pp. 33, 64–68, 72–73.

18. *Ibid.*, p. 72.

19. *Ibid.*, p. 78.

20. *Ibid.*, p. 65.

the slightest pretext," for the civilians "seek support from the people, the officer from the barracks; one employs prudence, the other, force."[21] Moreover, he recognized that "discontented or ambitious officers" could lend themselves to the conspiracies of others and could be used by opposing political factions.[22]

Américo Werneck found no satisfactory way to end these abuses. He could not support a revolt against the military-dominated government, for "revolt is an exception which cannot be erected into a system, or the constitution, congress, and the ballot box would serve no purpose at all."[23] Appealing to the officers' patriotism and self-interest, Werneck declared that if they realized how much evil they were doing the country they would cease, and he pointed out that "to introduce a dissolving element like politics into the army is to kill it."[24] According to him, everything should be "in favor of the officer, but everything against militarism."[25] He was not able, however, to win politically active officers over to these views. Werneck concluded "that only with the passage of time will the danger be warded off, and the normal functions of government and society be reestablished."[26]

In Congress, a large number of civilians opposed military participation in the affairs of the nation, though equally without success. Some of their strongest complaints were occasioned by military interference in state affairs and by infringements on civil liberties, especially on the freedom of the press, which remained one of the most sensitive areas both for them and for the officers.

21. *Ibid.*, p. 66.
22. *Ibid.*, pp. 67, 76.
23. *Ibid.*, p. 76.
24. Werneck, *O. Brazil*, p. 72.
25. *Ibid.*, p. 80.
26. *Ibid.*, p. 16.

To control military activities, some congressmen tried to limit the continually growing budget and size of the armed forces. These congressmen complained that the "deficit is enormous," that a third of the country's income was being spent on the armed forces, and that these "unproductive expenditures" were hurting the nation.[27] But nevertheless, the government succeeded in obtaining additional funds for the armed forces, even special appropriations in gold, at a time of inflation and deficit financing. Congressional efforts to decrease or limit the number of soldiers always ended in defeat.

The congressional opposition was also unsuccessful in its efforts to weaken the position of Marshal Floriano Peixoto. It was unable to force him to call a presidential election following Deodoro's overthrow late in 1891. According to Article 42 of the constitution, such an election must be held if the office of president became vacant less than two years after the president assumed power. Floriano's supporters maintained that this provision was not applicable during the first presidential term, due to the special circumstances of the first presidential election. Despite the hostility of the Marshal's friends, Congress did later pass a bill prohibiting him from running in the forthcoming presidential election. But Floriano vetoed this measure, and opponents of his like Admiral Custódio de Melo used this act as one justification for the Naval Revolt.[28]

Their inability to find a way to restrict the political pretensions and activities of the officers led to a feeling of frustration and disillusionment among many congressmen who had long favored the Republican ideal. On one occasion, a deputy who opposed the expense of an expanding army related a fable concerning a "spirited courser" who had failed to capture a "nim-

27. Session of August 29, 1892, Brazil, Congresso Nacional, *Annaes da Camara dos Deputados. Segunda sessão da primeira legislatura,* IV, 622; session of November 8, 1892, *ibid.,* VII, 139.

28. Mello, *Governo provisório,* II, 49–60, 306–12; Freire, *História da revolta,* I, 59–60.

ble roebuck." Therefore, the courser "allied himself with a strong and valiant lion," who, seating himself on the back of his ally, caught the roebuck. Then beastdom proclaimed the lion the conquering hero.[29] This story was well received in the legislature by many who had originally thought that the army would simply assist them in establishing a republic but instead found the officers attempting to dominate them.

Among the congressmen disillusioned by the infringements on civil liberty and the strong position of the armed forces were two old "historic" Republicans, signers of the Republican Manifesto of 1870. Joaquim Saldanha Marinho, born in 1817, and Cristiano Benedito Otôni, born in 1811, expressed great disappointment and sadness that the actual republic, for which they had labored so long, did not correspond to their "dreams."

As the first signatory of the 1870 manifesto and a Republican leader for many years, Saldanha Marinho occupied a highly respected position, although no longer a powerful one. His concern for civil liberties extended to the rights of men whose views he opposed, and he protested the confiscation of Eduardo Prado's *A illusão americana.*[30] Once, reminiscing about conditions under the empire, Saldanha Marinho was chided for complaining that the ministers no longer kept within the limits prescribed by law. He then retorted that such "reminiscences had become fashionable, because in my opinion, the present republic is much worse. I was a republican long before the 15th of November."[31] This, "certainly," was not the republic for which he had "braved the wrath of the emperor."[32]

29. Speech of Francisco da Veiga, September 4, 1891, Brazil, Congresso Nacional, *Annaes da Camara dos Deputados,* III, 129.

30. Prado, *A illusão americana,* p. 237.

31. Session of October 22, 1892, Brazil, Congresso Nacional, *Annaes do Senado Federal. Segunda sessão da primeira legislatura,* V, 47.

32. Session of June 22, 1892, *ibid.,* II, 35.

While Saldanha Marinho did support the manifesto of the thirteen generals and admirals in April of 1892, he remained firmly on the side of the government against a serious matter like the Naval Revolt of 1893–94. With many of his fellow congressmen, he manifested his "firm and loyal support for the president of the republic" and the "constitutional order of the republic" in this "most wretched instance of insubordination by a part of the armed forces."[33]

Another venerable Republican expressing severe doubts about the path pursued by the new republic was the sincere and forthright Cristiano Benedito Otôni, a prominent engineer, the first director of the Central Railroad, and a member of the imperial Senate. In a work describing the fall of the empire, he recalled his apprehension at the first manifestations of military solidarity. While he considered the officers' refusal to apprehend runaway slaves a noble one, for abolition was their only progressive ideal, he asserted that this refusal was partially inspired by their opposition to the Cotegipe ministry.[34] Until the eve of November 15, 1889, "the military did not discuss changing the form of government, or political reforms; they only cried out against alleged injustices, in which they saw a threat to their group position."[35]

Otôni also denied that the politicans under the empire were antagonistic toward the officers, holding, for example, that if the officers' salaries were low, those of public functionaries were also insufficient. He observed that the officers "were not sustaining an idea or political principle; they were not aspiring to any reform of general interest"; instead, their complaints were those of one group against all others in the nation.[36] Unlike some Republicans who had courted the officers

33. Manifesto to the Nation, *País*, September 15, 1891, p. 1.
34. Ottoni, *O advento da república no Brazil*, p. 84.
35. *Ibid.*, p. 94.
36. *Ibid.*, pp. 82–84.

and sympathized with their real or imaginary grievances during the latter days of the empire, Otôni had always been suspicious of the army.[37]

Otôni recalled participating in the overthrow of Pedro I in 1831. This, he claimed, was a popular movement, civilian in inspiration, to which the Rio de Janeiro army garrison had adhered through solidarity with the people.[38] In 1889, he seemed to be hoping that these circumstances would be repeated. The army was to be simply the immediate agent for the proclamation of the republic, called in at the last minute by the civilians, who were to remain in control.

The military predominance in government and the dangers to civil liberties that Otôni witnessed under the republic caused him great alarm for the future. Brazil did not need to be one of those "countries always on the alert, armed to the teeth." While he greatly admired the Swiss, whose constitution prohibited a standing army, he dared only to suggest that the Brazilian government reduce its army gradually and promote a system of small state militias, which would be "a guarantee for all, and a menace for no one." Unfortunately, the drastic increase in army size under the republic revealed a contrary intention on the part of the nation's new rulers. Otôni feared that such expansion, and the concessions granted the officers, would tend to "militarize the country."[39]

Following publication of these views, Otôni rarely spoke of military influence in government. Instead, his infrequent congressional speeches were generally confined to railroads, harbors, and other economic matters. He would not support military insurrections, even against a military regime. Otôni was one of the signers of a manifesto issued by a group of senators

37. See Ottoni, *Autobiographia de C. B. Ottoni*, pp. 345–46.
38. Ottoni, *O advento da republica no Brazil*, pp. 107–108.
39. *Ibid.*, pp. 124–26.

opposing the Naval Revolt as "a deranged ambition," and hoping "for the triumph of those sustaining the constitution and the established government."[40] Following the conclusion of this insurrection, Otôni, like Saldanha Marinho, demonstrated his support for Floriano's position by favoring the striking of a gold medal in honor of the United States and hemispheric solidarity.[41]

One younger Republican who objected to the political behavior of the officers but found it best to support the Floriano regime, was Felisbelo Firmo de Oliveira Freire, Republican governor of his native Sergipe, a member of the Constituent Assembly, and finance minister under Floriano during the Naval Revolt. Like other civilian intellectuals, he felt that the government was too sensitive to press criticism and that freedom of the press was more secure under the empire.[42]

As a Republican opposed to military domination in government, Felisbelo Freire was forced to deny Eduardo Prado's contention that the republic was responsible for "militarism" in Brazil. In his history of the first years of the republic, Freire claimed that "it was in the monarchical regime that the civil authority gave the first example of capitulation in the face of bayonets."[43] The principle of passive and unthinking obedience, against which the officers had rebelled, "no longer was a reality in the time of the empire."[44] Moreover, Freire maintained that in any case the Brazilian army never reached the depths of indiscipline of Spanish American armies, to which he as well as Eduardo Prado objected.[45]

Freire also emphasized the civilian role in establishing the

40. Telegram to State Governors, Rio de Janeiro, September 14, 1893, Arquivo do Instituto Histórico e Geográfico Brasileiro, L. 193, D. 5045.

41. Caldas, *A deshonra da república,* pp. 204–206.

42. Freire, *História constitucional,* II, 50–51.

43. *Ibid.,* I, 207.

44. *Ibid.*

45. *Ibid.,* II, 87.

republic, while recognizing, with Otôni, that without army aid it would have been utopian to attempt to overthrow the monarchy in 1889. Since the people had subsequently "adhered" to the republic, Freire maintained that this demonstrated that the Republican propaganda "had infiltrated the public spirit." Therefore, he viewed "the civil element as a factor of collaboration, although it did not constitute a material agent of the revolution."[46]

He realized that the civilian propagandists were "responsible" for the "military character of the revolution of November 15th," and that "the new regime would inevitably have to suffer the consequences of this."[47] However, he admitted that instead of disciplining the army, the Republican government had brought it still closer to the political arena.

Freire saw the strengthening of the executive as the correction for these military abuses, and he loyally supported Vice-President Floriano Peixoto against military uprisings. Unlike some civilians, who viewed Floriano as the greatest of the militarists, Freire served in the Marshal's cabinet during the tumultuous days of the Naval Revolt. For him, this was the only possible way to combat the political influence of the officers. While he regretted the "acts of violence" committed by the Floriano regime, he maintained that they were committed in self-defense against the "military *caudillismo*" which would destroy law and order.[48] Such measures were necessary to oppose "military indiscipline raised to the level of a class prerogative."[49] Instead of surrendering in the face of armed opposition, as had previous Brazilian governments, Floriano stood firm in defense of constitutionality.

Many civilian groups had been unsuccessful in their efforts

46. *Ibid.*, II, 5.
47. *Ibid.*, I, 372.
48. Freire, *História da revolta*, p. 64.
49. *Ibid.*, p. 65.

to limit the power of the officers. Rui Barbosa, the most outspoken critic of military predominance in government, had fled the country during the Naval Revolt. The congressional opposition had been unable to limit army size or budgets or the political activities of the officers. Some Republicans, like Cristiano Benedito Otôni, had objected to military influence in government without condoning instances of military indiscipline. While Otôni had supported the Floriano regime during the Naval Revolt, he lacked sufficient political strength to derive any benefit for civilian government from his stance. Younger Republicans, like Felisbelo Freire, who lent more active aid to the Marshal, might be successful. But a stronger power base was necessary, and this was offered by the Republicans from São Paulo.

CHAPTER VII

The Profit-Minded Paulistas *and the Floriano Government*

OF THE VARIOUS SEGMENTS of the articulate civilian population demonstrating dissatisfaction with the position of the officers in government, only one was able to dislodge them. These civilians, mainly large landowners from the economically powerful coffee-exporting state of São Paulo, had long favored the creation of a federal, Republican regime as in their own best interest. They now saw that a strong military government posed a threat to local autonomy and to their prosperity. During the first years of the republic, they strengthened their power base in São Paulo, built up their own local military force, and generally opposed the revolts and political disturbances which damaged the Brazilian government's credit abroad and hindered economic progress. When the Naval Revolt broke out, they were able to take advantage of the divisions within the armed forces, ally themselves with Floriano, who needed their state militia, and eventually gain control over the central government.

The large landholders of São Paulo took an active interest in the politics and government of their nation. Unlike the oligarchies of some other Latin American countries, they did not remain apart from the actual scene of political battle and rule by military proxy. Instead, they entered the political arena to defend their economic interests. They retained firm control over their state government and protected it against encroachments by the federal government, in part by building up a strong military force; the prosperous coffee planters controlled the men and the funds needed for the maintenance of a well-trained and well-equipped state "police force."

By the latter part of the nineteenth century, the divergences between the northern and southern parts of Brazil had deepened, and the south, which included São Paulo, had become dominant. After the end of the mining prosperity of the eighteenth century, the nation's economy had remained stagnant until the rise of coffee as a new export product. Social organization in the south underwent rapid changes, with increasing numbers of wage-earning laborers both on the coffee plantations and in the cities, growing European immigration, and agriculture based on small farms in the southernmost states. São Paulo, in particular, had become prosperous and its landed class wealthy.

Under the empire, the plantation owners in the south did not exercise political power commensurate with their economic importance. São Paulo thus naturally became the major home of the Republican movement. The imperial government, influenced largely by former slave-owning elements, some from the long decadent sugar economy, often showed little sympathy for administrative and other reforms required by the transformations in the south. For many *Paulistas* and other southerners, it was a federal regime with great local autonomy that promised to meet their needs.

The Republican Party of São Paulo, the best organized Republican grouping under the empire, advocated a federal regime. Alberto Sales, their chief theoretician, was the brother of Manuel Ferraz de Campos Sales, leading *Paulista* statesman and coffee planter. In Alberto Sales' writings, the benefits of this form of government are extolled almost to the point of separatism. Under a federal regime, each local center would "employ its own resources as best it thought," and "the elements of wealth which exist in the different localities, instead of all being drained off to the general treasury" of the imperial government, would remain to benefit each locality.[1] Moreover, São Paulo was "incontestably the only one giving to the imperial government without receiving."[2] Even under the "regime of the despotic centralization of the empire,"[3] São Paulo had advanced to the forefront of the nation, and Alberto Sales dwelt on the vast increase in agriculture, commerce, railroads, immigration, industry, and general prosperity which would result when the overwhelming proportion of São Paulo's revenues ceased to enter the imperial treasury. He advocated a form of separatism "as a means of arriving at federation," which would especially include the southern part of Brazil.[4] The coffee planters had learned the importance of government as an instrument of economic action, and they were aware that with state autonomy São Paulo would progress more rapidly and less of its wealth would flow into the coffers of the central government.

1. Alberto Salles, "Catecismo Republicano," in Luís Washington Vita, *Alberto Sales. Ideólogo da república* (São Paulo: Companhia Editôra Nacional, 1965), p. 193.

2. Alberto Salles, *A patria paulista* (Campinas: Typ. A Vapor da Gazeta de Campinas, 1887), p. 184.

3. *Ibid.*, pp. 148–49.

4. *Ibid.*, p. 294. See also Vita, *Alberto Sales. Ideólogo da república.*

Even before the founding of the republic in 1889, the *Paulistas* were intent on keeping control of their state government out of the hands of the officers. They had known of plans for the revolution of November 15 and were prepared to take action in São Paulo once the republic had been declared. According to Campos Sales, "the *Paulista* republicans closely followed the revolutionary movement and were informed of the details of occurring events" through letters, personal envoys, and telegraphic codes.[5] On the night of November 15, 1889, "the people of this capital [of São Paulo] gathered in a compact body in front of the Republican Club, acclaimed the provisional government of this state," a three-member junta, "without encountering the slightest resistance."[6] This junta, composed of two strong civilians and a compliant officer absent from the *Paulista* capital at the time, was recognized by the Deodoro government. São Paulo had set up its own Republican regime under civilian control, unlike many other states which were surprised by the overthrow of the empire and were forced to submit to military governors chosen by the central government.

During the early days of the republic, the *Paulistas* were anxious to preserve local autonomy. Their views were reflected in newspapers like the *Diário Popular,* which continued to proclaim the benefits of federalism and the "great principle of autonomy," and railed against the "dangers of parliamentarism" and a centralized government.[7] According to another local paper, São Paulo's government was perhaps "that with the greatest importance in all the vast territory of the Brazilian republic," and the state itself was one "most distinguished for

5. Campos Salles, *Da propaganda à presidencia,* p. 45.

6. *Relatório* of Prudente de Morais, in *O novo governo da república* (Rio de Janeiro: Imprensa Nacional, 1894), pp. 122–23.

7. *Diário Popular,* November 23, 1889, p. 1; December 2, 1889, p. 1; December 5, 1889, p. 1.

its orderly and progressive spirit" and its steady, fruitful economic labors.[8]

Only two weeks after the declaration of the republic the members of the ruling junta of São Paulo decisively informed the federal government of their desire to continue in control of the state, pointing out that São Paulo's "spirit of autonomy is well known." They emphasized their strong position within the state which was based on the "confidence that all social classes placed in the provisional government." In addition, they indirectly advised against any federal attempts to control São Paulo like some other states and pointed out that any such effort would cost the republic local support. But they politely promised to endeavor to secure popular acceptance of the governor to be nominated by the federal government.[9] The *Paulista* position was obvious; the state governor nominated by Marshal Deodoro da Fonseca several days later was Prudente de Morais, a member of the junta and a leading civilian Republican who would continue to defend his state's interest.

Prudente clearly expressed the *Paulista* desire for autonomy, and the intention to work for it, in a letter to the finance minister of the provisional government. Prudente declared that if the minister contributed "rapidly toward the decentralization of revenues—corresponding to the decentralization of services"—he would be "rendering the best and most important service to São Paulo, which, achieving this, will be able to live and develop itself with its own resources, without disturbing the central government—this is the supreme aspiration of this state."[10]

8. *Correio Paulistano*, June 4, 1890, p. 1.

9. Prudente de Morais, Francisco Rangel Pestana, and Joaquim de Souza Mursa to the Minister of the Interior, São Paulo, November 30, 1889, Arquivo Nacional, Secção dos ministérios, IJJ9 428.

10. Prudente to Rui Barbosa, São Paulo, September 29, 1890, copy in Prudente's handwriting, Prudente de Morais Papers.

This economic development would not be possible without political stability. Influential *Paulistas* like Campos Sales feared the "anarchy" which might arise out of the political violence of the times and the "discredit" into which Brazil was falling abroad.[11] As he later recalled, the "long series of grievous events and armed movements . . . disturbed the normal functioning of national life, causing the destruction of our credit abroad."[12] During peaceful times, São Paulo would be able to attract more European immigrants, enriching its agriculture and thereby the economy of the entire state.[13] The São Paulo government had become even more responsive to the interests of the coffee farmers under the federal republic, and it now took much more determined measures to promote the immigration of European laborers than had the imperial state government.

Great concern was expressed for the nation's finances, so seriously weakened by the military governments. The officers, unaccustomed to ruling a nation, did not always make the best administrators, and this contributed to civilian dissatisfaction. As one friend of Prudente de Morais related, many were deeply worried about "the credit of the Republic, so seriously jeopardized by the incapacity of the officers who have been governing us."[14] These economic considerations seem to have been of greater interest to the *Paulistas* than was any abstract principle of civil liberties or civilian rule.

In Minas Gerais, another economically powerful state in-

11. Manuel Ferraz de Campos Salles, *Cartas da Europa* (Rio de Janeiro: Typ. Leuzinger, 1894), p. 10; Campos Sales' speech, June 1, 1892, in Antonio Joaquim Ribas, *Perfil biographico do dr. Manoel Ferraz de Campos Salles, ministro da justiça do governo provisório, senador federal pelo estado de São Paulo* (Rio de Janeiro: Typ. Leuzinger, 1896), p. 462.

12. Campos Salles, *Da propaganda à presidencia*, pp. 52–53.

13. Manuel Ferraz de Campos Salles, *Manifesto ao estado de São Paulo* (São Paulo: Typ. do Diário Oficial, 1896), pp. 13–15; Campos Salles, *Cartas da Europa*, pp. 84, 93.

14. Guimarães Natal to Prudente, Goiás, June 20, 1894, Prudente de Morais Papers.

terested in coffee export, governmental leaders expressed similar concern for state autonomy and opposed the revolutions and military disturbances which damaged the economy. As in the case of São Paulo, the wealth of Minas Gerais was primarily agricultural. The mining region, once a great source of riches, was in decline, and the southern coffee area, a center of republicanism under the empire, was now ascendant. Since the establishment of the republic in 1889, the state government had remained in civilian hands, and local leaders expressed their belief in a large measure of state autonomy and political and economic stability. Residents of Minas Gerais like Américo Werneck could write that the officers' "intentions are disruptive and their pronouncements, rebounding in society, disturb families, promote the depression of the exchange rate, and cause losses of thousands of *contos* to frightened commerce, which sees in their acts a symptom of bad times or the latent prelude of revolt."[15] Like his *Paulista* colleagues, Minas Gerais' governor, Afonso A. Moreira Pena, had long been concerned with safeguarding state autonomy and maintaining stability, and he opposed revolutionary movements, those "most grievous political disturbances which weaken our institutions and compromise our credit."[16]

To help protect their own autonomy and fortify their position vis-à-vis the central government, the *Paulistas* concentrated on building up their own local military force. During the last years of the empire, governors and police chiefs urged drastic increase in the number of police troops, arguing that "the development of industries and the expansion of the railroads" had led to population growth requiring "a numerous police force," and that the existing force was grossly inadequate "for the most indispensable needs of policing the prov-

15. Werneck, *Erros e vicios*, p. 73.

16. Afonso Pena to Fernando Lobo, May 1, 1893, in Hélio Lobo, *Um varão da república. Fernando Lobo. A proclamação do regime em Minas, sua consolidação no Rio de Janeiro* (São Paulo: Companhia Editôra Nacional, 1937), p. 183.

ince."[17] But their incessant pleas went unheeded by the imperial government in Rio. With the arrival of the Republican federal regime, the governors of São Paulo gained the power to increase their forces. Prudente de Morais, the first Republican governor, could justify such expansion by the need to properly "guarantee order and public tranquillity" in this "revolutionary period."[18] As Campos Sales wrote Bernardino de Campos, the second governor of São Paulo, "our police force should be very well organized and disciplined, the command given to men of confidence," for "these men, under rigorous military discipline, will be a powerful safeguard in whatever eventuality."[19] Prudente later also advocated the formation of armed municipal forces of "good republicans," as further protection.[20]

17. Antonio de Queiroz Telles, Visconde de Parnahyba, *Exposição com que o exm. snr. Visconde de Parnahyba passou a administração da provincia de São Paulo ao exm. snr. dr. Francisco de Paula Rodrigues Alves, presidente desta provincia, no dia 19 de novembro de 1887* (São Paulo: Typographia a Vapor de Jorge Seckler & comp., 1888), p. 38; Salvador Antonio Moniz Barreto de Aragão, *Relatório apresentado ao illm. exm. snr. dr. Francisco de P. Rodrigues Alves presidente da provincia de São Paulo pelo chefe de policia interino o juiz de direito Salvador Antonio Moniz Barreto de Aragão, 1887.* (São Paulo: Typographia a Vapor de Jorge Seckler & comp., 1888), p. 25; Francisco de Paula Rodrigues Alves, *Relatório com que o exm. snr. dr. Francisco de Paula Rodrigues Alves passou a administração da provincia de São Paulo ao exm. snr. dr. Francisco Antonio Dutra Rodrigues 1º vice-presidente no dia 27 de abril de 1888* (São Paulo: Typographia a Vapor de Jorge Seckler & comp., 1888), *Anexos*, p. 14; Francisco Antonio Dutra Rodrigues, *Exposição com que ao exm. snr. dr. Pedro Vicente de Azevedo passou a administração da provincia de São Paulo o exm. snr. dr. Francisco Antonio Dutra Rodrigues 1º vice-presidente no dia 23 de junho de 1888* (São Paulo: Typographia a Vapor Baruel, Pauperio & comp., 1888), p. 15.

18. Prudente José de Moraes Barros, *Exposição apresentada ao dr. Jorge Tibiriçá pelo dr. Prudente J. de Moraes Barros 1º governador do estado de São Paulo ao passar-lhe a administração no dia 18 de outubro de 1890* (São Paulo: Typ. Vanorden & comp., 1890), p. 31.

19. Campos Sales to Bernardino, September 2, 1892, in Cândido Mota Filho, *Uma grande vida. Biográfia de Bernardino de Campos* (São Paulo: Companhia Editôra Nacional, 1941), p. 273.

20. Prudente to José Gabriel de Oliveira, Piracicaba, April 21, 1893, Prudente de Morais Papers.

All the states had police forces, but these had no military potential under the empire. Under the federal republic, however, states like Minas Gerais, Rio Grande do Sul, Bahia, and especially São Paulo increased the number of armed men. In 1888, the permanent police force of São Paulo numbered less than 500 men. Prudente de Morais raised the number of troops to 1,700. By the time of the outbreak of the Naval Revolt in 1893, the *Paulista* forces totaled approximately 3,000, organized into three infantry battalions equipped with machine guns and other modern equipment, one cavalry regiment, and a battalion of "firemen." Following the conclusion of the revolt, São Paulo would maintain its expanded, efficient armed force and would even secure a foreign training mission for its "police" long before the federal army received one. The *Paulistas* were aware that a powerful militia would give them increased leverage on the national scene, besides serving to protect their local interests. While some state governments, such as that of Rio de Janeiro, had to permit their police forces to be commanded by officers of the regular army, the *Paulistas* jealously guarded the independence of their large state army.[21]

Their concern in this regard was evident in their relations with the central government. Among the many incidents between the two governments, one specifically involved the São Paulo police. The war minister, Benjamin Constant, had rec-

21. Visconde de Parnahyba, *Exposição*, 1888, pp. 37–39; Moniz Barreto de Aragão, *Relatório*, 1888, pp. 25–29; Prudente de Moraes, *Exposição*, pp. 31–35; Ernani Silva Bruno, *História e tradições da cidade de São Paulo* (Rio de Janeiro: José Olympio, 1954), III, 1203; Pedro Dias de Campos, *A revolta de seis de setembro. (A acção de São Paulo). Esboço histórico* (Paris and Lisbon: Typographia Aillaud, Alves & Cia., 1913), p. 32; O. H. Dockery, "Police Force of Rio de Janeiro." January 18, 1892, in *Reports from the Consuls of the United States* (Washington: Government Printing Office, 1892), XXXIX, No. 142, p. 444; T. Oscar Marcondes de Souza, *O estado de São Paulo. Physico, político, económico e administrativo* (São Paulo: Estabelecimento Gráphico Universal, 1915), pp. 218–19; *Rio News*, June 18, 1895, p. 6; June 23, 1896, p. 7; July 2, 1896, p. 6; July 30, 1896, p. 5; August 17, 1897, p. 4.

ommended the nomination of an army captain, Tómas Alves, as commander of this state force. Alves, sure he would be given the post, left for São Paulo. While Campos Sales, the Minister of Justice in the provisional regime, was in public accord with the war minister's recommendation in order not to offend the government, he privately advised Prudente, then governor of São Paulo, against it.[22] The *Paulistas* vigorously defended the independence of their state force, and the captain was obliged to return to Rio.

A few months later, this same army officer secured a nomination from the war ministry to command the tenth cavalry regiment in São Paulo. It seems that the appointment came from Floriano Peixoto, the acting war minister, for the matter was decided during Benjamin Constant's absence. Alves was Floriano's man, for whom Floriano had secured the important position of commander of the civic guard during the last year of the empire.[23] Perhaps Floriano was seeking to extend his influence to São Paulo, and Prudente's hostile reaction to this ploy may have been one of the factors in their cool relations. Protesting vigorously, Prudente threatened to resign as governor of São Paulo if this nomination were not rescinded.[24] Campos Sales and Francisco Glicério, leading *Paulistas* and members of Deodoro's government, tried to assure Prudente that the nomination was made simply for service reasons and that "absolutely no one thought of causing you any displea-

22. Benjamin Constant to Campos Sales, December 11, 1889; Campos Sales to Prudente, Rio de Janeiro, December 12, 1889, and December 13, 1889, Prudente de Morais Papers.

23. Campos Sales and Francisco Glicério to Prudente, Rio de Janeiro, March 25, 1890, Prudente de Morais Papers; Floriano Peixoto to José Basson de Miranda Osório, Rio de Janeiro, August 5, 1889; August 8, 1889; November 15, 1889; and José Basson de Miranda Osório to Visconde de Ouro Prêto, Rio de Janeiro, December 15, 1889, Arquivo do Museu Histórico Nacional, P. 28, No. 13.

24. Prudente to Glicério, São Paulo, March 23, 1890, Prudente de Morais Papers.

sure," and another friend added that "São Paulo never will be deprived of its authority." But Prudente continued adamant until the *Paulistas* convinced the central government to revoke this nomination and send someone acceptable to them.[25]

Relations between the *Paulistas* and the Rio government were sometimes uneasy, for Marshal Deodoro da Fonseca did not always respect the boundaries of their state's autonomy. A small but illustrative incident concerned the granting of a concession to construct a second railroad linking the port of Santos with the interior of São Paulo. When Deodoro recommended that the concession be given to a certain not very promising company whose director was related to him by marriage, Prudente de Morais did not oblige. As governor of São Paulo, Prudente argued that the matter was so important and difficult that he would prefer nominating a commission of experts and then holding an open competition to decide the matter. Deodoro never secured his request.[26]

The *Paulistas* knew that Deodoro could threaten their position, and shortly before the opening of the Constituent Congress in November of 1890, Campos Sales wrote Prudente concerning the political action they should take. If they all worked together, they could assure their predominance in the state, and once a state constitution was approved and elections held, their rights would be protected. But the *Paulistas*, fully aware of Deodoro's political and military power, handled such matters with care and attempted to win his favor. In the same letter, Campos Sales spoke of a projected visit by Deodoro to São Paulo and urged Prudente to give him a "good reception,"

25. Campos Sales and Glicério to Prudente, Rio de Janeiro, March 25, 1890; Cesário Alvim to Prudente, March 26, 1890; Campos Sales to Prudente, March 27, 1890, Prudente de Morais Papers.

26. Glicério to Prudente, Rio de Janeiro, May 20, 1890; Deodoro to Prudente, May 21, 1890, and May 31, 1890; Prudente to Deodoro, São Paulo, June 8, 1890; Deodoro to Prudente, Rio de Janeiro, June 10, 1890, Prudente de Morais Papers.

for Campos Sales believed "that he will come away from there dazzled, and, like the man of emotions he is, he will devote all his affection to the *Paulistas,* giving us, consequently, a preponderant place in public affairs."[27]

With the end of the provisional government, relations between the *Paulistas* and the Deodoro government deteriorated rapidly. Prudente's candidacy for the presidency and the support given it by the *Paulistas* angered Deodoro. His chief minister, the Baron of Lucena, attempted to dislodge the São Paulo Republican Party from its position of prominence. For years, the party had worked for the creation of a federal republic, and now, as Campos Sales later recalled, the "autonomous life of the states" was being menaced by Deodoro, and their long-held desire "to destroy the oppressive apparatus of the centralized monarchy" was still unfulfilled.[28] They felt their state threatened by the central government, which went so far as to remove their governor a month after Deodoro's election as first constitutional president.

In a manifesto signed by Prudente de Morais, Campos Sales, Francisco Glicério, and Bernardino de Campos, by other important *Paulistas* leaders, and by the majority of the *Paulista* delegation in Congress, they charged that the Deodoro government had deliberately entered upon a policy of interference in the local affairs of São Paulo. Their governor had been dismissed without cause, and confidential agents had been appointed to all important posts in order to control the state. This, they said, was done because the *Paulista* delegation had voted against Deodoro for president.[29]

According to Prudente de Morais, much of the "explosion of hatred against São Paulo and especially against the *Paulista*

27. Campos Sales to Prudente, Rio de Janeiro, October 12, 1890, Prudente de Morais Papers.

28. Campos Salles, *Da propaganda à presidencia,* pp. 52, 78–79.

29. *Rio News,* March 17, 1891, p. 3.

republicans" was the result of his "being a *Paulista* considered and supported for President of the Republic." This was the cause of "the sudden, spiteful removal" of their governor and of "the organization of the reactionary government." Thus attacked, they must fight back, for their "cause" was that of the "autonomy and honor of São Paulo."[30]

While some *Paulistas* remained open to the possibility of a reconciliation with the Lucena ministry in return for various concessions, no such accord was achieved.[31] Tensions increased between Deodoro and his congressional opponents, and finally he unconstitutionally dissolved Congress on November 3, 1891. Furthermore, it seems that Deodoro intended to institute some constitutional reforms which would have strengthened the central government and weakened São Paulo's internal position and its influence within the union. These changes would have included the allotting of an equal number of seats in the Chamber of Deputies to all states, as was the case with the Senate, a measure which would benefit the northern states at the expense of the southern ones.[32]

Although the *Paulistas* had become some of the most outspoken opponents of Deodoro, who held Prudente largely responsible for the crisis, they were still powerless to act at this time. Instead, they could only wait until dissident military elements grouped themselves and overthrew Deodoro on November 23. Even then, the *Paulistas* lacked sufficient mili-

30. Prudente to Amador Simões, Águas do Lambarí, April 10, 1891, in José Benedicto Silveira Peixoto, *A tormenta que Prudente de Morais venceu!*, 2d ed. (Curitiba: Editôra Guaíra Limitada, 1942), p. 71.

31. Compare an unsigned article by Prudente de Morais, *Correio Paulistano*, May 18, 1902, p. 2, with article in *O Tempo*, June 3, 1902, p. 1; Campos Salles, *Da propaganda à presidencia*, pp. 60–61, 83–91; Barão de Lucena to Cesário Alvim, Rio de Janeiro, November 4, 1891, in Monteiro, *Pesquisas e depoimentos*, pp. 346–47.

32. Monteiro, *Pesquisas e depoimentos*, p. 358; Dunshee de Abranches, *Atas e atos do governo Lucena*, p. 113.

tary force to oust the state governor, who had been appointed by Deodoro earlier that year, and they were forced to request and await military assistance from the central government, now controlled by Marshal Floriano Peixoto.[33] The federal forces Deodoro had stationed in their state were more powerful than their own, and the *Paulistas* were dependent on Floriano's commands to the federal troops to regain control over their government.

Under the more competent Floriano regime, which generally respected São Paulo's autonomy, many *Paulistas* cooperated with the Marshal against armed threats to his government and to general political stability. They supported him when, following Deodoro's ouster, congressional opposition forces wanted a new presidential election. Francisco Glicério, who even served as government leader in the Chamber of Deputies, defended the regime against charges by dissident military leaders concerning the government's policy in Rio Grande do Sul, and so did Campos Sales.

Paulistas like Campos Sales wished to fortify the federal government against military disturbances and the danger of anarchy. But he ceased his support when Floriano went too far in his intervention in the states. If the central government persisted in interfering with state affairs, São Paulo itself might eventually be menaced. This was of greater concern to Campos Sales than was Floriano's infringements on civil liberties. Moreover, the Marshal's lack of moderation in dealing with his enemies seemed to encourage resistance and threaten political anarchy.[34] Two important *Paulista* desiderata—local

33. Campos Sales to Floriano, São Paulo, November 23, 1891; General Carlos Machado de Bittencourt to Floriano, São Paulo, November 23, 1891; November 24, 1891; Glicério, Campos Sales, Prudente, Bernardino de Campos to Floriano, São Paulo November 30, 1891, Arquivo Nacional, Cx 1206.

34. Campos Salles, *Da propaganda à presidencia*, pp. 98–99; Campos Salles, *Cartas da Europa*, pp. 28–31; Ribas, *Perfil biographico de Campos Salles*, pp. 451–52, 496.

autonomy and political stability—appeared to be in danger. Even after his split with Floriano, however, Campos Sales exemplified the cautious, nonviolent *Paulista* political procedure. Instead of joining the ranks of the Marshal's bitter critics, which would only "create new complications" and "assist or animate the pernicious elements of turmoil," Campos Sales took an extended trip to Europe, not to return until the outbreak of the Naval Revolt in September of 1893.[35]

During this most dangerous of the insurrections agitating the life of the young Brazilian republic, the *Paulista* leaders came to the aid of the Floriano government. Old grievances and disagreements were put aside in the face of such a serious military threat to the general peace of the nation and to São Paulo itself. The insurgents even attempted to attack the coffee port of Santos. The *Paulistas* could see that a military revolt was not the best way to achieve civilian government, especially when a *Paulista* was running for president; the insurgents were unlikely to let him assume power, should they triumph, but Floriano might, in exchange for their military and political support. Protesting "against this insane revolt, without a noble ideal that might justify it," Campos Sales returned from Europe to occupy his "post among those combating the revolt."[36] Fellow *Paulistas* like Prudente de Morais also abhorred this revolution and "the accursed Custódio de Melo."[37] In Congress, Prudente read a message of support for the government, arguing that history demonstrates that "the pronouncements and the revolts by armed troops against the authorities constituted by the national sovereignty . . . infalli-

35. Campos Sales to Coelho Rodrigues, Geneva, June 6, 1893, in Campos Salles, *Cartas da Europa*, pp. 30–31.

36. Campos Sales to Jorge Miranda, Paris, September 22, 1893, *ibid.*, p. 280; Introduction to *Cartas da Europa*, p. 33.

37. Prudente to Maria Amélia de Morais Silveira, Rio de Janeiro, September 10, 1893, in Silveira Peixoto, *A tormenta que Prudente de Morais venceu!*, p. 97.

bly produce anarchy and anarchy is the unfailing precursor of despotism."[38] Francisco Glicério continued to support Floriano in Congress, and Francisco Rangel Pestana, another *Paulista* leader, edited *O Tempo,* a strongly pro-government newspaper, during the revolt.

The governor of Minas Gerais, Afonso Pena, expressed the fears of civilians that should this military uprising succeed, others would follow, preventing civilian rule. He publicly opposed the Naval Revolt as a struggle "to decisively secure for the heads of the army and navy the power to appoint themselves the supreme arbiters of the nation." According to him, military despotism was "mainly due to the competition and rivalry of army and naval officers for the possession of power, each one controlling an armed force and striving to raise himself to the position of supreme arbiter of the established government and claiming to act under the constitution." He declared that those "who hope for the abolition of military despotism by military revolts" would be greatly deceived. Moreover, and most important, "revolutions, even when successful, are the cause of incalculable evil to the economic life of a nation." Continued revolts would mean "the complete destruction of public and private wealth and the ruin of the producing and laboring classes." If such a revolt, coming at the end of Floriano's term of office and just before a presidential election, were allowed to succeed, future presidents would never be able to govern securely.[39]

At the same time as the naval insurgents were menacing Rio de Janeiro, serving as a threat both to future civilian rule and to the Floriano government, the *Federalists* from the south were moving northward. They had left Rio Grande do Sul, invaded Santa Catarina and Paraná, and were fast approaching the southern boundary of São Paulo. "As the bar-

38. *País,* September 27, 1893, p. 1.
39. Manifesto of Afonso Pena, *País,* December 15, 1893, p. 1.

barians of a former age threw themselves, ravenous, upon the delights of Rome, so did the *Federalist* troops hasten toward the wealth of São Paulo," according to one longtime resident of São Paulo.[40] This state, situated between these two movements against the central government, held the balance of power.

The *Paulistas* were in a position to lend decisive aid to the Floriano regime. São Paulo's economic power had been translated into a capacity to employ armed force through its army, and São Paulo could decide the conflict between the federal government and the insurgents. The Floriano regime was dependent on São Paulo, and the *Paulistas* decided to throw their support to Floriano. With the state treasury in good shape, the state could and did lend large sums to the federal government. Before the termination of the Naval Revolt and the presidential election, Governor Bernardino de Campos reminded Floriano of the sum owed the state and of all the other war expenses São Paulo was assuming and called for an early payment. But Bernardino did not hesitate to cooperate fully with the central government. He purchased some arms from commercial establishments in São Paulo, inquired of Floriano concerning purchases abroad, and actively sought additional arms from Floriano to equip more *Paulista* troops.[41]

40. Ribas, *Perfil biographico de Campos Salles*, p. 527.

41. Bernardino to Floriano, São Paulo, January 10, 1894; January 12, 1894; January 18, 1894; January 23, 1894; January 25, 1894; January 27, 1894; February 3, 1894; February 4, 1894; February 23, 1894; Arquivo Nacional Cx 1195; Bernardino to Floriano, São Paulo, January 23, 1894, Arquivo Nacional, Cx 1209; Bernardino to General Bibiano Sérgio Macedo da Fontoura Constallat, São Paulo, February 7, 1894; February 16, 1894; March 3, 1894; Arquivo Nacional, Cx 1195; Bernardino to General Constallat, São Paulo, February 8, 1894, Arquivo Nacional, Cx 1209; Colonel J. J. Jardim to Floriano, Santos, January 10, 1894; January 11, 1894; January 12, 1894; January 15, 1894; March 3, 1894; April 10, 1894; Arquivo Nacional, Cx 1195; Captain Lauro Muller to General Constallat, São Paulo, March 3, 1894; March 4, 1894; March 9, 1894; Arquivo Nacional, Cx 1195; Captain Lauro Muller to Floriano, São Paulo, February 13, 1894, Arquivo Nacional, Cx 1209; Mello, *O governo provisório*, II, 39. See also Dias de Campos, *A revolta de seis de setembro. (A acção de São Paulo)*.

The *Paulistas* already had a large number of men under arms, and Bernardino de Campos raised additional troops through the landowners of São Paulo, who had numerous workers at their disposal. With the cooperation of *Paulista* leaders like Prudente de Morais, he asked "the local chiefs" to "send, with all possible brevity, the contingents they could obtain to the state capital, where they will be uniformed, armed, and instructed, to defend our state against the invasion of barbarians with which it is menaced."[42] These troops proved to be not only crucial in deciding the conflict but also valuable in enforcing São Paulo's will later on.

The governor of the other economically powerful coffee state, Minas Gerais, took the lead in pressing Floriano for elections. While the Naval Revolt was still raging, Governor Afonso Pena attempted to convince Floriano of the wisdom of holding the presidential elections scheduled for March 1, 1894. In late January of 1894, he called Floriano's attention to this "matter of the greatest political importance" and requested him to limit the extent and duration of the state of siege, so that it would "not impede the holding of elections" or give any pretext to those who supposed that the presidential election would be prevented. Otherwise, the people would view Floriano's "government as aspiring to a dictatorship." People "in revolutionary epochs" carry out "generally unreasonable action" and tend to believe any charges of usurpation which are leveled against those heading the government.[43] In this way, Afonso Pena was warning Floriano of a possible reaction if the election was not held and Prudente was not elected.

42. Prudente to José Gabriel de Oliveira, Piracicaba, January 28, 1894, in Gastão Pereira da Silva, *Prudente de Moraes. O pacificador* (Rio de Janeiro: Zélio Valverde, [1937]), p. 197.

43. Afonso Pena to Floriano, Ouro Prêto, January 23, 1894. Arquivo Nacional, Cx 1209.

At this crucial juncture, with the naval insurgents still threatening the capital and the *Federalists* rapidly approaching the southern borders of São Paulo, the presidential election of March 1, 1894, was held, and a leading *Paulista*, Prudente de Morais, was chosen. With much of the country under a state of siege and the southern part of the nation in insurgent hands, a civilian who had long opposed military control in government would not have won so easily if Floriano had actively opposed his candidacy. But in February and March of 1894, the *Federalist* threat was at its peak and the Marshal was dependent on *Paulista* aid.

A diverse group of civilians had long wished to secure civilian rule through the election of a civilian as chief magistrate. In July of 1893, before the outbreak of the Naval Revolt, a large group of senators and deputies, led by Francisco Glicério of São Paulo, met to organize an all-inclusive political party, the Federal Republican Party, and to prepare for the presidential elections. The party embraced all major state groupings. Their program was not merely to defend the constitution and constitutional liberties but also to "secure the authority of the states, scrupulously maintaining their rights, which are as sacred as those of the union," and "to raise the public credit."[44] On September 25, 1893, during the Naval Revolt, the party convention unanimously chose Prudente de Morais as its presidential candidate. Another civilian, Manoel Vitorino Pereira of Bahia, was selected as the vice-presidential candidate. In 1890, Deodoro had forced him to resign as governor of his state, after he had forbidden a demonstration in honor of one of Deodoro's officer-brothers, who then became the next governor. Manoel Vitorino was naturally no friend of military rule.

Floriano had never evinced any fondness for Prudente, even

44. *O novo governo da república*, p. 227.

when both had been supported by elements opposing Deodoro's election in 1891. Since the constitution forbade Floriano himself from running for the presidency, some of his friends attempted a constitutional revision, but they could not obtain the necessary congressional approval and the only legal alternative was another candidate. It has been said that beginning in April of 1893, Floriano had constantly attempted to learn who would be the civilians' candidate. When it seemed likely that Prudente would be chosen, Floriano objected and offered his assistance to Rangel Pestana, another *Paulista.* Other civilians were also approached, including Gabriel de Toledo Piza e Almeida, a *Paulista* serving as Brazil's representative in Paris. But the *Paulistas* remained united and loyal to Prudente.[45] While Floriano never came out in favor of Prudente's candidacy, he did not overtly oppose him. However, Colonel Manuel Prescíliano de Oliveira Valadão, Floriano's political confidant and former secretary, then chief of the Rio de Janeiro police, sent telegrams to the state governors and district military commanders suggesting the candidacy of another officer, Lauro Sodré. But the officers were not united, and Sodré declined to run.[46] Despite his refusal, Sodré did receive a number of votes when the presidential election took place as scheduled on March 1, 1894. But Prudente de Morais was elected the first civilian president of Brazil, in order to, as he termed it, "initiate the civilian, or truly republican, government."[47]

Although Floriano had not prevented Prudente's election,

45. See Silveira Peixoto, *A tormenta que Prudente de Morais venceu!*, p. 101; Pereira da Silva, *Prudente de Moraes. O pacificador*, pp. 39–41; José Maria dos Santos, *A política geral do Brasil*, p. 334.

46. Tobias Monteiro, *O presidente Campos Salles na Europa. Com uma introducção e cinco retratos* (Rio de Janeiro: F. Briguiet & Cia., 1928), Lii; Interview with Lauro Sodré, *Jornal do Comércio*, January 31, 1895, p. 1.

47. Prudente to Antonio Mercado, Piracicaba, March 7, 1894, Prudente de Morais Papers.

many civilians were fearful that military elements might keep Prudente from occupying the presidency once the Naval Revolt had ended and the *Federalist* insurgents were on the defensive. For months, newspapers from one end of the country to another reported military plots and rumors that Floriano would retain control of the government and proclaim a dictatorship. So persistent were these rumors that they were even repeated in foreign newspapers. And Prudente received anonymous warnings that Floriano would not permit him to take office.

Floriano did seem to be attempting to fortify his position. When the Naval Revolt collapsed, he did not end the state of siege, and he kept some opponents in jail for many more months. Additional arms were purchased in Europe, troops were forcibly recruited, and numerous military appointments were made. In August of 1894, Campos Sales, concerned by Floriano's course of action, wrote Bernardino de Campos from Rio that "the political situation is not very good; for the present, it continues very bad."[48]

Some of Prudente's friends urged him to compromise with those military elements supporting Floriano and to ally himself with others. From Paris, Gabriel Piza wrote Prudente stressing the need to compromise, to come to terms with the officers if necessary, in order to stay in office. Only with a strong, stable, economically sound government would Brazil be able to deal effectively with the European powers. "If, for whatever irregular motive, your administration does not arrive at its normal termination (revolt, resignation, assassination), we will be giving testament declaring Brazil bankrupt and the republic destroyed and lost." Since "politics, being full of relativity, does not admit perfection," it would be

48. Campos Sales to Bernardino, Rio de Janeiro, August 26, 1894, in Mota Filho, *Uma grande vida. Biográfia de Bernardino de Campos*, p. 268.

"perfectly licit to compromise a little with such elements, which, poorly directed, can pervert the republic and disrupt the country." In this connection, Piza cited the examples of the Cotegipe ministry which "had prolonged the life of the monarchy" when menaced by military conflicts and of the French government's skill in handling the Boulanger affair to insure a Republican, loyal, and disciplined army.[49]

Prudente did compromise. In choosing his ministry, he was careful not to antagonize Floriano. Besides being "competent," he wrote, the new ministers could "not signify hostility toward the Marshal, who continues irascible"; and Prudente appointed a finance minister who was "highly esteemed" by Marshal Floriano, besides inspiring general confidence. But Prudente could still write that "the situation continues fraught with apprehension and the murmurs of our pessimistic friends are great."[50]

Prudente de Morais was also well aware of the divisions within the armed forces which facilitated his ascension to power. While some army officers seemed to have been plotting to keep Floriano in office, others signified their refusal to comply with such plans. And the weakened navy, as could be expected, opposed Floriano's remaining in control. Still, some officers favorable to Prudente were being transferred from Rio de Janeiro. Therefore, although Prudente could say that letters from Rio told him that Floriano "was backing down before the opinion and resistance, especially of Barbosa Lima," the officer-governor of Bahia, he continued to be anxious.[51]

49. Gabriel Piza to Prudente, Paris, September 24, 1894, Prudente de Morais Papers.

50. Prudente to Bernardino, Rio de Janeiro, November 11, 1894, in Silveira Peixoto, *A tormenta que Prudente de Morais venceu!*, p. 129.

51. Prudente to Bernardino, Piracicaba, October 22, 1894, in *ibid.*, pp. 123–24; cf. Tobias Monteiro, *O presidente Campos Salles na Europa*, Lvi-Lvii; Medeiros e Albuquerque, *Minha Vida. Memorias*, I, 228–29.

A few years later, after his split with Prudente, Vice-President Manoel Vitorino recalled that "it was very late" for Floriano to "realize his political plans," for he lacked sufficient "capable personnel for the attainment of his ends."[52] While Floriano was still extremely popular among certain army sectors, he could not command a sufficiently strong body of armed forces to illegally prevent Prudente from occupying the presidency. Furthermore, Floriano was infirm and did not have sufficient energy to attempt such a move. Perhaps this illness was the reason Floriano did not attend Prudente's inaugural, although Prudente's supporters construed this as further evidence of the Marshal's hostility. If the armed forces had been united, some other officer, less popular than Floriano, might have been able to lead them against Prudente. However, they were divided.

Despite last-minute rumors of a military movement, Prudente was inaugurated on schedule on November 15, 1894, without military incident. A few days later he could write Bernardino that "the new situation is being inaugurated under good auspices; I received congratulations and adherence from everywhere and from all groups, including officers here and in the states. The *clouds* are disappearing and the horizon is becoming clear," although up to the "last minute" Floriano and his people had been active and intriguing.[53] While Prudente's presidency would not be free from clashes with military elements, the government was now basically in civilian hands.

One group of civilians, composed principally of representatives from the economically powerful state of São Paulo, had profited from the divisions among the armed forces and had

52. Manoel Victorino Pereira, *Manifesto político* (São Paulo: Typ. de Carlos Jeep & Cia., 1898), p. 26.

53. Prudente to Bernardino, Rio de Janeiro, November 18, 1894, in Silveira Peixoto, *A tormenta que Prudente de Morais venceu!*, p. 135.

managed to take direct political control out of the hands of the officers. The *Paulistas* opposed military predominance, for the resultant instability endangered economic growth and prosperity and state autonomy. They could see that a successful military uprising would only encourage future revolts and would leave the government in military hands. Instead of directly attacking the officers in the Floriano government, the *Paulistas* tended to cooperate and compromise when necessary. During the Naval Revolt, they gave decisive aid to the Floriano regime, mainly through their state militia, and were able to secure the election of one of their most antimilitary colleagues, Prudente de Morais, as president. But success was in doubt until the very end, and Prudente's presidency would be a time of continued struggles to impose effective civilian rule.

CHAPTER VIII

Prudente de Morais and the Consolidation of Civilian Rule

DURING THE PRESIDENCY of Prudente de Morais, altercations between civilians and officers continued. But civilians were now able to use the divisions within the armed forces to consolidate their control over the government. Through compromise where necessary, support of certain military factions, and firmness at the right times, Prudente maintained himself in power. When the opposition of dissatisfied officers and of politicians attempting to use military grievances for their own ends culminated in an unsuccessful and poorly conceived effort to assassinate him, Prudente was able to increase his support and to move more forcibly against his opponents. Having secured his position and established civilian rule, he peacefully passed the presidency to a fellow *Paulista* at the conclusion of his term.

Prudente's inauguration was widely hailed as the end of

military rule and the beginning of a better era. Newspapers like *A Notícia* declared that "finally the hour has arrived to return to its scabbard the sword that has been defending the Republic"; up to this point the nation had been governed "the way an army is commanded," but now "the people have invested a man of the law, a civilian statesman, with the executive mandate."[1] Even the *País*, which had long supported Floriano, and which would later come to oppose Prudente, greeted him as "for everyone, a candidate of the nation."[2] An opponent of military rule like Américo Werneck could see Prudente as "the depository of public confidence," who would inaugurate a civilian government.[3] Poems were even written in honor of Prudente to link his name with peace, hailing him as the "shepherd" or the "Moses" desired by the people to end the period of fighting dominated by "warriors."[4] But such a state of virtual euphoria and unaniminity could not long endure, for Prudente would soon have to take specific actions which would antagonize some segments of the population.

Once in power, the *Paulistas* under Prudente de Morais attempted to consolidate their position, and their policies alienated a section of the population, which in part sought to rally about the name of Floriano Peixoto and also to take advantage of divisions within the armed forces. But the *Paulistas* and other civilian elements in the government were more successful in utilizing the disunity of the armed forces. Besides controlling the allocation of government funds and jobs, these civilians skillfully played off the various military factions against each other, taking care to strengthen the position of anti-Floriano officers.

In his efforts to consolidate civilian rule and end military

1. *Noticia*, November 16, 1894, p. 1.
2. *País*, November 15, 1894, p. 1.
3. Werneck, *Erros e vicios*, p. 80.
4. João Dunshee de Abranches Moura, *Pela paz ao dr. Prudente de Moraes.* (Rio de Janeiro: Off. de Obras do Jornal do Brasil, 1895).

demonstrations, with their adverse economic effects, Prudente sought to reduce the size of the armed forces, diminish military expenses, and control the political activities of the officers. The number of troops in the army early in 1896 (approximately 16,500) was less that in early 1893 (18,052), before the outbreak of the Naval Revolt and the resulting increase in recruitment.[5] Yet according to the law of 1895 fixing the number of troops for the coming year, the army should have had 28,160 men instead of approximately 16,500. Thus, while Prudente was not able to secure a legal reduction of the number of enlisted men below 28,000, he kept the army much smaller in actuality. According to his war minister, "there is no necessity to maintain a numerous army under normal conditions for the country."[6] But Prudente could not diminish the number of officers as easily as that of the troops, and in 1896 the officers still totaled 3,352, as against the 1,516 prescribed by law.[7] At least he managed during his entire term in office to hold the number of officers and troops to approximately these figures.

Shortly before the end of his term of office, Marshal Floriano Peixoto had contracted for eight new warships in Europe, besides purchasing large quantities of munitions. Prudente de Morais was unable to cancel all the ship contracts, but he did secure a delay in their completion to help the exhausted treasury. Finally several of the ships, still in Europe, were sold to the Japanese government and to the United States.[8]

5. Brazil, Ministério da Guerra, *Relatório apresentado ao presidente da República dos Estados Unidos do Brazil pelo marechal Bernardo Vasquez, ministro de estado dos negocios da guerra em maio de 1896* (Rio de Janeiro: Imprensa Nacional, 1896), p. 74; Brazil, Ministério da Guerra, *Relatório apresentado ao vice-presidente da República dos Estados Unidos do Brazil pelo general de brigada Francisco Antonio de Moura, ministro de estado dos negocios da guerra em abril de 1893.* (Rio de Janeiro: Imprensa Nacional, 1893), p. 62.

6. Brazil, Ministério da Guerra, *Relatório, 1896*, p. 5.

7. *Ibid.*, p. 74.

8. Frank D. Hill, January 26, 1898, *Reports from the Consuls of the United States* (Washington: U. S. Government Printing Office, 1898), LVII, 510; Piza to

Efforts were also made to professionalize the army, creating a general staff system similar to that of European armies for the "work of organization and regulation of the diverse services" of the army.[9] And sentiment in favor of a small but well-organized and professional army was fostered.[10]

Prudente's choice of war ministers reflected his intention to depoliticize the army, for he chose generals who were committed to civilian rule. It has been noted that many officers favored a less politically oriented officer corps, and Prudente now strengthened this faction and facilitated their efforts to impose such views. In keeping with their earlier records, war ministers like General Bernardo Vasques, minister from November, 1894 to November, 1896, and Marshal Carlos Machado de Bittencourt, minister in 1897, worked to restore military discipline. In 1893, the year before the presidential election, General Vasques had declared that he was and would remain "opposed to rule by the sword" and that it was "absolutely necessary that a civilian name be voted in the coming election, that a patriotic, learned, upright, circumspect, just citizen, *a civilian citizen*, be elected."[11]

Marshal Bittencourt, one of the relatively few *Paulista* army officers,[12] was so strongly opposed to military intervention in

---

Prudente, Paris, December 5, 1894; January 20, 1895; Prudente de Morais Papers; *Jornal do Comércio*, January 20, 1898, p. 1; *Rio News*, January 18, 1898, p. 5; March 22, 1898, p. 4; Monteiro, *O presidente Campos Salles na Europa*, Lxii; some of the munitions contracts are found in the Arquivo Nacional, Cx 1202.

9. Ministério de Guerra, *Relatório, 1896*, p. 4.

10. See Gabriel Salgado, in *Cidade do Rio*, November 18, 1896, p. 2.

11. Bernardo Vasques, "Aos meus concidadãos," Rio de Janeiro, April 17, 1893, in Múcio Teixeira, *A revolução do Rio Grande do Sul. Suas causas e seus effeitos* (Pôrto Alegre: Typ. Jornal do Comércio, 1893), p. 311.

12. Thus under-representation of the *Paulistas* in the national army may have stemmed from a *Paulista* disdain for an army career, the absence of a need for the educational opportunities the army provided, or a lack of active army recruiting in São Paulo. It was closely related to *Paulista* antimilitary feelings. Under the federal regime São Paulo continued to maintain one of the largest

state political affairs that in 1891, following Floriano's accession to power, he had tried to resist the Marshal's efforts and those of the *Paulistas* to overturn their state government. At that time, he telegraphed Floriano that he "could only maintain the constituted authority [in São Paulo] if the 24th battalion is not withdrawn from here, as the adjunct general has just ordered me."[13] When Campos Sales informed him that a commission was going to invite the governor of São Paulo to resign, he again telegraphed Floriano, for he did "not wish to be involved in the politics of the state, so I ask you to give orders on the way I should face this question and the measures I should take."[14] But, since the intention of the federal government was to depose the state governor, his orders were reaffirmed, and he complied, despite his disapproval of such political military undertakings. A general who was loath to overthrow governments was most welcome as war minister under Prudente. And when Bittencourt assumed office he declared that "a soldier should have no politics; he should think only of performing his duty to his country. I know very well that there are divergent opinions; but they are confined to a small group, and with slight effort I hope in a short time to see them entirely disappear."[15]

Starting with his first days in office, Prudente removed many of Floriano's appointees and filled positions with men more in accord with his policies. Such acts angered Floriano and many of his supporters, who could see that Prudente was weakening their position and strengthening that of rival fac-

---

and best-organized state forces, and many army officers, viewing the army as a national unifying force and perhaps jealous of these state armies, objected to them.

13. General Carlos Machado de Bittencourt to Floriano, São Paulo, November 23, 1891, Arquivo Nacional, Cx 1206.

14. Bittencourt to Floriano, São Paulo, November 24, 1891, Arquivo Nacional, Cx 1206.

15. *Rio News*, May 25, 1897, p. 4.

tions. Prudente's ministerial choices included civilians like Amaro Cavalcanti, one of Floriano's strongest opponents. Numerous army officers holding governmental posts lost them. In a letter written late in November of 1894 to an officer-friend who had been director of the Central Railroad, Floriano expressed his hostility toward his successors, bitterly noting that they had coveted and secured these positions and that "they are executing their plan and it seems to me that it is going *very well.* Poor country!!!"[16] Prudente was utilizing the divisions within the officer corps to improve the position of those more favorable to him and to strengthen their loyalty. In so doing, he evoked tremendous hostility from Floriano's people, but these no longer controlled the government apparatus, and, because of the fragmentation of the armed forces, they could not amass sufficient power to stop him.

Prudente actually succeeded in cowing some politically minded officers, as can be seen in a Club Militar resolution passed only a few months after he had assumed office. Despite their admiration for Floriano Peixoto, the members of the Club Militar voted against sending a special greeting to the Marshal on his birthday. As the interim president of the Club argued, "this act is imprudent in view of how past occurrences and manifestations to Marshal Floriano Peixoto appeared to the government, giving rise to . . . acts which contributed to

16. Floriano Peixoto to Colonel Vespasiano de Albuquerque, November 28, 1894, in possession of Colonel Ademir Guimarães (Rio de Janeiro). A similar letter of disappointment was written to console a friend whom Floriano had rewarded for his service as governor of Rio de Janeiro during the Naval Revolt with a diplomatic post in Vienna, but whose appointment the Senate under Prudente had refused to confirm. Floriano lamented that "the spirit of miniature sordid politics had set up court in that edifice," and that "the bravest and most resolute laborers against the revolt are now the *spiteful ones*, the *criminals*" (Floriano Peixoto to José Tomás da Porciúcula, Rio de Janeiro, November 27, 1894, in Afonso Arinos de Melo Franco, *Um estadista da república* [*Afrânio de Melo Franco e seu tempo*] [Rio de Janeiro: José Olympio, 1955], I, 260–61).

weakening the military"; therefore, it would "be very prudent not to awaken the attention of the government and give rise to its taking precautions, even though unfounded ones."[17]

The divisions within the armed forces and the difficulties besetting the civilian regime became most apparent when the government attempted to bring peace to Rio Grande do Sul. Passions kindled by this struggle and by the Naval Revolt could not be easily quenched. Those officers who had fought for the Floriano government were unwilling to countenance an amnesty they thought too favorable to the rebels. But Prudente was determined to pursue such a policy, for he could profit from a peace permitting Floriano's military rivals to re-enter the armed forces, thus maintaining the disunity of the army and reducing its political strength. Furthermore, for the security of civilian rule and of his own regime, Prudente de Morais had to end the fighting in Rio Grande as quickly as possible. Continued warfare was straining the treasury, promoting additional instability, and necessitating the maintenance of a large army. Moreover, the separatist and monarchist tendencies in the struggle seemed to be growing stronger.[18] But many insurgents seemed anxious to cease fighting if they could obtain certain guarantees.[19] War-weariness in Rio Grande and in the country as a whole strengthened the peace sentiment.

Despite these considerations, Prudente moved slowly, for he knew that some regarded him as favorable to the rebels. In his

17. Atas of Club Militar, meeting of April 29, 1895.

18. See Gabriel Piza to Prudente, Paris, June 10, 1896, Prudente de Morais Papers; Prudente interview in *Jornal do Brasil*, December 15, 1894, p. 1; Eduardo Prado to Gaspar da Silveira Martins, n.p., November 17, 1895, in José Júlio Silveira Martins, *Silveira Martins* (Rio de Janeiro: São Benedicto, 1929), pp. 401–402.

19. See interview with General Salgado, *Jornal do Brasil*, April 22, 1895, p. 1; interview with Silva Tavares, *Notícia*, March 27, 1895, p. 1; interview with Berford Guimarães, *Correio de Tarde*, March 2, 1895, p. 1.

own draft of his inaugural address, he had castigated the military revolts tormenting the young republic, including Deodoro da Fonseca's coup d'état of November 3, 1891, the uprising at the Santa Cruz fortress, and the troubles of April 10, 1892, as well as the *Federalist* and naval insurrections. But Quintino Bocaiúva, editor of the *País*, rewrote this section of the address, and his version citing only the Naval Revolt became the official text.[20]

As Campos Sales, his fellow *Paulista*, warned Prudente, the Floriano people would try to convince everyone "that your government is one of reaction against those who fought the revolt and defended the republic."[21] Recognizing the strength of this opposition and the unlikelihood of the passage of an amnesty bill at this time, Prudente did not wish to press the matter. He preferred that the limited amnesty project presented by Campos Sales not "appear with the responsibility of the government," and the bill was defeated.[22] In his message to Congress, Prudente stressed that elements from the Naval Revolt had joined the revolution in the south, and that "this struggle cannot terminate without the submission of its promoters" to the institutions of the nation.[23] Many Rio newspapers, such as the *Jornal do Comércio*, the *Gazeta da Tarde, Cidade do Rio*, and the *Jornal do Brasil*, misinterpreted this message as a stern refusal to seek an amnesty. The *Gazeta da Tarde* even accused "*the fat nonentities of the purple earth*" (referring to the rich coffee-producing soil in São Paulo), "this

20. Drafts in Prudente de Morais Papers. For a different version of Quintino's modification of Prudente's original message, see Manoel Victorino Pereira, *Manifesto político*, pp. 32–33.

21. Campos Sales to Prudente, São Paulo, February 16, 1895, Prudente de Morais Papers.

22. Prudente to Campos Sales, Rio de Janeiro, May 21, 1895, in Silveira Peixoto, *A tormenta que Prudente de Morais venceu!*, p. 146.

23. *Notícia*, May 4, 1895, p. 1.

insignificant minority which governs the country," of wishing to continue the war.[24]

At the same time that he made these concessions to the anti-insurgent elements, Prudente began more strenuous efforts to secure peace. A month after his message to Congress, Prudente nominated a new army commander in Rio Grande, General Inocêncio Galvão de Queiroz, who would soon negotiate a peace settlement. These efforts were strengthened by the defeat of the *Federalists* in the last major encounter of the revolution, a battle in which Admiral Saldanha da Gama was killed. Despite financial problems, internal dissensions among the insurgents, and his acknowledgment of the virtual impossibility of victory, Saldanha had fought on, not believing Prudente or the *Paulistas* would favor a just pacification settlement.[25] With his death, effective rebel resistance came to an end, the general desire for peace was strengthened, and the possibility of attaining a settlement was improved, for Saldanha had been considered a monarchist with whom there could be no compromise. On June 29, 1895, five days after Saldanha's death, his great adversary Floriano Peixoto died peacefully on a farm outside the capital. Although Floriano's partisans would continue to oppose the Prudente government, Floriano's death may also have contributed to the termination of the Rio Grande conflict.

The admitted strategy of General Galvão, Prudente's new army commander in Rio Grande do Sul, was to "separate the republicans hostile to the government of Júlio de Castilhos from the monarchists led by Saldanha da Gama and Gaspar

24. *Gazeta da Tarde*, May 25, 1895, p. 2.

25. Saldanha da Gama to Carlos Landares, Montevideo, October 9, 1894; November 20, 1894; December 12, 1894; Serviço Geral da Marinha, Box 70, Ministério da Marinha; Saldanha da Gama to Rui Barbosa, Montevideo, October 5, 1894, Arquivo da Casa de Rui Barbosa, Pasta Luís Felipe de Saldanha da Gama.

Martins."[26] He extended an invitation to General João Nunes da Silva Tavares, one of the main *Federalist* leaders, for a peace conference. During a mutual cessation of hostilities the conference was held, and General Tavares declared his willingness to lay down his arms if the insurgents were effectively guaranteed all their constitutional rights by the central government, if the positivist-oriented constitution of Rio Grande, which gave overwhelming power to the executive, would be reconstituted in line with the federal constitution, and if the *Federalists* were to receive some indemnities.

Such terms were not completely acceptable. From the beginning, Governor Júlio de Castilhos of Rio Grande do Sul had opposed Galvão's meeting with Tavares, arguing that pacification could come only "from the real submission of the rebels," and he warned Prudente that "Galvão's attitude is becoming more and more imprudent and dangerous every time."[27] Prudente consulted with various statesmen about the pacification proposals, and many said that the federal government had no right to interfere in the organization of state governments.[28] While Prudente assured Castilhos that the federal regime would never agree that the state constitution be changed, Castilhos continued to accuse Galvão of acting illegally and requested the general's removal. Furthermore, Castilhos argued that a rapid military campaign would completely settle the problem.[29] Prudente refused to agree to Cas-

26. General Galvão to Prudente, Pelotas, June 30, 1895, Prudente de Morais Papers.

27. Castilhos to Prudente, Pôrto Alegre, July 4, 1895; July 23, 1895; Prudente de Morais Papers.

28. See resumés by Prudente of opinions of Ubaldino do Amaral, July 23, 1895; Manoel Vitorino, July 25, 1895; Campos Sales, July 25, 1895; Pinheiro Machado, n.d.; Leopoldo de Bulhões to Prudente, Senate, July 31, 1895, Prudente de Morais Papers.

29. Prudente to Castilhos, Rio de Janeiro, August 2, 1895; Castilhos to Prudente, Pôrto Alegre, August 3, 1895; Prudente de Morais Papers. See also Castilhos to Prudente, Pôrto Alegre, August 24, 1895; August 27, 1895; August 30, 1895; Prudente de Morais Papers.

tilhos' demands, although two months after the passage of the amnesty bill Galvão was removed from his command in Rio Grande for having supported the former insurgents' demands too strenuously.

A modified amnesty bill was finally voted by Congress in October of 1895. To help secure passage of this bill, Prudente tried to rush the collection of rebel arms in Rio Grande. He also threatened to resign the presidency. Although an unconditional amnesty project was defeated, Prudente did manage to cut from three to two years the time lapse before the rebel officers could return to active service.

Through concessions to both the rebels and their opponents, Prudente had ended the fighting in Rio Grande, which had necessitated the maintenance of a large and expensive army and had kept the country in an unsettled state. Although the president had thus attempted to mollify the pro-Floriano officers who wished to prevent an unconditional amnesty and to delay the final peace, they remained dissatisfied with the Prudente regime, which they accused of favoring the former rebels. Many such opposition elements now looked to Júlio de Castilhos for assistance. The former insurgents, on the other hand, were coming to support the Prudente government. In two years they would be readmitted to military ranks, and Prudente would be assured an additional counterweight to the pro-Floriano elements. Some days after the amnesty bill was passed, another group of anti-Floriano officers, those whom the Marshal had forcibly retired in April of 1893 for having published a manifesto calling on him to hold presidential elections, were returned to active service. Such a fractious and mutually suspicious military was not very likely to move against Prudente.

Some military elements continued to demonstrate their hostility toward the government, despite Prudente's skillful use of military divisions to maintain civilian control. Much of this resistance was centered in the Military School in Rio de Janeiro. Many of the pupils continued to suspect the government of sympathizing with Floriano's opponents in the Naval Revolt and in the Rio Grande do Sul conflict. By themselves, these students could never bring sufficient military pressure against the government to displace it, but they could perhaps create sufficient agitation and unrest to precipitate intervention by the regular armed forces. Some of Prudente's opponents tended to support them, contributing to the general turmoil. But Prudente dealt firmly with the cadets, thereby impressing other, more powerful military elements with his will and capacity to defend his regime.

Early in 1895, students at the Military School celebrated the anniversary of the termination of the Naval Revolt with a demonstration basically hostile to the government and to the director of the school. With the support of the war minister and Prudente, the director ordered some infantry and cavalry forces to take control, and, when the demonstrations continued he closed the school and dismissed a large number of pupils.[30] While in itself the Military School presented only a minor threat to the stability of the government, any hesitation in putting down insubordination there could only encourage insubordination elsewhere, and at the time pacification in Rio Grande had not yet been assured.

The *País*, under Quintino Bocaiúva, who had long been a supporter of Marshal Floriano Peixoto and his policies, as shown by his modification of Prudente's inaugural address, immediately came to the defense of the school. This leading newspaper deplored "the unfortunate events of which so many

30. General Joaquim Mendes Ourique Jacques to General Bernardo Vasques, Rio de Janeiro, March 14, 1895; March 16, 1895, Arquivo do Ministério da Guerra, 2ª seção, Documentos diversos, Cx 132; *Gazeta de Noticias*, March 15, 1895, p. 2; March 16, 1895, p. 1; March 17, 1895, p. 1; *Diário de Noticias*, March 16, 1895, p. 1; *País*, March 16, 1895, p. 1; *Jornal do Comércio*, March 18, 1895, p. 1; *Jornal do Brasil*, March 19, 1895, p. 1.

and so noble boys were victims—faithful soldiers of the republic, and most enthusiastically dedicated to it." It opened a subscription for the expelled pupils, although the government was providing them with transportation home.[31] A columnist in a pro-government newspaper argued that the *País*, by saying that the government abused these pupils and that it would soon "dissolve one battalion, and later the national army," was "presenting the government as an adversary of the army" and was again summoning this body "into active politics, in which it cannot enter as a corporation except through the vile door of revolution."[32]

Another sympathizer with the military cadets was the popular Francisco Glicério, one of the *Paulista* leaders. With the election of Prudente de Morais, the political unity of this group also had begun to weaken. Glicério had worked more closely with Floriano Peixoto than any of the others, and he tended to gravitate toward the ranks of Floriano's followers who were dissatisfied with Prudente's more conservative policies. He seemed to be spending more time in Rio de Janeiro than in São Paulo and perhaps was losing some of his original political base, while turning more to military elements for support.

These divisions among the *Paulistas* became more apparent when the cadets of the Military School expressed their hostility to the government. Campos Sales wrote Prudente that he "wholeheartedly applauded your measures affecting the Military School," for in this way "a difficulty, if not a danger was removed," since "those people, with the heat that Benjamin [Constant] bequeathed them, thought they could govern the world."[33] But Glicério wrote to Prudente requesting that the

31. *País*, March 17, 1895, p. 1.

32. "Cousas políticas," *Gazeta de Noticias*, March 26, 1895, p. 1.

33. Campos Sales to Prudente, Aguas Virtuosas, March 28, 1895, Prudente de Morais Papers.

expelled pupils of the Military School be readmitted, in addition to permitting them "to accompany the burial of Floriano, in uniform."[34] However, Prudente refused to reinstate them, holding that "this would mean the re-establishment of indiscipline, anarchy, and constant disturbances of the order in this capital."[35] Glicério then fostered a congressional bill to readmit these students. As Campos Sales later wrote, during this period "no politician out of power had personal prestige equal to that attained by Glicério in that phase of national politics."[36]

Relations between Prudente and Glicério continued to deteriorate. While Prudente had appeared to be cooperating with Glicério, he had come to consider him one of the leaders of the "Jacobins," the vehement Republicans who hated him and his policies and who, "as soon as they feel they have enough forces to substitute for me some *general,* who will carry out the strong *politics* of the Marshal [Floriano], will not postpone it until the following day."[37]

A subsequent incident involving the Military School precipitated the final breach between Glicério and Prudente, as well as a schism in the Federal Republican Party. Citing conditions in Uruguay and the request of the army commander in Rio Grande do Sul for additional arms, the government ordered a large number of guns removed from the Military School. But the pupils, charging the government with an attempt to disarm them, mutinied, arrested their commander, and armed themselves. Soon they were forced to surrender. Pupils there and at the military school in Ceará, which had

34. Glicério to Prudente, Rio de Janeiro, July 3, 1895, Prudente de Morais Papers.

35. Prudente to Glicério, Rio de Janeiro, July 3, 1895 (draft), Prudente de Morais Papers.

36. Campos Salles, *Da propaganda à presidencia,* pp. 128–29.

37. Prudente to Bernardino, Rio de Janeiro, January 10, 1896, in Mota Filho, *Uma grande vida. Biográfia de Bernardino de Campos,* p. 272.

also mutinied in sympathy with the cadets in Rio, were expelled. While Glicério, playing upon *Paulista* interests, requested Prudente to avoid "any clash, any disturbance which at this time could lead to a definitive financial disaster," José Joaquim Seabra of Bahia, an old enemy of Floriano, introduced a motion in Congress to nominate a commission to congratulate Prudente for reestablishing order after the sedition in the Military School.[38] Glicério maintained that he opposed any movement of indiscipline, but he argued against this motion as an attempt to divide the party. On May 29, 1897, the day after the motion was rejected, the *Jornal do Comércio* announced that it considered itself authorized to declare that Glicério no longer interpreted the sentiments of the government in Congress.[39]

Four days later, Glicério was defeated in the election for president of the Chamber of Deputies. In his move against Glicério, who received support from the followers of Júlio de Castilhos in Rio Grande do Sul, Prudente counted most heavily on the aid of the representatives of São Paulo, Minas Gerais, Pernambuco, and Bahia. He telegraphed the governor of Minas Gerais requesting continued support from the *Mineiro* congressmen, arguing that the vote in the Chamber against the motion supporting his actions in the Military School incident "meant an incitement to new revolts."[40] With the aid of other state governors whom he requested to ensure the votes of their congressional representatives, the defeat of Glicério was assured. This policy of relying on state governors to provide congressmen favorably disposed toward the central

38. Glicério to Prudente, Rio de Janeiro, May 26, 1897, Prudente de Morais Papers.

39. A copy of the announcement which appeared in the *Jornal do Comércio* is found in Prudente's handwriting in the Prudente de Morais Papers.

40. Prudente to President of Minas Gerais, Rio de Janeiro, May 29, 1897, Prudente de Morais Papers.

government, while in return the central government refrained from interfering in the states, had been termed the "politics of the governors" and would be characteristic of the oligarchic First Republic, which extended to 1930.

In São Paulo, Glicério found little support, for the *Paulista* politicians basically agreed with Prudente's more conservative policies, which tended to safeguard their position and which were more likely to insure political stability. As Campos Sales reported to Prudente, Glicério was "isolated, without a single adhesion from the local directories," and "the entire state is with us. . . . altogether, the result we have obtained leaves nothing to be desired."[41] In São Paulo, the elections of December 1, 1897, and March 1, 1898, resulted in "the complete crushing of Glicério" even in Campinas, his home territory.[42]

The schism in the Federal Republican Party made apparent the shift in power which had been under way since the beginning of Prudente's administration. Some of his enemies even accused him of having transferred control from the Republicans who had proclaimed the republic to elements of the old monarchical regime. While strongly opposed to the monarchy, the *Paulistas* revealed interests contrary to those of many urban, military, and less propertied elements which had participated in the early phases of the Republican government.

The *Paulistas'* interests were still basically agricultural, not urban or industrial. The first years of the republic were an exceptionally favorable period for the coffee growers, with abundant credit for financing the opening of new land and an expanding international market for their coffee, since Asian sources were encountering blights. By 1900–1901, more than three times as many coffee trees were in production in

41. Campos Sales to Prudente, São Paulo, July 10, 1897, Prudente de Morais Papers.

42. Campos Sales to Prudente, São Paulo, March 22, 1898, Prudente de Morais Papers.

São Paulo than had been in 1890–91.[43] Brazilian coffee production had risen from 3.7 million bags in 1880–81, to 5.5 million bags in 1890–91, and to 16.3 million bags in 1901–2.[44] The *Paulista* leaders defended and fostered agriculture, which for them constituted the prime source of Brazil's wealth. The industrial development of São Paulo had not yet gathered force, and the industrialists calling for government protection and aid in the name of economic nationalism rarely included *Paulistas*. Prudente's finance minister even thought industrial development was prejudicing agriculture by attracting into the cities labor and capital which was necessary to agriculture.[45]

The heterogeneous urban groups could contribute to the social and political unrest of the period, but they did not have the strength to overthrow or basically modify the Prudente government. While many of them had supported Deodoro and Floriano, for the imperial regime had neglected their interests, they did not supply the power necessary to sustain these administrations. Instead, Deodoro and Floriano had maintained their control basically through the force of arms.

With the world economic crises of 1893 and 1897, and the fall in coffee prices which was partially due to the excessive expansion of coffee plantations, the exchange rate had fallen. Dependent on many imported items, from basic foodstuffs to various manufactured goods, the urban groups suffered economic hardship resulting from the depreciation of the exchange rate and the concomitant rise in prices. The coffee

43. V. D. Wickizer, *The World Coffee Economy, with Special Reference to Control Schemes* (Stanford: Food Research Institute, Stanford University, 1943), p. 139.

44. Celso Furtado, *The Economic Growth of Brazil: A Survey from Colonial to Modern Times* trans. Ricardo W. de Aguiar and Eric Charles Drysdale (Berkeley: University of California Press, 1963), p. 193. A bag of coffee contains 60 kilos or approximately 132 pounds.

45. See Nícia Villela Luz, *A luta pela industrialização do Brasil (1808–1930)* (São Paulo: Difusão Européia do Livro, 1961), pp. 96–117, 157–75.

planters, in contrast, fared far better. While their exports now earned smaller quantities of foreign currency, each unit of this money bought a larger amount of local currency.

The coffee planters were able to pass on resulting losses, but the urban, middle-class sectors were directly affected, and unrest increased. The urban groups were hardest hit by inflation and by the Prudente government's discouragement of industrial expansion. Many of these same urban elements had also suffered financial losses resulting from the *encilhamento,* the large credit and currency expansion and investment bubble during the provisional government, which also contributed to a boom-and-bust psychology. While some *Paulista* landowners profited from this expansion, they were generally alarmed by the loose credit procedures. The landowning elements continued to consider political stability essential for their prosperity, and they vigorously opposed any urban agitation.

Like some Republicans under the empire, a number of Prudente's opponents now thought they might benefit by military unrest. Discontented urban elements, some die-hard monarchists, and various ambitious politicians all encouraged dissident military elements to move against the government.

Some of Prudente's most bitter enemies were the "Jacobins," the extreme nationalists and vehement Republicans who glorified Floriano's memory and who vituperatively attacked any departure from the Marshal's policies. Noting with astonishment and relish "the modification that is apparent in everything," a close associate of Rui Barbosa, who had remained abroad after the Naval Revolt was over, declared that "those most displeased with the situation are the fanatical elements of the 'Jacobins,' who carried out the atrocities of the *major* [Floriano]."[46] As Prudente's term in office pro-

46. Tobias Monteiro to Rui Barbosa, Rio de Janeiro, January 6, 1895, Arquivo da Casa de Rui Barbosa, Pasta Tobias do Rêgo Monteiro.

gressed, they grew more dissatisfied with his actions and more vehement in their opposition, virtually calling on the armed forces to move against him. Their views are well reflected in *O Jacobino,* a violently Republican and nationalistic newspaper which also defended the urban workers and which was somewhat sporadically published in Rio de Janeiro during Prudente's presidency. Continually praising Floriano for his patriotism, nationalism, and republicanism, this journal accused Prudente of nullifying his predecessor's policies, which he had promised to follow, of dismissing masses of Floriano's civilian and military appointees, and of moving against the army. *O Jacobino* denounced the reduction in army and navy size as a danger to the nation and urged "the army to be alert and oppose the passage of any such law which is a threat to its existence."[47] During the major military-political incidents of the period, such as those relating to the Military School, this journal actively opposed Prudente, his tenacious persecution of the "brave youth of the national army," and the "dictatorial act of the government closing the glorious Military School."[48] Even an opponent of Prudente who agreed that Floriano's policies were no longer being followed, and that "all the great social reforms that we won on November 15, 1889," were being destroyed, could criticize the Jacobins, that "ardently republican element" which first "agitates and finally conspires" against the government.[49]

Opposition elements like the Jacobins realized that Prudente was using the disunity within the armed forces to weaken their political position. They accused him of seeking to govern the nation by creating dissension in the army and navy,

47. *Jacobino,* November 18, 1894, p. 3.

48. *Jacobino,* April 6, 1895, p. 1; June 12, 1895, p. 1.

49. Joaquim Francisco Assis Brazil, *O attentado de 5 de novembro de 1897 contra o presidente da república. Causa e effeitos* (São Paulo: Casa Vanordem, 1909), pp. 48, 53.

but they were powerless to stop him. All they could do was attempt to stimulate military discontent and incite military elements to move against the government.

This disunity within the armed forces offered opportunities for attempts at manipulation by the various opponents of the government. These enemies of Prudente often pointed to a supposed monarchist danger, of which Prudente was presumed to be insufficiently aware, and called upon the army to save the republic. A monarchist threat also provided many officers with the opportunity to speak out.

The Club Militar, the spokesman for many of the most politically active officers, published an antimonarchist "pact of solidarity to resist at all costs any attempt to change" the institutions of the republic which were menaced by subversive groups. Moreover, they declared "that the destinies of the republic are identified with their very military honor," and that the army could not play a role of "political passivity," as some groups desired.[50] In addition to the unusually large number of officers who signed this manifesto, many others pledged their solidarity. While a few officers published statements opposing "meetings and military manifestos," viewing them as "incompatible with military discipline," the vast majority disagreed and thought they had the right to defend the republic as they wished.[51] However, civilians in government resented such assertions and the implication that Prudente was not sufficiently concerned with the monarchist peril. A few days later Prudente felt obliged to issue rejoinders that the "monarchist propaganda does not have the importance attributed to it."[52]

50. *País,* March 22, 1896, p. 1.

51. See statements published in *País,* March 23, 1896, p. 1; March 24, 1896, p. 1; March 25, 1896, pp. 1–2; March 26, 1896, p. 1; March 27, 1896, pp. 1–2; March 28, 1896, p. 1; March 29, 1896, pp. 1–2; March 30, 1896, p. 1.

52. Prudente to Governor of Maranhão, Rio de Janeiro, March 27, 1896, Prudente de Morais Papers.

While the government could not publicly censure a statement of support for the republic, Prudente's brother, a federal senator from São Paulo, sponsored an article attacking "such demonstrations of military officers." A newspaper he edited proclaimed that "a soldier has no politics," and that if the situation were actually so dangerous, "it is because our military men have not conformed in their practice to this great principle of public order. The soldiers, as soldiers, have no right to any preference as to the form of government: it is their duty to be faithful to their constitutional mission. When the sovereign nation clothed them in its uniform as its defenders, it conferred upon them no right to be its rulers."[53]

The existence of an actual monarchist danger is debatable, but a number of monarchists did attempt to provoke military discontent and gain support from some military factions. Under the Prudente regime, there were fewer restrictions on the monarchists' activities than under Deodoro or Floriano; they set up centers in Rio de Janeiro and São Paulo, published newspapers, issued manifestoes, organized a political party, and instituted a more active propaganda campaign. At the meeting of the Club Militar at which the antimonarchist motion was adopted, officers spoke of "attempts at bribery" and even presented "documents corroborating the subversive efforts of the enemies of the republic."[54] In one manifesto to the nation, a group of leading statesmen of the empire described how the "new regime was born in uniform in order to afflict even its only and true authors, the army," which once had been well treated but now, like the navy, suffered grievous wrongs.[55] Eduardo Prado argued that the army, which had

53. *Rio News*, April 7, 1896, p. 6.

54. *País*, March 22, 1896, p. 1.

55. Visconde de Ouro Prêto, João Alfredo Correia de Oliveira, Domingos de Andrade Figueira, Lafayette Rodrigues Pereira, Carlos Affonso de Assis Figueiredo, "À nação brazileira," *Comércio de São Paulo*, January 14, 1896, p. 1.

created the republic, was being gravely damaged by the unpatriotic Republicans and was even "considered troublesome by its very child." The republic was "slowly destroying it through fear that it would repent" of its earlier deed and was "reducing its size and prestige, because, as the republican masters say—the republic does not need an army."[56] Like some Republicans under the empire, Prado was playing on perennial military fears of dissolution or enfeeblement and calling on the officers to move against the government to save the nation.

Campos Sales, the governor of São Paulo, was aware that the monarchists' existence and scheming provided opportunities for others to injure the government, and that some monarchists were trying to foster and use military dissension. For these reasons he wanted their activities limited. In 1896, he closed the monarchist center in São Paulo, although he admitted that "the monarchists here cannot amass strength, because their very leaders are heartily divided." But it was "certain that they have never appeared so bold as now," and Campos Sales feared they might foster and take advantage of "an atmosphere of unrest," unless the Republicans remained alert. "The process," he said, "is not new; this was the way we caused the monarchy to fall."[57] Some months later, he wrote Prudente that he should take action against the monarchists throughout the nation and suspend their newspapers and meetings. While Campos Sales did "not fear that the monarchists can destroy the republic," they were "moving toward revolutionary processes." Moreover, Brazil's "financial credit will not become secure abroad while it is supposed there that reactionary elements here are powerful." Again he reminded

56. Eduardo Prado (pseud. Graccho), *Salvemos o Brazil* (Rio de Janeiro: September 25, 1899), p. 10.

57. Campos Sales to Prudente, São Paulo, October 28, 1896, Prudente de Morais Papers.

Prudente that the Republicans now controlling the government "should not do what the monarchists did, heedlessly letting their regime fall."[58] Campos Sales, like many others, was feeling the effects of events in the interior of the northeast—the Canudos affair and the rising antimonarchist sentiments it produced.

In the backlands of the state of Bahia, far from the concerns of the European-oriented Brazilians dealing with the central government, a dissident local movement had developed. This movement may have been the result of the religious fanaticism of a group isolated and alienated from the Brazilian society of the seaboard, or it may have been partially an outgrowth of local political rivalries and insubordination, but it was not a centrally controlled or subsidized monarchist uprising. An expedition sent by the state governor against Canudos, the base of Antônio "Conselheiro" and his followers, was easily defeated. Then the governor appealed for help to the central government, and two subsequent expeditions composed of federal and state troops were sent against the religious fanatics led by Antônio "Conselheiro." But these expeditions were poorly organized and were led by men unfamiliar with the terrain, the nature of the enemy, or his mode of fighting, and they were repelled with great losses. In the distant southern cities many sincerely thought that this struggle posed a serious threat to Republican institutions and involved prominent monarchists; others seized upon it for political gain.

During this period, the federal government was in the hands of Vice-President Manoel Vitorino Pereira, who sought to gain increasing political power through cooperation with dissident military elements. In November of 1896, Prudente had been forced to undergo an operation and then spend a

58. Campos Sales to Prudente, São Paulo, April 2, 1897, Prudente de Morais Papers.

number of months convalescing, away from the capital. The vice-president, perhaps believing he would finish out Prudente's term, made a number of policy and personnel changes. Until he had become acting president, Manoel Vitorino had not expressed noticeably pro-military sentiments. But once in power, he attempted to win military support, granting the officers certain favors and attempting to weaken the position of those loyal to the president. Two weeks after Prudente passed the control of the government over to Manoel Vitorino, General Bernardo Vasques, Prudente's severe and disciplined war minister, was replaced. Numerous changes were also made in the naval ministry. Though he was aware of this threat to his position, Prudente was too ill to return immediately. When he felt that he had recovered his health sufficiently, and friends advised him that the time was ripe for a return, he left for Rio, without notifying Manoel Vitorino, although the vice-president had previously requested that he be informed when the president was going to return.[59] Having been displaced from power, Manoel Vitorino remained one of Prudente's most vehement opponents and turned increasingly to dissident military elements.

A few days after Prudente reassumed control of the government, news arrived of the defeat of the third expedition against Canudos and the death of its commander, the fiery Colonel Antônio Moreira César, who had been extremely popular among his fellow officers. An antimonarchist outburst greeted this news, and the government itself seemed in danger. The offices of three monarchist journals were destroyed, and Gentil de Castro, partial owner of two of them, was assassinated by a small group of officers. Two leading monarchists, the Viscount of Ouro Prêto and Afonso Celso, barely escaped

59. See Manoel Vitorino to Bernardino de Campos, Rio de Janeiro, January 14, 1897; Rodrigues Alves to Prudente, Rio de Janeiro, February 1, 1897; Prudente to Bernardino, Teresópolis, February 27, 1897, Prudente de Morais Papers.

with their lives. With such ferocious Republican sentiment rampant, the government was either unable or unwilling to risk any defense of these monarchists. Pro-Prudente newspapers, however, like the *Jornal do Comércio* were protected by the police.[60]

Emotions were at a savage pitch, and many felt that the republic was in the gravest danger. Some opposition papers like the *República* continued to assert that the backwoodsmen at Canudos must be receiving aid from the outside, for "they do not have sufficient resources to do what these hordes are doing"; this journal also maintained that monarchists had been seen sending arms destined for Canudos through Minas Gerais.[61] Rumors continued to circulate that foreigners were training the rebels, who were said to have much imported equipment, or that prominent monarchists were fighting among them. For example, one officer in Bahia excitedly telegraphed the Minister of War that he had seen a letter sent to Canudos addressed to a former naval insurgent and that the letter contained news of arms shipments for Antônio "Conselheiro." Prudente was well aware that this particular former naval officer was working peacefully in Rio de Janeiro at the time.[62] Even Campos Sales questioned whether the followers of Antônio "Conselheiro" could defeat "organized courageous troops led by commanders of the greatest prestige and proven ability" without outside aid.[63]

Although the unsuccessful Moreira César expedition had

60. See Feliciano Gonzaga to José Carlos Rodrigues, Rio de Janeiro, March 16, 1897, Seção de Manuscritos da Biblioteca Nacional, I–3, 2, 88; Tobias Monteiro to Rodrigues, Rio de Janeiro, March 16, 1897, Seção de Manuscritos da Biblioteca Nacional, I–3, 3, 63.

61. *República*, February 20, 1897, p. 1; February 21, 1897, p. 1; February 22, 1897, p. 1.

62. Captain João Luis de Castro e Silva to Minister of War, Monte Santo, August 4, 1897; unsigned statements in handwriting of Amaro Cavalcanti, Prudente de Morais Papers.

63. Campos Sales to Prudente, São Paulo, March, 1897, Prudente de Morais Papers.

been organized by the vice-president, Prudente was subject to accusations of lacking patriotism and of destroying the army. Prudente was actually not joking when he said, as a friend reported, that he was "afraid of being considered a monarchist (*sebastianista*)," for he thought "excessive the zeal of those individuals who live to find themselves surrounded by monarchists and to discover conspiracies every minute."[64] While Prudente and his ministers denied the existence of a serious monarchist danger to the republic, many officers felt that he was not acting decisively enough and was permitting the army to be decimated. Following the defeat of the Moreira César expedition, the Club Militar sent a commission to seek information from the government on this disaster, and its members continued to be hostile.

Prudente had so far been able to maintain himself in power because the diverse elements within the armed forces had never been able to unite against him. But the officers might succeed in forgetting their differences if they thought that the army's very existence was at stake in Canudos and that the government was not moving to meet this grave threat. Prudente's opponents, such as Vice-President Manoel Vitorino, attempted to play upon such army fears. Shortly after the Club Militar had questioned Prudente on the defeat of the Moreira César expedition against Canudos, Manoel Vitorino wrote the Club that Moreira César had warned the government against reducing "the garrison in the capital and principal cities of the country," for he had been convinced that this was being done "in obedience to the plan of dispersing the troops in order better to facilitate the execution of monarchist purposes and plans." Manoel Vitorino declared that "to avenge the death of the distinguished officer [Moreira César]

64. Tobias Monteiro to José Carlos Rodrigues, Rio de Janeiro, March 16, 1897, Seção de Manuscritos da Biblioteca Nacional, I–3, 3, 63.

I will be at their side [the officers] here or at the theater of battle, whenever my presence is needed."[65] Aware of such efforts to stimulate military fears and force Prudente from office, Joaquim Nabuco held that, "if the work against Prudente continues, he will not find even a small boat on which to flee, at the first sign from Manoel Vitorino."[66]

Certain monarchists, such as Eduardo Prado, also attempted to take advantage of the Canudos affair to stir up further army discontent. Denying that the monarchists had "the slightest responsibility, direct or indirect, in the revolt of Antônio Conselheiro," he held the Republican government responsible for the army defeats, as it had "disorganized the army and the national defense, to the point of exposing the bravery of the Brazilian soldier to disasters of that magnitude."[67]

As the Canudos campaign continued, Prudente's military opponents grew bolder. General Arthur Oscar, commander of the fourth expedition against Canudos, sent messages to opposition newspapers about the enemy's skill in using excellent arms. He even queried rhetorically, "Who furnishes those arms and munitions in such abundance? Through where do they pass to arrive in Canudos?"[68] Of course, the defeated third expedition had abandoned all its modern equipment to the opponents. The Club Militar voted unanimously to reprimand the *Jornal do Comércio* for its "great amount of ill will toward the illustrious commander," as this newspaper had not

65. Manoel Vitorino to Club Militar, Rio de Janeiro, March 7, 1897, in Caneca (pseud.), *Attentado de cinco de novembro. Artigos de Caneca publicados na "Gazeta de Noticias" sobre o "Despacho" do juiz Affonso de Miranda* (Rio de Janeiro: Imprensa Nacional, 1898), p. 85.

66. Joaquim Nabuco to João Alfredo Corrêa de Oliveira, Rio de Janeiro, n.d., *Revista do Instituto Histórico e Geográfico Brasileiro* Vol. 257 (October–December, 1962), p. 205.

67. Eduardo Prado, speech at Santos, March 18, 1897, *Collectaneas* (São Paulo: Escola Typographica Salesiana, 1904), III, 111–12.

68. *País*, August 21, 1897, p. 1.

approved all of his actions. The club members reaffirmed their "solidarity with all those heroically . . . fighting in Canudos for the Republic."[69] The military clubs of Salvador and Pôrto Alegre also adopted resolutions endorsing the general's conduct.[70]

Victory was essential for the existence of the government. Prudente appointed a new, trustworthy war minister, Marshal Machado de Bittencourt, an exponent of civilian rule, and sent him to Bahia. While he had kept the war minister chosen by Vice-President Manoel Vitorino for some time, so as not to further antagonize his opponents, this general's press activities led to his forced resignation. Prudente now told Marshal Bittencourt, "what we need is complete victory with all possible speed." Prudente was careful not to offend army sensitivities at this crucial juncture, and he refused to support certain members of his government who would have reduced army size.[71] He knew that the army was fighting as though the destiny of the republic were at stake in Canudos and to redeem its honor. And victory finally was achieved in October of 1897.

The army had done poorly at Canudos, and it attempted to redeem itself by finding a scapegoat. Some officers now attacked Prudente as their enemy and sought to dislodge him. Some of his civilian opponents, also hoping to force him from office, worked to stimulate this military hostility, which posed a grave threat to the security of his administration. But military disunity, assiduously fostered by Prudente, was too great to be overcome. Moreover, Prudente was finally able to achieve a victory in Canudos which assuaged army passions

69. *Ibid.*
70. *Rio News*, August 31, 1897, p. 4.
71. Prudente to Bittencourt, Rio de Janeiro, September 18, 1897; October 2, 1897; Bittencourt to Prudente, Monte Santo, October 3, 1897, Prudente de Morais Papers.

and wounded military honor. Some officers realized that the army's fighting abilities could not be improved without government aid, and, during the Canudos struggle, Prudente had been careful to appear in complete agreement with this goal.

The hostility of certain military elements, heightened by civilian opposition groups, the dramatic split of the political party which had supposedly ruled the nation in unity, and the emotional turmoil of the Canudos affair culminated in an assassination attempt against Prudente de Morais. But the poor judgment of the military and civilian opposition elements who planned this assault only enabled Prudente to strengthen his position.

While rumors of conspiracies against the president had continued to circulate ever since the first days of his term, when many expected Marshal Floriano Peixoto or his supporters to seize control, no overt attacks against the government had been made. Movements such as those in the Military School, which might have provided the opportunity for further agitation and disorders leading to open revolt, had been quickly put down.

In the convulsive atmosphere of the Canudos campaign, violent press attacks against Prudente de Morais had increased. The *País*, which had long played upon the officers' fear that the president might dissolve the army, now cried out more strongly against this alleged threat. Prudente had drastically reduced the size of the armed forces from their high point under Floriano. Quintino Bocaiúva, editor of the *País*, lamented in private that "we are without an army and a navy. All the services are more or less in disorder and the colossal expenditures are always on the increase."[72] In the press, he accused Prudente of harming the army, "the pillar of the

72. Quintino Bocaiúva to Gabriel Cruz, Santa Helena, State of Rio de Janeiro, March 31, 1897, Arquivo do Museu Histórico Nacional (uncatalogued).

Republic," and of moving against those officers who applauded Floriano and his policies.[73] While he defended himself from government charges of instigating military revolts, he continued to attack Prudente's treatment of the armed forces as a danger to the republic and as part of a conspiracy for "the discrediting, the dispersal, and the annihilation" of the army, in much the same way as he had once denounced the imperial government.[74] The *Jacobino,* which had long opposed Prudente's policies, used more violent language, reviling the "corrupting and unpatriotic policies of this sickly imbecile called Prudente de Morais" and his attempts to annihilate the army. It assailed "the plan of restoring the monarchy . . . with the entire knowledge and frank protection of the *fazendeiro* of Piracicaba [Prudente]"[75]

This vituperative campaign resulted in tragedy. On November 5, 1897, the day of the welcome celebration for the victorious troops returning from Canudos, a soldier mounted the presidential reviewing stand and fired at Prudente. He missed, but in the struggle to disarm the would-be assassin war minister Machado de Bittencourt was stabbed and killed.

Amidst the general mourning for Marshal Bittencourt, who was hailed as having given his life to protect his chief, Prudente de Morais moved swiftly against his enemies. They had gone too far and had left themselves open to harsh reprisals. A state of siege was proclaimed, and opponents, including congressmen, were arrested. Crowds wrecked the offices of newspapers like the *Jacobino* which had been highly critical of the president. During the state of siege, Prudente also ordered the Club Militar closed, and he had sufficient military support to enforce this decision when some officers questioned it.

73. *País,* June 21, 1897, p. 1.
74. *País,* June 24, 1897, p. 1; June 26, 1897, p. 1; August 12, 1897, p. 1.
75. *Jacobino,* May 8, 1897, p. 1.

Some of Prudente's supporters argued that the young soldier who had killed Marshal Bittencourt was just an instrument in a far-reaching conspiracy, and the police report brought out connections to many prominent politicians. The soldier, Marcelino Bispo, recalled that he "liked to read the newspaper the *Jacobino*," and that, since he was "fanatically devoted to the memory of Marshal Floriano Peixoto, Deocleciano's [the editor's] language delighted him." In their conversations, Deocleciano Martyr told him that "the government persecuted the army" and that "the Canudos affair was created by the government for the purpose of bringing back the monarchy." Then Deocleciano told him that the "way to forestall all these evils" was "to assassinate the President of the republic." Bispo related that Deocleciano had encouraged him and had provided him with weapons for the assassination.[76] Finally Deocleciano Martyr admitted his part, and he also described a secret meeting in the Club Militar with a group of officers, who had been involved in the uprising at the Military School, to conspire against the government and Prudente.[77] According to Deocleciano and other witnesses, a number of prominent men were involved in the assassination attempt. Deocleciano said that Francisco Glicério knew of the plot and that Manoel Vitorino was aware of the plans, although he never committed himself. The police report closed with an accusation of Manoel Vitorino and several congressmen, but Prudente never arrested them.[78] The prominent opposition leaders were now discredited, and as long as they

76. "Depoimento de Marcellino Bispo," November 13, 1897, in Vicente Neiva, *Attentado de cinco de novembro. Relatório do dr. Vicente Neiva 1º delegado auxiliar e diversas peças do inquerito* (Rio de Janeiro: Imprensa Nacional, 1898), pp. 56–61.

77. "Depoimento de Deocleciano Martyr," November 28, 1897, *ibid.*, pp. 72–79.

78. For Manoel Vitorino's bitter rejoinder to this police report and his attack on the Prudente government, see Manoel Vitorino Pereira, *Manifesto político.*

were not prosecuted they would have no cause to seek revenge.

Opponents of Prudente had failed to gauge the strength of his support and had gone too far, thus facilitating his efforts to consolidate his position. They had miscalculated public sentiment and had unsuccessfully attempted murder instead of following the more accepted pattern of stirring up discontent, applying pressure, and forcing a bloodless toppling of the government. The remainder of Prudente's term in office was peaceful.

Strong measures were eventually followed by moderate ones. Several months after the assassination attempt, some sentiment was expressed on behalf of the president's opponents who were still in prison. In his diary Prudente showed indignation and resentment when the federal Supreme Tribunal accepted a petition of *habeas corpus* for those adversaries he had exiled to a prison colony in the far north, but he complied with the court's wishes.[79] Near the end of his term in office, the Chamber of Deputies rejected a motion to permit the trial of the deputies named in connection with the attempted assassination. By that time, a new president had been elected, and, as has often occurred in Brazil, direct political clashes were being muffled.

The Club Militar remained closed until well into the next elected regime. In March of 1898, the president of the club had convoked a general meeting, but the war minister reminded him that the club had been officially closed the previous year. The club's president held that the Club Militar was not obligated to obey, since it was a "purely private association," not a "dependency of the War Ministry"; he also pointed out that the state of siege under which the club had been closed had expired, citing articles of the federal consti-

79. See Prudente de Morais diary, March 5, 1898; March 26, 1898; Prudente de Morais Papers.

tution in reference to his position.[80] Once again, an officer was placing his own constitutional interpretations against his superiors' instructions, refusing to obey an order of which he disapproved. This could not be tolerated by a civilian government. He was placed under house arrest for four days, and a guard was stationed at the door of the club. The Club Militar itself met and voted to take the matter to the courts, which three years later permitted it to reopen.[81]

By this show of force against the Club Militar, Prudente demonstrated that he would willingly move against such military opposition and that he had sufficient support within the armed forces to enforce these measures. As he wrote a friend, "*my* officers are quiet now, after verifying that the government has sufficient energy and force to arrest even generals."[82]

Prudente designated Campos Sales, governor of São Paulo, as his successor. While some of Prudente's opponents were favorably inclined towards Campos Sales, there was actually very little difference between the two *Paulistas* on most important matters, although Campos Sales was more careful, antagonizing fewer people and displaying no obviously anti-military feelings. Although the opposition forces ran their own candidate, Lauro Sodré, an officer-politician and a follower of Floriano Peixoto, the government candidate won, as was to be the case until 1930. Civilian power seemed assured for the next few decades.

80. General Francisco Antônio de Moura to General João Nepomuceno de Medeiros Mallet, Rio de Janeiro, March 6, 1898; March 9, 1898; Arquivo do Ministério da Guerra, 2a seção, Diversos, Cx 109.

81. General João Thomaz Cantuaria to General João Nepomuceno de Medeiros Mallet, Rio de Janeiro, March 5, 1898; March 8, 1898; March 10, 1898; Arquivo do Ministério da Guerra, 2a seção, Diversos, Cx 109; diary of Prudente de Morais, March 5, 1898; March 7, 1898; March 8, 1898; March 9, 1898; March 10, 1898; March 11, 1898; Prudente de Morais Papers; *País*, March 5, 1898, p. 3; Atas of Club Militar, session of reopening club, July 14, 1901.

82. Prudente to Antonio Mendes, Rio de Janeiro, March 20, 1898, in Silveira Peixoto, *A tormenta que Prudente de Morais venceu!*, p. 285.

In November of 1898, Prudente peacefully handed the presidency over to Campos Sales. Unlike the situation four years earlier, there were no rumors of impending military movements or threats to depose the new president.

During the administration of Prudente de Morais civilian control in government had been secured. Through a skillful use of the divisions within the armed forces, Prudente had maintained himself in office and had reduced military political power to such a point that it would not seriously menace his successors. Although the Brazilian armed forces would remain in a position to influence government policy, direct military rule and successful military uprisings would not occur for years to come.

Conclusion

DURING THE LATTER PART of the nineteenth century, the Brazilian armed forces gained a position of power and influence in the political life of the nation, and in 1889 they took command of the government. But their lack of unity enabled civilians to regain control. While numerous civilians demonstrated dissatisfaction with military involvement in political affairs, only one group, composed primarily of large landowners from the economically powerful coffee-exporting state of São Paulo, succeeded in removing the officers from the government.

Before the establishment of the republic in 1889, neither the officers nor the *Paulistas* had enjoyed such political power, but during the latter years of the empire both were gaining strength and becoming more dissatisfied with the imperial regime. São Paulo was the center of the dominant coffee economy and an area which was undergoing rapid development.

However, the imperial government did not devote sufficient attention to problems arising from economic and social changes in this region. The São Paulo Republican Party, the best organized Republican group in the nation, advocated a federal regime.

Army officers also felt neglected by the imperial government. Stimulated by the Paraguayan War, which had led to an enlarged and increasingly self-conscious army, the officers complained bitterly of government abuses. Through a series of minor incidents, the army officers demonstrated their increasing political self-consciousness and their dissatisfaction with the government's treatment of their interests. Finally, incited by dissident civilian elements, they overthrew the monarchy and stepped into the power void left by its sudden demise.

During the provisional Republican regime, the officers were basically in control of the nation. Although civilian Republicans participated in the government they had helped to establish, they could not exercise decisive influence on matters of importance to the officers or prevent them from infringing on civil liberties. The liberty of the press in particular remained a point of conflict between them. In most of the states, as in the central government, officers wielded the crucial power. While the primarily civilian Constituent Congress often clashed with Marshal Deodoro da Fonseca, the provisional president, the congressmen were unable to force basic modifications in the government or elect a civilian as first constitutional president of the republic. The officers dominated the government, for theirs had been the arms which overturned the monarchy and then maintained the stability of the republic.

The officers' involvement in politics and in movements against the government reflected a widespread view that such activities lay within their legitimate sphere of action. Under the republic, officers continued to rail against the doctrine of "passive obedience" and to view civilian politicians with a jaundiced eye, disdainful of their capacities to rule the nation and distrustful of their intentions toward the armed forces. The officers constantly claimed the right to speak out on any issue of importance to them. Moreover, they wished to expand the size of the armed forces and increase the military budget. Many felt that the armed forces must wield a "moderating power," similar to that once held by the emperor, over the republic they had helped to establish and for whose destiny they were therefore responsible. In the exercise of such a right, they could go as far as revolution if they considered this the only way to "save the republic." Other officers, influenced by positivist thought, tended to justify such activities as necessary to regenerate the nation and bring "progress" to the republic. The belief in the right and duty of the armed forces to guard Brazil's destiny presupposed the officers' active participation in the political process. When attitudes such as these were coupled with the divisions within the armed forces, the result was the seemingly interminable revolts and military demonstrations of the first few years of the republic.

The armed forces were far from united. The solidarity which had enabled them to topple the monarchy was only apparent. The officers controlling the government were opposed by diverse military factions that also struggled among themselves. Deodoro da Fonseca, the first president, Floriano Peixoto, who helped to overthrow Deodoro and then assumed the presidency, and Benjamin Constant, the idol of the younger positivist-inclined officers, each commanded a group of followers. Moreover, friction occurred between the younger, better educated officers and their older colleagues, who had not attended the theoretically oriented military schools and had not been influenced by Benjamin Constant and other positivists. Within the navy, similar divisions began to become evident; the naval officers seemed to be grouping themselves about such prestigious leaders as the impulsive and competent Eduardo Wandenkolk, the politically ambitious Custódio de Melo, and the disciplined and severe Saldanha da Gama. The traditional jealousies and rivalries between the two major branches of the armed forces were heightened by the discriminatory treatment the naval officers felt they were receiving from the army-dominated government. These hostilities first led to demonstrations by naval officers and finally exploded in the most serious military revolt of the period, the Naval Revolt of 1893–94. During this rebellion, which basically pitted the army against the navy, naval divisions again became evident, and the tensions and lack of effective cooperation between leading naval officers contributed to the failure of the insurrection. This naval movement, combined with a regional revolt in the south of Brazil, provided one civilian group with the opportunity to gain control of the government.

Large numbers of civilians, from vigorous defenders of civil liberties to disillusioned Republicans and bickering congressmen, had objected to military predominance, but most of these groups were helpless. The most sensitive issue for civilians was that of civil liberties, for the officers often appeared blind to demands for freedom of expression on the part of others, although they were vigorously hostile to any criticisms of their own activities. Congressional opponents of military expansion were unable to limit the size of the armed forces or their budget. A vehement critic of the officers' political pursuits like Rui Barbosa was forced to flee the Floriano regime during the Naval Revolt. Rui was a political liberal enamored of civil liberties and sincerely aroused when these were attacked by the military government, but he was also a personal enemy of Floriano Peixoto. Like some other opponents of military government, Rui did not rule out military means to end a military regime, and he sympathized with the Naval Revolt. Not all civilians realized that military rule could not be ended through military revolt. Even those who had learned this lesson often remained frustrated in their attempts to remove the officers from government without resorting to revolution, for they lacked the necessary power base for applying political leverage against the military government.

The monarchists, the most vitriolic critics of the officers' political activities, were unable either to drive them from power or to use them to gain control for themselves. Through their maneuvers, the monarchists helped persuade additional civilians and officers to support the Floriano government. The sympathy of some monarchists for the Naval Revolt helped convince various Republicans of the need to aid the Marshal in order to prevent the success of a military uprising in which they detected a danger to the republic. Some monarchists were coming to see that the monarchy lacked popular appeal and that only military force could restore the crown. But they were unable to use the divisions within the armed forces and to persuade some officers to move against the republic. They failed in a few half-hearted attempts to instigate a military counterrevolt during the first days of the republic, and they were unable to turn the Naval Revolt into a monarchist-controlled movement. Nor did they succeed in diverting military discontent into monarchist channels under the civilian presidents who followed Floriano. While the armed forces lacked cohesion, the number of monarchist sympathizers within their ranks was slight, and the monarchists could not supply the necessary inducements or benefits to attract wider support. They were attempting to repeat the tactics employed by some Republicans against the monarchy in 1889 which had helped to lead to a military-dominated government. But the republic enjoyed much wider support, and powerful groups like the *Paulistas* would never permit a return to a regime they believed had neglected their interests.

This entrepreneurial group based on landed wealth considered stability the key to profit. The unrest and incipient anarchy resulting from incessant military demonstrations during the first years of the republic were endangering the economic growth of their state. Under the federal regime, for which they had long labored, São Paulo's revenues remained largely at home. *Paulista* economic power was translated into a capacity for the effective exercise of force through the creation of a local army. With the expansion of the *Paulista* militia, this landed class was better able to defend state autonomy and exert greater pressure on the national scene.

The *Paulista* approach to the problem of achieving civilian rule was to take advantage of military divisions, to support the group controlling the government against opposing military factions, and to demand as their price the return of power to civilians. The Naval Revolt provided them with their greatest opportunity, for it forced the officers in the government to depend upon *Paulista* military and political aid. While civilians like Cristiano Benedito Otôni and Felisbelo Freire had also realized that the officers could not be removed from their position of authority through armed force, and had assisted Floriano against the naval insurgents, they lacked the power of the *Paulistas* to extract concessions for civilian rule. Through their support of Marshal Floriano Peixoto, the *Paulistas* maintained the power of the government to put down such rebellions, helping to discourage future uprisings, and they preserved a government over which they could then gain possession. The São Paulo militia, dominated by the coffee planters who supplied the necessary funds and labor, provided Floriano with essential military support against the *Federalists* and naval insurgents. While the *Federalists* were steadily advancing northward early in 1894 and approaching the southern boundary of São Paulo, and the naval insurgents were holding out in the harbor of Rio de Janeiro, Prudente de Morais, a leading Paulista and a strong believer in civilian rule, was elected president.

During his term of office, Prudente employed the divisions within the armed forces to consolidate civilian rule. He cut down on army size, decreased military expenses, and strengthened the position of less politically minded officers. When hostile military elements like the Military School cadets attempted to threaten him, he moved swiftly and vigorously, impressing more powerful military groups with his determination and ability to remain in power. But when compromise was necessary, as in the achieving of peace in Rio Grande do Sul, he moved slowly and carefully, while also playing off opposing military factions like Floriano's supporters and those sympathetic toward the insurgents. Although various hostile elements, including monarchists and some urban, middle-class groups, tried to take advantage of military discontent to unseat Prudente, they lacked sufficient strength and skill for success, and they could not unite the armed forces against the president. When various opposition groups miscalculated public sentiments and fostered an assassination attempt against Prudente, he was able to take forceful action against his enemies and solidify his own position. Both the armed forces and the civilians were divided. But one civilian group, the *Paulistas,* possessed the necessary cohesion and economic and military power to play successfully on military disunity to achieve control over the government and preserve it.

The Brazilian "military" was far from monolithic, and civilians found in this disunity their source of strength. The landed oligarchy of São Paulo, concerned as they were with the maintenance of stability and anxious to control the republic for which they had struggled, replaced military rule with civilian rule. By creating an armed force of their own, they were able to play a decisive role during the critical days of the Naval Revolt of 1893–94. They wisely shunned attempts to overthrow the military faction in power by siding with rival military groups, and, in exchange for their crucial support, Prudente de Morais was allowed to be elected the first civilian president of the Republic of Brazil in 1894. The armed forces were then unable to unite to prevent Prudente from assuming the presidency or consolidating civilian rule. Although the Brazilian armed forces would continue to influence political decisions, civilians would rule the nation until 1930.

Bibliography

RELATIVELY LITTLE DOCUMENTARY MATERIAL relating to the first years of the republic has yet been published. Manuscript materials, therefore, assume major importance, and these may be difficult to consult. The papers of many statesmen of the First Republic have remained in the hands of their families, and access to them depends on circumstances. While the documentary collections in public archives are generally open to scholars, researchers may encounter difficulties arising from the frequently disorganized state and inadequate staffs of the archives.

Among printed sources, some of the most useful are memoirs, such as the apologia by Campos Sales, *Da propaganda à presidencia* (São Paulo: Typ. A Editôra, 1908); the innumerable contemporary pamphlets and political literature of the period; published collections of letters, such as those by Rui Barbosa in *Mocidade e exilio: Cartas,* edited by Américo Jacobina Lacombe (São Paulo: Companhia Editôra Nacional, 1934), in *Cartas da Inglaterra* (São Paulo: Livraria Academica, 1929); and firsthand accounts of key events, such as that of the Naval Revolt by Admiral Custódio José de Melo, *O governo provisório e a revolução de 1893,* 2 vols. (São Paulo: Companhia Editôra Nacional, 1938), and that by the anonymous author of *Notas de um revoltoso* (Rio de Janeiro: Typ. Moraes, 1895). Also valuable are newspapers of the period like the *Jornal do Comércio* and accounts of foreign travelers, like Max Leclerc, *Cartas do Brasil,* trans. Sérgio Milliet (São Paulo: Companhia Editôra Nacional, 1942).

MANUSCRIPT SOURCES

Arquivo da Casa de Rui Barbosa.[1]

Arquivo do Club Militar (minutes of meetings).

Arquivo do Instituto Histórico e Geográfico Brasileiro.

Arquivo do Instituto Histórico e Geográfico de São Paulo (São Paulo).

Arquivo do Ministério da Guerra.

Arquivo do Ministério da Marinha.

Arquivo do Serviço de Documentação Geral da Marinha.

Arquivo Histórico do Ministério das Relações Exteriores.

Arquivo do Museu Histórico Nacional.

Arquivo do Museu Imperial (Petrópolis).

Arquivo do Museu Paulista (São Paulo).

Clodoaldo da Fonseca Papers, in possession of Sr. Roberto Piragibe da Fonseca.

Floriano Peixoto Collection. Arquivo Nacional do Brasil, Cx 1194–1209.

José Carlos Rodrigues Collection. Seção de Manuscritos da Biblioteca Nacional.

1. Unless otherwise indicated, these archives are in Rio de Janeiro.

Joaquim Saldanha Marinho Collection. Arquivo do Estado de Guanabara.

Prudente de Morais Papers, formerly in possession of Sr. Odálio Amorim and now in the Instituto Histórico e Geográfico Brasileiro.

United States Government Diplomatic Archives. National Archives (Washington, D.C.).

PRINTED SOURCES

Abranches Moura, João Dunshee de, ed. *Actas e actos do governo provisório: Copias authénticas dos protocollos das sessões secretas do conselho de ministros desde a proclamação da república até a organisação do gabinete Lucena, acompanhadas de importantes revelações e documentos.* Rio de Janeiro: Imprensa Nacional, 1907.

—— (pseud. Barão de S. Bibiano). *Cartas de um sebastianista—satyras em verso.* Rio de Janeiro: Off. de Obras do Jornal do Brasil, 1896.

——, ed. *O golpe de estado. Atas e atos do governo Lucena. (Obra póstuma).* Rio de Janeiro: Oficinas Gráficas do Jornal do Brasil, 1954.

——. *Governos e congressos da República dos Estados Unidos do Brazil 1889 a 1917.* São Paulo: M. V. Abranches, 1918.

——. *Pela paz ao dr. Prudente de Moraes.* Rio de Janeiro: Off. de Obras do Jornal do Brasil, 1895.

——. *A revolta da armada e a revolução rio grandense. Correspondencia entre Saldanha da Gama e Silveira Martins.* 2 vols. Rio de Janeiro: M. V. Abranches, 1914.

Abreu, João Capistrano de. *Ensaios e estudos (Crítica e história).* 1ª–3ª séries. Rio de Janeiro: Sociedade Capistrano de Abreu, Livraria Briguiet, 1931–39.

Abreu, Modesto de. *Estilo e personalidade de Euclides da Cunha, estilistica d' "Os sertões."* Rio de Janeiro: Editôra Civilização Brasileira, 1963.

Alba, Víctor. "Dever y haber del militarismo ibero-americano," *Combate,* I (September and October, 1958), 24–30.

———. "Las psicologías del militar," *Combate,* I (November and December, 1958), 7–13.

———. "El ejército y la defensa nacional," *Combate,* I (January and February, 1959), 18–25.

———. "El ejército y la sociedad," *Combate,* I (March and April, 1959), 14–24.

———. "Em busca de soluciones," *Combate,* I (May and June, 1959), 29–39.

Albuquerque, Américo. *Floriano Peixoto. O consolidador da república. Escorso Biographico.* Rio de Janeiro: Typ. Moreira Maximino & Co., 1894.

Alencar, Alexandrino Faria de. *Aquidiban. Histórico do combate de 16 de abril de 1894 em aguas de Santa Catharina.* Montevideo, n.p., 1895.

Alencar, Araripe, Tristão de. *Tasso Fragoso. Um pouco de história do nosso exército.* Rio de Janeiro: Biblioteca do Exército, 1960.

Alexander, Robert J. "The Army in Politics," in *Government and Politics in Latin America.* Edited by Harold Eugene Davis. New York: The Ronald Press Company, 1958.

———. "Brazilian Tenentismo," *Hispanic American Historical Review,* XXXVI (May, 1956), 229–42.

Almeida, Tito Franco de. *Monarchia e monarchistas.* Pará: Typ. de Tavares Cardoso & C., 1895.

Alves, Arthur. *Lauro Müller perante e exército e o exército perante a nação.* Rio de Janeiro: Club Militar, 1919.

Amorim, Annibal. *Viagens pelo Brazil.* Rio de Janeiro: Livraria Garnier, [1909].

Andréa, Júlio. *A marinha brasileira: Florões de glórias e de epopéias memoráveis.* Rio de Janeiro: Artes Gráficas C. Mendes Junior, 1955.

Andrews, Christopher Columbus. *Brazil: Its Condition and Prospects.* 3rd ed. New York: D. Appleton & Company, 1891.

Andrzejewski, Stanislaw. *Military Organization and Society.* London: Routledge & Kegan Paul, Ltd., 1954.

Araripe Júnior, T. A. *Funcção normal do terror nas sociedades cultas. Capítulo para ser intercalado na história da república brazileira.* Rio de Janeiro: Typ. Universal de Laemmert & C., 1891.

Artigos epizodicos publicados durante o ano de 1891. Rio de Janeiro: Na Séde de Apostolado Pozitivista do Brazil, January, 1892.

Assis Brazil, Joaquim Francisco. *O attentado de 5 de novembro de 1897 contra o presidente da república. Causa e effeitos.* São Paulo: Casa Vanordem, 1909.

———. *Democracia representativa do voto e do modo de votar.* 4th ed. Rio de Janeiro: Imprensa Nacional, 1931.

———. *Dictadura, parlamentarismo, democracia.* Rio de Janeiro: Livraria Ed. Leite Ribeiro, 1927.

———. *Os militares e a política.* 2d ed. São Paulo: Empreza Gráfica Léon Orban, 1929.

Assis Cintra. *Bernardino de Campos e seu tempo.* São Paulo: Ed. Cupolo Ltda., 1953.

Ata da sessão do Club Militar de 9 de novembro de 1889. Coleção de pactos de sangue e mensagens recebidos por Benjamin Constant. Rio de Janeiro: Gab. Fotocartográfico do Ministerio da Guerra, 1939.

Azevedo, Asdrúbal Guyer de. *Os militares e a política.* Barcelos, Portugal: Biblioteca da Grande Revolução Branter, 1926.

Azevedo Machado, M. A. *Histórico da proclamação da Repúbilca dos Estados Unidos do Brazil. Apontamentos e noticias da imprensa do Rio de Janeiro.* 2d ed. Rio de Janeiro: Typ. a Vapor de J. A. Borges, 1889.

Baleeiro, Aliomar. *Rui, um estadista no ministério da fazenda.* Rio de Janeiro: Casa de Rui Barbosa, 1952.

Bandeira, Sebastião. *Quinze de novembro. "Contestação á Suetonio."* Rio de Janeiro: Typ. do Jornal do Comércio, 1898.

Barbosa Lima Sobrinho. *Desde quando somos nacionalistas?* Rio de Janeiro: Editôra Civilização Brasileira, 1963.

Barbosa, Rui. *Os actos inconstitucionais do congresso e do executivo ante a justiça federal.* Rio de Janeiro: Companhia Impressora, 1893.

———. *Antologia.* Edited by Luís Viana Filho. Rio de Janeiro. Casa de Rui Barbosa, 1953.

———. *Campanhas jornalístics. República (1893–1899).* Vol. VIII of *Obras seletas.* Rio deJaneiro: Casa de Rui Barbosa, 1956.

———. *Cartas de Inglaterra.* São Paulo: Livraria Academica, 1929.

———. *A ditadura de 1893. Jornal do Brazil.* Vol. XX, Tomo IV, of *Obras completas de Rui Barbosa.* Rio de Janeiro: Ministério de Educação e Saude, 1949.

———. *Finanças e política da república. Discursos e escriptos.* Rio de Janeiro: Companhia Impressora, 1892.

———. *Mocidade e exílio. Cartas.* Edited by Américo Jacobina Lacombe. São Paulo: Companhia Editôra Nacional, 1934.

———. *Queda do império. Diário de Notícias.* Vol. XVI, Tomo I–III, of *Obras completas de Rui Barbosa.* Rio de Janeiro: Ministério da Educação e Saude, 1947.

———. *Rui Barbosa e o exército. (Conferência as classes armadas).* Rio de Janeiro: Casa de Rui Barbosa, 1949.

Barreto, Plinio. "Eduardo Prado e seus amigos (Cartas inéditas)," *Revista do Brazil,* I, No. 2 (February, 1916), 173–97.

Barros, Pedro de. *Cartas monarchistas.* Rio de Janeiro: Ed. Domingos de Magalhães, 1895.

Barroso, Gustavo. *História militar do Brasil.* São Paulo: Companhia Editôra Nacional, 1935.

Basbaum, Leoncio. *História sincera da república. De 1889 a 1930.* 3 vols. São Paulo: Edições LB, 1962.

Bastos, Humberto. *Rui Barbosa. Ministro da independência económica do Brasil.* Rio de Janeiro: Casa de Rui Barbosa, 1949.

Bello, José Maria. *História da república (1889–1954).* 4th ed. São Paulo: Companhia Editôra Nacional, 1959.

Bennet, Frank. *Forty Years in Brazil.* London: Mills & Boon, Ltd., 1914.

Bernárdez, Manuel. *El Brasil. Su vida, su trabajo, su futuro.* Buenos Aires: n.p., 1908.

Bettencourt Machado, José. *Machado of Brazil: The Life and Times of Machado de Assis.* New York: Brameirca, 1953.

Biblioteca do Jornal do Brazil. *Episodios da revolta de 6 de setembro. Fusilados em Sepetiba e horores de Magé. Narrativas publicadas pelo Jornal do Brasil.* Rio de Janeiro: Jornal do Brasil, 1895.

Bijos, Gerardo Majella. *O Clube Militar e seus presidentes.* Rio de Janeiro: n.p., 1960.

Boehrer, George C. A. "The Brazilian Republican Revolution: Old and New Views," *Luso-Brazilian Review,* III (Winter, 1966), 43–57.

———. *Da monarquia à república. História do Partido Republicano do Brasil (1870–1889).* Translated by Berenice Xavier. Rio de Janeiro: Ministério da Educação e Cultura, Serviço de Documentação, 1954.

Boiteux, Henrique. *Os nossos almirantes.* 6 vols. Rio de Janeiro: Imprensa Naval, 1915.

Boraston, John Maclair. "Brazil in 1898," *Journal of the Manchester Geographic Society,* XIV, 321–54.

El Brasil en 1910. Rio de Janeiro: Typ. Jornal do Comércio de Rodrigues & Cia., 1910.

Brazil. *Constituição da República dos Estados Unidos do Brazil. Acompanhadas das leis organicas publicadas desde 15 de novembro de 1889.* Rio de Janeiro: Imprensa Nacional, 1891.

———. *Constituinte. Annaes do Congresso Nacional.* 2 vols. Rio de Janeiro: Imprensa Nacional, 1891.

———. Department of Foreign Affairs. *Correspondence exchanged with the Legation of Portugal and the Legation of Brasil at Lisbon in regard to the surrender of the insurgent refugees on board the Portuguese corvettes "Mindello" and "Affonso de Albuquerque."* Rio de Janeiro: Typ. Leuzinger, 1894.

———. Ministério da Guerra. *Relatório.* 1888–98. Rio de Janeiro: Imprensa Nacional, 1888–98.

———. Ministério da Marinha. *Relatório.* 1892–97. Rio de Janeiro: Imprensa Nacional, 1892–97.

Brazil Militar. 1895–96.

Bruce, G. J. *Brazil and the Brazilians.* New York: Dodd, Mead & Co., 1914.

Bruno, Ernani Silva. *História e tradições da cidade de São Paulo.* 3 vols. Rio de Janeiro: José Olympio, 1953–54.

Buarque, Felício. *Origens republicanas. Estudos de gênese política em refutação ao livro do sr. dr. Affonso Celso. O imperador no exilio.* Recife: Francisco Soares Quintas, Livraria Internacional, [1894].

Bureau of the American Republics. *United States of Brazil.* Washington, D.C.: United States Government Printing Office, 1901.

Caldas, Honorato Candido Ferreira. *Apotheose do almirante Saldanha da Gama. Documentos e traços históricos de sua carreira militar e vida publica. Epopéas de dor e homenagens civicas, nacionaes e estrangeiras, tributadas á sua memoria.* Rio de Janeiro: Typ. Alex. Villela, 1896.

———. *A deshonra da república.* 2d ed. Rio de Janeiro: Imprensa Montenegro, 1895.

———. (pseud. Kleber). *A legalidade de 23 de novembro. Coordenação didactica de tres elementos syntheticos: Secção militar d'O Combate, documentos históricos, Congresso Nacional comprehendido de novembro de 1891 a setembro de 1892.* Rio de Janeiro: n.p., 1892.

———. *O marechal de ouro. Consagração histórica da morte tragica de inclyte marechal Carlos Machado de Bittencourt, ministro da guerra, lição fecundo de civismo, lealdade e valor, a 5 de novembro de 1897.* Rio de Janeiro: Typ. Popular, 1898.

Calogeras, João Pandiá. *A History of Brazil.* Translated by Percy Martin. Chapel Hill: University of North Carolina Press, 1939.

———. *Problemas de governo.* 2d ed. São Paulo: Companhia Editôra Nacional, 1936.

Camargo, Joracy. *O consolidador da república.* Rio de Janeiro: Departmento Nacional de Propaganda, 1939.

Camêu, Francolino and Peixoto, Arthur Vieira. *Floriano Peixoto. Vida e governo.* Rio de Janeiro: Officinas Gráficas da A Norte, 1925.

Campos, Porto, M. E. de. *Apontamentos para a história da República dos Estados Unidos do Brazil.* Rio de Janeiro: Imprensa Nacional, 1890.

Campos Salles, Manuel Ferraz de. *Cartas da Europa.* Rio de Janeiro: Typ. Leuzinger, 1894.

———. *Da propaganda à presidência.* São Paula: Typ. A Editôra, 1908.

———. *Manifesto ao estado de São Paulo.* São Paulo: Typ. do Diário Oficial, 1896.

Caneca (pseud.). *Attentado de cinco de novembro. Artigos de Caneca publicados na "Gazeta de Notícias" sobre o "Despacho" do juiz Affonso de Miranda.* Rio de Janeiro: Imprensa Nacional, 1898.

Cardoso, Leontina Licínio. *Licínio Cardoso, seu pensamento, sua obra, sua vida.* Rio de Janeiro: Ed. Zélio Valverde, 1944.

Cardoso, Vicente Licínio, and others. *À margem da história da república (Ideaes, crenças, e affirmações).* Rio de Janeiro: Edição do Annuario do Brazil, [1924].

Carmil, Renato. Assemblea Fluminense. *O caso de Campos. Os adeptos de Floriano Peixoto. A scisão do Partido Republicano Fluminense. Pareceres apresentados e discursos pronunciados pelo deputado Carmil Renato na sessão extraordinario de abril de 1899.* Rio de Janeiro: Typ. Jornal de Comércio, 1899.

Carneiro, Daví. *O Paraná e a revolução federalista.* São Paulo: Atena Editôra, [1944?]

Carvalho, Affonso de. *Viagem pelo Brasil.* Rio de Janeiro: Editôra Guanabara, [1935].

Carvalho, João Manuel de. *Reminiscencias sobre vultos e factos do império e da república.* Amparo: Typ. do Correio Amparense, 1894.

Carvalho, José Carlos de. *O livro da minha vida. Na guerra, na paz e nas revoluções (1847–1910).* Rio de Janeiro: Typ. do Jornal do Comércio, de Rodrigues & C., 1912.

Carvalho, Leitão de. *O exército e a república.* Rio de Janeiro: n. p., 1939.

Castro, Sertório de. *A república que a revolução destruio.* Rio de Janeiro: Freitas Bastos & Cia., 1932.

Cavalcanti, Amaro. *Política e finanças.* Rio de Janeiro: Imprensa Nacional, 1892.

———. *Regime federativo e a república brazileira.* Rio de Janeiro: Imprensa Nacional, 1900.

———. *Responsabilidade civil do estado.* Rio de Janeiro: Laemmert, 1905.

Celso, Affonso. Affonso Celso de Assis Figueiredo, Conde de. *Aos monarchistas.* Rio de Janeiro: Livraria Moderna, 1895.

———. *Contradictas monarchicas.* Rio de Janeiro: Livraria Moderna, 1896.

———. *Um invejado.* 2 vols. Rio de Janeiro: Livraria Moderna, 1894–95.

———. *Porque me ufano do meu paiz. Right or wrong my country.* Rio de Janeiro: Laemmert & C., 1901.

Centenário de Júlio de Mesquita. São Paulo: Anhambi, 1964.

Chagas, João. *De bond. Alguns aspectos da civilisação brazileira.* Lisbon: Livraria Moderna, 1897.

Chamberlain, George. "A Letter from Brazil," *Atlantic Monthly,* XC (December, 1902), 821–31.

Civis (pseud.). *O militarismo e a consolidação da república.* Bahia: Imprensa Economica, 1893.

Clowes, William Laird. *Four Modern Naval Campaigns.* London and New York: Unit Library Limited, 1902.

Coêlho Rodrigues, A. *A república na América do Sul ou um pouco de história e crítica offerecido aos Latino-Americanos.* 2d ed. Einsiedeln, Switzerland: Typ. dos Estabelecimentos Benzinger, & Co., 1906.

Comércio de São Paulo. 1895–96.

Congresso de história da revolução de 1894. *Anais do primeiro congresso de história da revolução de 1894: Comemorativo ao cinqüentenario do cérco da Lapa.* Curtiba: Empreza Gráfica Paranaense Ltd., 1944.

Cooper, Clayton Sedgwick. *The Brazilians and their Country.* New York: Frederick A. Stokes Co., 1917.

Cordeiro, José Pedro Leite. *Esboça do papel desempenhado, durante a revolução de 1894 pelo dr. Bernardino de Campos, presidente do estado de São Paulo.* Belo Horizonte: n.p., 1946.

Corrêa, José Augusto. *A revolução no Brazil e o opusculo do Vis-*

conde de São Boaventura. Lisbon: Typ. da Companhia Nacional Editôra, 1894.

Corrêa, Inocêncio Serzedello. *Uma figura da república. Páginas do passado.* 2d ed. Rio de Janeiro: Freitas Bastos, 1959.

Corrêa da Costa, Sérgio. *A diplomacia do marechal. (Intervenção estrangeira na revolta de armada).* Rio de Janeiro: Ed. Zélio Valverde, 1945.

Correia, Leóncio. *A verdade história sobre o 15 de novembro.* Rio de Janeiro: Imprensa Nacional, 1939.

Correio do Povo. 1889.

Costa, Dídio Iratim Afonso da. *Saldanha. Almirante L. Ph. de Saldanha da Gama.* Rio de Janeiro: Serviço de Documentação Geral da Marinha, 1957.

Costa, Emília Viotti da. "Sôbre as origens da República." *Anais do Museu Paulista* XVIII (1964), 63–120.

———. "A proclamação da República." *Anais do Museu Paulista* XIX (1965), 169–207.

Cruz Costa, João. *Contribuição a história das idéias no Brasil (O desenvolvimento da filosofia no Brasil e a evolução histórica nacional).* Rio de Janeiro: José Olympio, 1956.

———. "Os desenganos na política republicana," *O Estado de São Paulo,* March 20, 1947, pp. 14–15.

———. *O positivismo na república. Notas sobre a história do positivismo no Brasil.* São Paulo: Companhia Editôra Nacional, 1956.

Cunha, Euclydes da. *Contrastes e confrontos.* Oporto: Emprêsa Litteraria e Typographica, 1907.

———. *À margem da história.* 6th ed. Oporto: Livraria Lollo & Irmão, 1946.

———. *Rebellion in the Backlands.* Translated by Samuel Putnam, from *Os sertões.* Chicago: University of Chicago Press, 1944.

Cunha Mattos, Ernesto Augusto da. *Defeza do general de divisão Ernesto Augusto da Cunha Mattos na summario de culpa a que responde por denuncia do dr. subprocurador do Districto Federal.* Rio de Janeiro: Typ. G. Leuzinger & Filho, 1893.

Cunninghame-Graham, Robert B. *A Brazilian Mystic, Being the*

Life and Miracles of Antonio Conselheiro. London: William Heinemann, 1920.

Dantas Barreto, Emydio. *Conspirações.* Rio de Janeiro: Livraria Francisco Alves, 1917.

———. *Impressões militares.* Rio de Janeiro: Leuzinger & Cia., 1910.

Dantas, Francisco Clementino de San Tiago. *Dois momentos de Rui Barbosa.* Rio de Janeiro: Casa de Rui Barbosa, 1949.

Dean, Warren. "The Planter as Entrepreneur: The Case of São Paulo," *Hispanic American Historical Review,* XLVI (May, 1966), 138–52.

———. "São Paulo's Industrial Elite. 1890–1960" Unpublished Ph.D. dissertation, University of Florida, 1964.

A década republicana. 8 vols. Rio de Janeiro: Companhia Typ. do Brazil, 1899–1901.

Denis, Pierre. *Brazil.* Translated by Bernard Miall. New York: Charles Scribner's Sons, 1911.

Denúncia (Pôrto Alegre). 1888.

Deodoro 1827–1927. Rio de Janeiro: Typ. de A Encadernadora S. A., 1929.

Desmoulins, C. *A logica das revoluções. Apreciação da crise política actual.* N.p., 1897.

Diário de Notícias. 1889.

Diário Oficial. 1889–98.

Diário Popular. (São Paulo). 1888–89.

Dias, Arthur. *The Brazil of Today.* Nievelles, Belgium: Lanneau & Despret, [1907?].

———. *Nossa marinha. Notas sobre o renascimento da marinha de guerra do Brasil no quatriennio de 1906 a 1910.* Rio de Janeiro: Officinas Gráficas da Liga Marítima Brazileira, 1910.

Dias de Campos, Pedro. *A revolta de seis de setembro. (A acção de São Paulo). Esboço histórico.* Paris and Lisbon: Typographia Aillaud, Alves & Cia., 1913.

Dockery, O. H. "Police Force of Rio de Janeiro," *Reports from the Consuls of the United States,* XXXIX, No. 142, January 18, 1892. Washington: Government Printing Office, 1892.

———. "The United States of Brazil," *Reports from the Consuls of the United States*, XXXII, No. 114, Rio de Janeiro, January 27, 1890. Washington: Government Printing Office, 1890.

Domville-Fife, Charles W. *The United States of Brazil.* London: Francis Griffiths, 1910.

Dourado, Angelo. *Os voluntarios do martyrio. Factos e epizodios da guerra civil.* Pelotas: Typ. a Vapor da Livraria Americano, 1896.

Dutra Rodrigues, Francisco Antonio. *Exposição com que ao exm. snr. dr. Pedro Vicente de Azevedo passou a administração da provincia de São Paulo o exm. snr. dr. Francisco Antonio Dutra Rodrigues 1° vice-presidente no dia 23 de junho de 1888.* São Paulo: Typographia a Vapor Baruel, Pauperio & comp., 1888.

Ekirch, Arthur A., Jr. *The Civilian and the Military.* New York: Oxford University Press, 1956.

Escobar, Wenceslau. *Apontamentos para a história da revolução de 1893.* Pôrto Alegre: Officinas Gráphicas do Globo, 1920.

Estado de São Paulo. 1888–98.

Faoro, Raymundo. *Os donos do poder. Formação do patronato político brasileiro.* Rio de Janeiro: Editôra Globo, 1958.

Ferreira Vianna Filho (pseud. Suetonio). *Biographia do senador general Quintino Bocayuva (Chefe da propaganda republicano).* Rio de Janeiro: Typ. da Comp. de Lot N do Brasil, 1900.

———. *O antigo regimen (Homens e coisas) por Suetonio. Com um prefacio de Quintino Bocayuva.* Rio de Janeiro: Cunha & Irmão, 1896.

Fialho, Anfrisio. *História da fundação da república no Brazil.* Rio de Janeiro: Typ. Universal de Laemmert & Cia., 1891.

As finanças do manifesto. Refutação. Colleção de artigos publicados em O Debate. Rio de Janeiro: Imprensa Nacional, 1898.

Finer, Samuel E. *The Man on Horseback: The Role of the Military in Politics.* New York: Frederick A. Praeger, 1962.

Fitzgibbon, Russell H. "Measurement of Latin American Political Phenomena: A Statistical Experiment," *American Political Science Review* (June, 1951), 517–23.

———. "Revolution: Western Hemisphere." *South Atlantic Quarterly*, LV (July, 1956), 263–79.

Fleiuss, Max. *História administrativa do Brasil.* São Paulo: Companhia Melhoramentos de São Paulo, 1922.

Fonseca Hermes, Djalma da and Fonesca Hermes, J. S. da, Jr. *Fonseca Hermes e a livro 'Deodoro. A espada contra o imperio' R. Magalhaes, Jr., Carta aberta ao autor.* Rio de Janeiro: Papelaria Natal, 1958.

Forjaz, Pimental Augusto Eugenio Duarte Pereira de. *Portugal e Brazil: apontamentos para a história do nosso conflicto com a República dos Estados Unidos do Brazil.* Lisbon: Typ. Castro Irmão, 1894.

Frances, May. *Beyond the Argentine: or, Letters from Brazil.* London: W. H. Allen & Co., 1890.

Freire, Felisbello Firmo de Oliveira. *História constitucional da República dos Estados Unidos do Brasil.* Vols. I and III, Rio de Janeiro: Typ. Aldina, 1894–95; Vol. II, Rio de Janeiro: Typ. Moreira Maximino, Chagas & C., 1894.

———. *História da revolta de 6 de setembro de 1893.* Rio de Janeiro: Cunha & Irmãos, 1896.

Freitas, Leopoldo de. *História militar do Brasil.* São Paulo: Livraria Magalhães, 1911.

Freyre, Gilberto. *The Mansions and Shanties. (Sobrados e mucambos).* Translated by Harriet de Onís. New York: Alfred A. Knopf, 1963.

———. *Nação e exército.* Rio de Janeiro: José Olympio, 1949.

———. *New World in the Tropics: The Culture of Modern Brazil.* New York: Alfred A. Knopf, 1959.

———. *Ordem e Progresso. Processo de desintegração das sociedades patriarcal e semipatriarcal no Brasil sob o regime de trabalho livre. Aspectos de um quase meio seculo de transição do trabalho escravo para o trabalho livre, e da monarquia para à república.* 2 vols. Rio de Janeiro: José Olympio, 1959.

———. *Perfil de Euclydes e outros perfis.* Rio de Janeiro: José Olympio, 1944.

Furtado, Celso. *The Economic Growth of Brazil. A Survey from*

Colonial to Modern Times. Translated by Ricardo W. de Aguiar and Eric Charles Drysdale. Berkeley: University of California Press, 1963.

Gazeta de Notícias. 1889–92.

Graça Aranha, José Pereira de. *Machado de Assis e Joaquim Nabuco. Comentários e notas à correspondência entre estes dois escritores.* 2d ed. Rio de Janeiro: F. Briguiet Cia., 1942.

Guanabara, Alcindo. *História da revolta de 6 de setembro de 1893.* Rio de Janeiro: Typ. e Papelaria Mont'Alverne, 1894.

———. *A presidencia de Campos Salles. Política e finanças,* 1898–1902. Rio de Janeiro: Laemmert & C., 1902.

Guesdes, Pelino. *Biographia de Amaro Cavalcanti, ministro da justiça e negocios interiores.* Rio de Janeiro: Typ. Leuzinger, 1897.

———. *Marechal Bittencourt (A victima do dever).* Rio de Janeiro: Typ. Leuzinger & C., 1898.

Gutteridge, William. *Armed Forces in New States.* London: Oxford University Press, 1962.

Hambloch, Ernest. *His Majesty the President.* London: Methuen & Co., 1935.

Haring, Clarence H. *Empire in Brazil: A New World Experiment with Monarchy.* Cambridge, Mass.: Harvard University Press, 1958.

Hasslocher, Germano. *A verdade sobre a revolução.* Pôrto Alegre: Edição da Livraria Mazeron, 1894.

Hill, Frank D. "The World's Production and Consumption of Coffee," *Reports from the Consuls of the United States,* LVII, No. 215, January 26, 1898. Washington: Government Printing Office, 1898.

———. *Diplomatic Relations between the United States and Brazil.* Durham: Duke University Press, 1932.

Hillard, Henry W. *Politics and Pen Pictures at Home and Abroad.* New York and London: G. P. Putnam's Sons, 1892.

Howard, Michael, ed. *Soldiers and Governments: Nine Studies in Civil-Military Relations.* Bloomington, Ind.: Indiana University Press, 1959.

Humphrey, Alice R. *A Summer Journey to Brazil.* London: Bonnell, Silva & Co., 1900.

Humphreys, Robert A. "Latin America: The Caudillo Tradition," in *Soldiers and Governments: Nine Studies in Civil-Military Relations.* London: Eyre & Spottiswoode, 1957.

Huntington, Samuel P. ed. *Changing Patterns of Military Politics.* New York: The Free Press of Glencoe, Inc., 1962.

———. *The Soldier and the State: The Theory and Politics of Civil-Military Relations.* Cambridge, Mass.: The Belknap Press of Harvard University Press, 1964.

Ilha Moreira, Antônio. *Proclamação e fundação da república.* Rio de Janeiro: Imprensa Nacional, 1947.

Império. 1896.

Jaceguay, Arthur Silveira da Motta. *De aspirante à almirante.* 4 vols. Rio de Janeiro: Typ. do Jornal do Comérico, 1907–13.

———. *O dever do momento. Carta à Joaquim Nabuco.* Rio de Janeiro: Typ. Leuzinger, 1897.

———. *Organização naval. Artigos publicados na Revista Brazileira e Jornal do Commercio em 1896.* Rio de Janeiro: Typ. Leuzinger, 1896.

———. *Sobre a reforma compulsoria.* Estado do Rio: Typ. da Companhia Industrial Santa Rita, 1905.

Jacobino. 1894–97.

Jane, Lionel Cecil. *Liberty and Despotism in Spanish America.* London: Clarendon Press, 1929.

Janowitz, Morris. *The Military in the Political Development of New Nations: An Essay in Comparative Analysis.* Chicago and London: University of Chicago Press, 1964.

Jerram, Charles S. *Armies of the World.* New York: New Amsterdam Book Company, 1900.

Johnson, John J. *The Military and Society in Latin America.* Stanford: Stanford University Press, 1964.

———. *Political Change in Latin America: The Emergence of the Middle Sectors.* Stanford: Stanford University Press, 1958.

———, ed. *The Role of the Military in Underdeveloped Countries.* Princeton: Princeton University Press, 1962.

Jornal do Brasil. 1893–95.

Jornal do Comércio. 1889–98.

Kerwin, Jerome G., ed. *Civil-Military Relations in American Life.* Chicago: University of Chicago Press, 1948.

Kidder, Rev. D. P. and Fletcher, Rev. James C. *Brazil and the Brazilians.* Boston: Little Brown & Co., 1879

Klein, Herbert S. "David Toro and the Establishment of 'Military Socialism' in Bolivia," *Hispanic American Historical Review,* XLV (February, 1965), 25–52.

Kling, Merle. "Towards a Theory of Power and Political Instability in Latin America," *Western Political Quarterly,* IX (March, 1956), 21–35.

Klinger, Bertoldo. *Parada e desfile duma vida de voluntârio do Brazil na primeira metade do século.* Rio de Janeiro: Emprêsa Gráfica O Cruzeiro, 1958.

Lacerda, Paulo de. *Confettis políticos.* São Paulo: Typ. Ladeira S. Francisco, 1894.

Lacombe, Américo Jacobina, ed. *Rio-Branco e Rui Barbosa.* Rio de Janeiro: Imprensa Nacional, 1948.

Lafayette, Pedro. *Saldanha da Gama.* 2 vols. Rio de Janeiro: Editôra Souza, 1959.

LaFeber, Walter. *The New Empire: An Interpretation of American Expansion, 1860–1898.* Ithaca: Cornell University Press, 1963.

———. "United States Depression Diplomacy and the Brazilian Revolution, 1893–1894," *Hispanic American Historical Review,* XL (February, 1960), 107–18.

Lagarrigue, Jorge. *A ditadura republicana segundo Augusto Comte.* Translated by J. Mariano de Oliveira. Rio de Janeiro: Apostolado Pozitivista do Brasil, 1897.

Leclerc, Max. *Cartas do Brasil.* Translated by Sérgio Milliet. São Paulo: Companhia Editôra Nacional, 1942.

Leitão de Carvalho, Estevão. *Dever militar e política partidária.* São Paulo: Companhia Editôra Nacional, 1959.

Lemos, Miguel. *O calendario pozitivista.* Rio de Janeiro: Apostolado Pozitivista do Brazil, February, 1890.

———. *Constituição sem constituinte.* Rio de Janeiro: Na Sede Central do Apostolado Pozitivista do Brazil, 1890.

———. *A liberdade de profissões i o regulamento para o serviço domestico.* Rio de Janeiro: Tip. Central de Evaristo Costa, February, 1890.

———. *A secularização dos cemiterios.* Rio de Janeiro: Tip. Central de Evaristo Costa, March, 1890.

———. *A separação da igreja do estado. Os dias santificados.* Rio de Janeiro: Tip. Central de Evaristo Costa, March, 1890.

Lemos, Miguel and Teixeira Mendes, Raymundo. *Bazes de uma constituição politica ditatorial federativa para a república brazileira.* Rio de Janeiro: Na Sede do Apostolado Pozitivista do Brazil, January, 1890.

———. *Representação enviado ao Congresso Nacional propondo modificações no projecto da constituição apresentado pelo governo e contendo como annexo o opusculo "Razões contra a lei de grande naturalisação."* Rio de Janeíro: Na Sede do Apostolado Pozitivista do Brasil, December, 1890.

———. *A ultima crise. O golpe d'estado de 3 novembro e a revolução de 23 do mesmo mez.* 2d ed. Rio de Janeiro: Na Sede Central do Apostolado Pozitivista do Brasil, 1891.

Levy, Scavarda. "A Escola Naval através do tempo," in Brazil, Ministério da Marinha, *Subsídios para a história marítima do Brasil,* XIV. Rio de Janeiro: Serviço de Documentação Geral da Marinha, 1955.

Leyland, John. "The Naval Lessons of the Brazilian Revolt," *United Service Magazine,* CXXX (August, 1894), 426–35.

Lieuwen, Edwin. *Arms and Politics in Latin America.* New York: Frederick A. Praeger, 1961.

———. "The Changing Role of the Military in Latin America," *Journal of Inter-American Studies,* III (October, 1961), 559–69.

Lima Figueirêdo, José de. *Brasil militar.* Rio de Janeiro: n. p., 1944.

Lins, Alvaro. *Rio-Branco (O Barão do Rio Branco) 1845–1912.* 2 vols. Rio de Janeiro: José Olympio, 1945.

Lins, Ivan. *História do positivismo no Brasil.* São Paulo: Companhia Editôra Nacional, 1964.

Lins de Barros, João Alberto. *Memórias de um revolucionário.* Rio de Janeiro: Editôra Civilização Brasileiro, 1953.

Lobo, Hélio. *Um varão da república. Fernando Lobo. A proclamação do regime em Minas, sua consolidação no Rio de Janeiro.* São Paulo: Companhia Editôra Nacional, 1937.

Lopes, Luis Arthur. "Eu fui cadete da Escola Militar da Praia Vermelha de 1889," *Revista do Clube Militar,* No. 158 (January–March, 1961), 37–44.

Lopes, Murilo Ribeiro., ed. *Rui Barbosa e a marinha.* Rio de Janeiro: Casa de Rui Barbosa, 1953.

Lopes, Theodorico and Torres, Gentil. *Ministros da guerra do Brasil (1808–1950).* 4th ed. Rio de Janeiro: Borsoi, 1950.

Lopes, Trovão. *Lopes Trovão no Congresso Nacional Assemblea Constituinte.* Rio de Janeiro: Companhia Impressora, 1891.

Luís, Pedro. *Militarismo e república (Critica e história).* São Paulo, n.d.

Luz, Fabio and Carneiro, Daví. *A invasão federalista em Santa Catarina e Paraná (Comentários e anotações).* Vol. VI of *Floriano. Memórias e documentos.* Rio de Janeiro: Imprensa Nacional, 1941.

Luz, Nícia Villela. *A luta pela industrialização do Brasil (1808 à 1930).* São Paulo: Difusão Européia do Livro, 1961.

———. "O papel das classes médias brasileiras no movimento republicano," *Revista de História,* No. 57, (January–March, 1964), 13–27.

Lyra, Heitor. *História da queda do império.* 2 vols. São Paulo: Imprensa Nacional, 1964.

McAlister, Lyle N. "Civil-Military Relations in Latin America," *Journal of Inter-American Studies,* III (July, 1961), 341–50.

———. "Recent Research and Writings on the Role of the Military in Latin America," *Latin American Research Review,* I (Fall, 1966), 5–36.

McCloskey, Michael B. "The United States and the Brazilian Naval Revolt," *The Americas,* II (January, 1946), 296–321.

Macedo, Roberto. *A administração de Floriano.* Vol. V. of *Floriano. Memórias e documentos.* Rio de Janeiro: Serviço Gráfico do Ministério da Educação, 1939.

Magalhães, João Batista. *A evolução militar do Brasil. (Anotações para a história).* Rio de Janeiro: Biblioteca do Exército, 1958.

Magalhães, Olyntho Maximo de. *Centenário do presidente Campos Sales; commentários e documentos sobre alguns episódios do seu governo pelo ministro das relações exteriores de 1898 a 1902.* Rio de Janeiro: Irmãos Ponzetti, 1941.

Magalhães Júnior, Raymundo. *Deodoro. A espada contra o império.* 2 vols. São Paulo: Companhia Editôra Nacional, 1957.

———. *Machado de Assis. Funcionário público. (No império e na república).* Rio de Janeiro: Ministério da Viação e Obras Públicas, Serviço de Documentação, 1958.

———. *Rui. O homen e o mito.* Rio de Janeiro: Editôra Civilização Brasileira, 1964.

Manchester, Alan K. "Brazil in Transition," *South Atlantic Quarterly,* LIV (April, 1955), 167–76.

———. *British Preëminence in Brazil: Its Rise and Decline.* Chapel Hill: University of North Carolina Press, 1933.

Marcondes de Souza, T. Oscar. *O estado de São Paulo. Physico, político, económico e administrativo.* São Paulo: Estabelecimento Graphico Universal, 1915.

Martin, Percy Alvin. "Causes of the Collapse of the Brazilian Empire," *Hispanic American Historical Review,* IV (February, 1921), 4–48.

Medeiros e Albuquerque, José Joaquim de. *Minha vida. Memórias.* 2d ed. Rio de Janeiro: Calvino Filho, 1933–34.

Meivarida Azevedo, H. C. de. *Confronto da república e da monarchia.* São Paulo: n.p., 1902.

Mello, Custódio José de. *Apontamentos para a história da revolução de 23 de novembro de 1891.* Rio de Janeiro: n.p., 1895.

———. *O governo provisório e a revolução de 1893.* 2 vols. São Paulo: Companhia Editôra Nacional, 1938.

Mello, N. M. de Braga. *Joaquim Saldanha Marinho e a primeira república. (Ensaios).* Rio de Janeiro: Lito Tipo Guanabara, 1960.

Melo Franco, Afonso Arinos de. *Um estadista da república. (Afrânio de Melo Franco e seu tempo).* 3 vols. Rio de Janeiro: José Olympio, 1955.

Melo, Higino de Bastos. *O Brasil de hoje.* Rio de Janeiro: Papelaria Niemeyer, 1905.

Mendes de Almeida, Fernando (pseud. Marcio). *Semana Política. (Presidencia Prudente de Moraes). Vol. I (Novembro de 1894 a junho de 1896).* Rio de Janeiro: Officinas Graphicas do Jornal do Brasil, 1916.

Mendonça, Lúcio de. *Caricaturas instantâneas.* Rio de Janeiro: Ed. A Noite, 1939.

Miguel-Pereira, Lucia. *Machado de Assis. (Estudo crítico e biográfico).* 2d ed. São Paulo: Companhia Editôra Nacional, 1939.

Miranda Azevedo, A. C. de. *Discurso proferido na Camara dos Deputados do Congresso Nacional, em sessão de 15 de setembro de 1902. (Confronto da república e da monarchia).* São Paulo: Typ. do Diário Official, 1902.

Monarchistas restauradores. Quatro especies distinctas. Duas palavras incisivas (Fragmentos de um livro). Rio de Janeiro: Officinas d'O Tempo, 1893.

Moniz Barreto de Aragão, Salvador Antonio. *Relatório apresentado ao illm. exm. snr. dr. Francisco de P. Rodrigues Alves presidente da provincia de São Paulo pelo chefe de policia interino o juiz de direito Salvador Antonio Moniz Barreto de Aragão, 1887.* São Paulo: Typographia a Vapor de Jorge Seckler & comp., 1888.

Moniz de Aragão, Pedro. "Canudos e os monarquistas," *Revista do Instituto Histórico e Geográfico Brasileiro,* 237 (October–December, 1957), 85–131.

———. "Cartas de Conde de Nioac ao conselheiro João Alfredo," *Revista do Instituto Histórico e Geográfico Brasileiro,* 258 (January–March, 1963), 243–99.

———. "Cartas do conselheiro João Alfredo à Princessa Isabel," *Revista do Instituto Histórico e Geográfico Brasileiro,* 260 (July–September, 1963), 339–412.

———. "Cartas de D. Luís a João Alfredo," *Revista do Instituto*

Histórico e Geográfico Brasileiro, 240 (July–September, 1958), 343–49.

———. "Cartas de Joaquim Nabuco a João Alfredo," *Revista do Instituto Histórico e Geográfico Brasileiro*, 257 (October–December, 1962), 201–209.

Monteiro, Tobias. *Pesquisas e depoimentos para a história*. Rio de Janeiro: Francisco Alves & Cia., 1913.

———. *O presidente Campos Salles na Europa. Com uma introducção e cinco retratos*. Rio de Janeiro: F. Briguiet & Cia., 1928.

Moraes, Evaristo de. *Da monarchia para a república (1870–1889)*. Rio de Janeiro: Ed. Athena, [1937].

Moraes Barros, Prudente José de. *Exposição apresentada ao dr. Jorge Tibiriçá pelo dr. Prudente J. de Moraes Barros 1º governador do estado de São Paulo ao passar-lhe a administração no dia 18 de outubro de 1890*. São Paulo: Typ. Vanorden & comp., 1890.

Morse, Richard M. *From Community to Metropolis: A Biography of São Paulo, Brazil*. Gainesville: University of Floirda Press, 1958.

Mota Filho, Cândido. *Uma grande vida. Biográfia de Bernardino de Campos*. São Paulo: Companhia Editôra Nacional, 1941.

Moura, A. Lourival de. *As forças armadas e o destino histórico do Brasil*. São Paulo: Companhia Editôra Nacional, 1937.

Moura, Francisco Amyntar de Carvalho. *A republicanisação do Brazil perante a história*. Recife: Typ. Manoel de Figueiroa de Faria & Filho, 1891.

Moura, Hastimphilo de. *Da primeira à segunda república*. Rio de Janeiro: Irmãos Pongetti, 1936.

Müller, Lauro. *Os ideas republicanos*. Rio de Janeiro: F. Briguiet & Cia., 1912.

Nabuco, Carolina. *The Life of Joaquim Nabuco*. Translated by Ronald Hilton. Stanford: Stanford University Press, 1950.

Nabuco, Joaquim. *Agradecimento aos pernambucanos*. 2d ed. London: Abraham Kingdom & Newnham, 1891.

———. *Balmaceda. A intervenção estrangeira durante a revolta de 1893*. São Paulo: Instituto Progresso Editorial, [1949].

———. *Cartas à amigos.* Edited by Carolina Nabuco. Vols. XIII and XIV of *Obras Completas de Joaquim Nabuco.* São Paulo: Instituto Progresso Editorial, 1949.

———. *O dever dos monarchistas. Carta ao almirante Jaceguay.* Rio de Janeiro: Typ. Leuzinger, 1895.

———. *Minha formação.* Rio de Janeiro: José Olympio, 1957.

———. *Porque continuo a ser monarchista. Carta ao Diário do Commercio.* London: Abraham Kingdom & Newnham, 1890.

———. *Reposta as mensagens do Recife e Nazareth.* 2d ed. Rio de Janeiro: Typ. Leuzinger & Filho, 1890.

Neeld, Reginald Rundell. *Diary of the Revolution at Rio de Janeiro, Brazil. Kept by Commander Neeld, H. M. S. "Beagle," September 6th, 1893 to March 14th, 1894.* Portsmouth, England: Charpentier & Co., 1895.

Neiva, Vicente. *Attentado de cinco de novembro. Relatório do dr. Vicente Neiva 1º delegado auxiliar e diversas peças do inquerito.* Rio de Janeiro: Imprensa Nacional, 1898.

Neves, Edgard de Carvalho. *Afirmação de Euclides da Cunha. Ensaio e crítica.* [1960?].

Nobre, Fernando. *Um grande diplomata brasileiro nos Estados Unidos. Salvador de Mendonça. (Ensaio biográfico).* São Paulo: Livraria Martins Editôra, [1954].

Nogueira Cobra, Amador Pereira Gomes. *Brios de gente armada (Páginas republicanas na história do Brazil).* São Paulo: Beccari, Jannini & Cia., [1924?].

Notas de um revoltoso. (Diário de bordo). Documentos authenticos publicados pelo "Commercio de S. Paulo" Rio de Janeiro: Typ. Moraes, 1895.

O novo governo da república. Rio de Janeiro: Imprensa Nacional, 1894.

Nun, José. "The Middle-Class Military Coup," in *The Politics of Conformity in Latin America.* Edited by Claudio Veliz. London and New York: Oxford University Press,1967.

Oakenfull, J. C. *Brazil in 1911.* London: Butter & Tanner, Frome and London, 1912.

Um official da armada. *Política versus marinha.* Paris: Imprimerie Français-Etrangère, n.d.

Oliveira, Franklin de. *Revolução e contra-revolução no Brasil.* Rio de Janeiro: Editôra Civilização Brasileira, 1962.

Oliveira Lima, Manuel de. *O movimento da independência. O império brasileiro (1821–1889).* São Paulo: Edições Melhoramentos, 1962.

Oliveira Martins, Joaquim Pedro. *O Brazil e as colonias portuguezas.* Lisbon: Livraria de Antonio Maria Pereira, [1893?].

Oliveira Vianna, F. J. *O occaso do império.* São Paulo: Companhia Melhoramentos de São Paulo, [1925].

Ordens do Dia revolucionarias (Santa Catharina, Paraná e Rio Grande do Sul). Organisadas por um capitão-secretario do exército liberador. Rio de Janeiro: Companhia Typographica do Brazil, 1897.

Ottoni, Christiano Benedicto. *O advento da república no Brasil.* Rio de Janeiro: Typ. Perseverança, 1890.

———. *Autobiographia de C. B. Ottoni.* Rio de Janeiro: Typ. Leuzinger, 1908.

Ourique, Jacques. *O drama do Paraná. Episódios da tyrannia do marechal Floriano Peixoto.* Buenos Aires: n.p., 1894.

———. *O marechal Hermes da Fonseca. Sua eleição à presidencia da república. Estudo político.* Rio de Janeiro: Typ. Jornal do Commercio, 1910.

———. "A revolução de 15 de novembro," *Jornal do Comércio,* January 4, 1890, p. 2, and January 5, 1890, p. 2.

———. "A revolução de 6 de setembro," *Correio da Tarde,* 1895–96.

Ouro Prêto, Visconde de. Affonso Celso de Assis Figueiredo. *Advento da dictadura militar no Brasil.* Paris: F. Pichon, 1891.

———. *A marinha d'outr'ora (Subsídios para a história).* Rio de Janeiro: Livraria Moderna, 1894.

País. 1887–98.

Paiva, Alfredo. *A mentira republicana.* Juiz de Fora: Typ. Pereira, 1892.

———. *Questões políticas e sociaes.* Juiz de Fora: Typ. A Vapor de Leite Ribeiro & C., 1891.

Palha, Américo. *Soldados e marinheiros do Brasil.* Rio de Janeiro: Biblioteca do Exército, 1962.

Parnahyba, Antonio de Queiroz Telles, Visconde de. *Exposição com que o exm. snr. Visconde de Parnahyba passou a administração da provincia de São Paulo ao exm. snr. dr. Francisco de Paula Rodrigues Alves, presidente desta provincia, no dia 19 de novembro de 1887.* São Paulo: Typographia a Vapor de Jorge Seckler & comp., 1888.

Paula Cidade, Francisco de, ed. *Cadetes e alunos militares através dos tempos.* Rio de Janeiro: Biblioteca do Exército Editôra, 1961.

Peixoto, Arthur Viera. *Biographia do marechal Floriano Peixoto.* Vol. I of *Floriano. Memórias e documentos.* Rio de Janeiro: Serviço Gráfico do Ministério da Educação, 1939.

Peixoto, Dermeval. *Memórias de um velho soldado.* Rio de Janeiro: Biblioteca do Exército, 1960.

Peixoto, Floriano. *Mensagem dirigida ao Congresso Nacional pelo marechal Floriano Peixoto por occasio de abrir-se a 2ª sessão ordinario da 1ª legislativa.* Rio de Janeiro: Imprensa Nacional, 1892.

Peixoto, Silveira. *No tempo de Floriano.* Rio de Janeiro: Ed. A Noite, 1940.

Peixoto, Silvio. *Início do período presidencial.* Vol. IV of *Floriano. Memórias e documentos.* Rio de Janeiro: Serviço Gráfico do Ministério da Educação, 1939.

Pereira, Manoel Victorino. *Manifesto político.* São Paulo: Typ. de Carlos Jeep & Cia., 1898.

Pereira, Teotônio Freire e Franca. *A pátria nova. Estudo literário, crítico e histórico do Brasil sob o dominio da república.* Recife: Typ. d'O Norte, 1890.

Pereira da Silva, Gastão. *Prudente de Moraes. O Pacificador.* Rio de Janeiro: Zélio Valverde, [1937].

Pereira da Silva, Luiz José. *Floriano Peixoto. Traços biográphicos.* Rio de Janeiro: Fauchon e comp., 1894.

Pimentel, Adriane Xavier de Oliveira. *Capitulação de Tijucas 19 de janeiro de 1894. Defensa proferida perante o conselho de guerra.* Rio de Janeiro: Typ. Leuzinger, 1894.

Pinheiro, Xavier. *Marechal Floriano (O consolidador da república brasileira). Commemoração ao V anno da sua morto. Culto civico de Xavier Pinheiro e de republicanos florianistas intransigentos.* Rio de Janeiro: Laemmert & C., 1900.

Piragibe da Fonseca, Roberto. "Um estadista da primeira república. Clodoaldo da Fonseca," *Revista Verbum,* XXI (December, 1964), 303–56; XXII (March–June, 1965), 63–135.

Pires, Aurelio. *Homens e factos de meu tempo.* São Paulo: Campanhia Editôra Nacional, 1939.

Pires, Homero. *Anglo-American Political Influences on Rui Barbosa.* Translated by Sylvia Medrado Clinton. Rio de Janeiro: Casa de Rui Barbosa, 1949.

Prado, Eduardo Paulo da Silva. *Annullação das liberdades políticas. (Commentario ao 4° art. 90 da constituição da república).* São Paulo: Livraria Civilização. 1897.

———. *A bandeira nacional.* São Paulo: Escola Typographica Salesiana, 1903.

———. *Collectaneas.* 4 vols. São Paulo: Escola Typographica Salesiana, 1904–1906.

——— (pseud. Frederico de S.). *Fastos da dictadura militar no Brazil.* 3rd ed. [Lisbon]: n.p., 1890.

———. *A illusão americana.* 2d ed. Paris: Armand Colin Cie., 1895.

——— (pseud. Graccho). *Salvemos o Brazil.* Rio de Janeiro: September 25, 1899.

Prado, Nazareth. *Antonio Prado no império e na república. Seus discursos e actos colligidos e apresentados por sua filha Nazareth Prado.* Rio de Janeiro: Briguiet & Cia., 1929.

Prado Junior, Caio. *História económica do Brasil.* 8th ed. São Paulo: Editôra Brasiliense, 1963.

Prudente de Moraes. O primeiro centenário do seu nascimento. (1841–1941). São Paulo: Typ. Revista dos Tribunais, 1942.

Ramírez, Engenio. *Nuestras fronteiras. La República de los Estados Unidos del Brasil.* Buenos Aires: n.p., 1917.

Rangel Pestana, Francisco (pseud. Thomas Jefferson). *Notas republicanas. I. A reacção e os novos partidos. II. A política do marechal Floriano Peixoto.* Rio de Janeiro: n.p., 1898.

Ray, T. Bronson. *Brazilian Sketches.* Louisville: Baptist World Publishing Co., 1912.

Rebouças, Andre. *Diário e notas autobiográficas.* Rio de Janeiro: José Olympio, 1938.

Rei, Januário João del. *A intendência militar através dos tempos.* Rio de Janeiro: Companhia Editôra Americana, 1955.

República. 1871.

A república brazileira. Rio de Janeiro: Biblioteca Militar, 1939.

Republicano. 1884.

Revista do Club Militar. Ano xi, No. 48. Numero especial de celebração do cincocentenario do Club Militar, June 26, 1937.

Revista Federal. 1886–87.

Ribas, Antonio Joaquim. *Perfil biographico do dr. Manoel Ferraz de Campos Salles, ministro da justiça do governo provisório, senador federal pelo estado de São Paulo.* Rio de Janeiro: Typ. Leuzinger, 1896.

Ribeiro, Atanagildo Barata. *Sonho no carcere. Dramas da revolução de 1893 no Brazil.* Rio de Janeiro: Casa Mont'Alverne, 1895.

Ribeiro de Andrada, Antonio Carlos. *Bancos de emissão no Brazil.* Rio de Janeiro: Livraria Leite Ribeiro, 1923.

Rio Branco, Barão do. *Discursos. Obras do Barão do Rio Branco.* IX. Rio de Janeiro: Ministério das Relações Exteriores, 1948.

Rio News. 1888–98.

Rodrigues Alves, Francisco de Paula. *Relatório com que o exm. snr. dr. Francisco de Paula Rodrigues Alves passou a administração da provincia de São Paulo ao exm. snr. dr. Francisco Antonio Dutra Rodrigues 1° vice-presidente no dia 27 de abril de 1888.* São Paulo: Typographia a Vapor de Jorge Seckler & comp., 1888.

Rodrigues, José Honório., ed. *Correspondência de Capistrano de Abreu.* Rio de Janeiro: Instituto Nacional do Livro, 1954.

Romero, Sylvio. *Parlamentarismo e presidencialismo na república brasileira. (Cartas ao conselheiro Ruy Barbosa).* Rio de Janeiro: Companhia Impressora, 1893.

Rosa, Othello. *Júlio de Castilhos. I parte. Perfil biographico. II parte. Escriptos políticos.* Pôrto Alegre: Livraria do Globo, 1928.

Roscof (pseud.). *Notas del Brasil.* Buenos Aires: n.p., 1917.

Sabóia, Edith. "Francisco Rangel Pestana. (Notas biográficas por ocasião do centenário do seu nacimento, 1839–1939)," *Revista do Arquivo Municipal* (São Paulo), LXI (September–October, 1939), 23–42.

Salles, Alberto. *A patria paulista.* Campinas: Typ. A Vapor da Gazeta de Campinas, 1887.

Salles, Antonio Carlos de. *O idealismo republicano de Campos Salles.* Rio de Janeiro: Zélio Valverde, [1944].

Salles Sousa. *Os echos da liberdade. Critica sobre o governo Prudente. Apreciação sobre o estado do paiz, dos factos ocorridos no governo Rodrigues Lima.* Bahia: Typ. Diário da Bahia, 1896.

Santos, Eduardo. "Latin American Realities," *Foreign Affairs,* XXXIV (January, 1956), 244–57.

Santos, José Maria dos. *Bernardino de Campos e o Partido Republicano Paulista. Subsídios para a história da república.* Rio de Janeiro: José Olympio, 1960.

———. *A política geral do Brasil.* São Paulo: J. Magalhães, 1930.

———. *Os republicanos paulistas e a abolição.* São Paulo: Livraria Martins, 1965.

Santos, Noronha. *A revolução de 1891 e suas consequências.* Vol. II of *Floriano. Memórias e documentos.* Rio de Janeiro: Serviço Gráfico do Ministério da Educação, 1939.

São Boaventura, Visconde de. *O Brazil actual.* Lisbon: José Bastos, 1895.

Schurz, William Lytle. *Brazil: The Infinite Country.* New York: E. P. Dutton & Co., 1961.

Seabra Fagundes, M. *As forças armadas na constituição.* Rio de Janeiro: n.p., 1955.

Seixas, Demétrio. *O golpe d'estado de 15 de novembro. (Ao exército e à armada).* Pôrto Alegre: Typ. da Livraria Americana, 1890.

Sena, Ernesto. *Deodoro. Subsídios para a história. Notas de um reporter.* Rio de Janeiro: Imprensa Nacional, 1913.

Serpa, Phocion. *Visconde de Taunay. Ensaio biográfico.* Rio de Janeiro: Publicações da Acadêmica Brasileira, 1952.

Silva, Cyro. *Floriano Peixoto. O consolidador da república.* São Paulo: Editôra Edaglit, 1963.

———. *Quintino Bocayuva. O patriarca da república.* São Paulo: Editôra Edaglit, 1962.

Silva Herzog, Jesús. "Las juntas militares de gobierno," *Cuadernos americanos,* XLV (July–August, 1949), 7–13.

Silvado, Americano Brasilio. *A nova marinha. Resposta a "Marinha d'outr'ora" do sr. Afonso Celso de Assis Figueiredo (Ex. Visconde de Ouro Preto).* Rio de Janeiro: Typ. Lith. Carlos Schmidt, 1897.

Silveira, Urias Antonio da. *Galeria histórica da revolução brasileira de 15 de novembro de 1889 que occasionou a fundação da República dos Estados Unidos do Brasil.* Rio de Janeiro: Typ. Universal de Laemmert & Co., 1890.

Silveira Martins, José Júlio. *Silveira Martins.* Rio de Janeiro: Typ. São Benedicto, 1929.

Silveira Peixoto, José Benedicto. *A tormenta que Prudente de Morais venceu!* 2d ed. Curitiba: Editôra Guaíra Limitada, 1942.

Simmons, Charles Willis. "Deodoro da Fonseca. Fate's Dictator," *Journal of Inter-American Studies,* V (January, 1963), 45–52.

———. *Marshal Deodoro and the Fall of Dom Pedro II.* Durham, N.C.: Duke University Press, 1966.

———. "The Rise of the Brazilian Military Class, 1870–1890," *Mid-America,* XXXIX (October, 1957), 227–36.

Smith, Carleton Sprague. *Os livros norte-americanos no pensamento de Rui Barbosa.* Rio de Janeiro: Imprensa Nacional, 1945.

Soares, Carlos (pseud. Marius). *Perfil biographico do marechal Floriano Peixoto.* Pará: E. Papelaria de Alfredo Silva & Cia., 1893.

Sodré, Lauro. *Crenças e opiniões.* Belém: Typ. do Diário Official, 1896.

———. *A evolução política do Brasil.* Rio de Janeiro: n.p., 1906.

———. *A proclamação da república.* Rio de Janeiro: Serviço Gráfico do Ministério da Educação, 1939.

Sodré, Nelson Werneck. *Formação da sociedade brasileira.* Rio de Janeiro: José Olympio, 1944.

———. *Formação histórica do Brasil.* São Paulo: Editôra Brasiliense, 1962.

———. *História militar do Brasil.* Rio de Janeiro: Editôra Civilização Brasileira, 1965.

———, ed. *Narrativas militares. Seleção, organização e notas biográficas.* Rio de Janeiro: Biblioteca do Exército, 1959.

Soromenho, Castro. *A guarda nacional da capital federal e a revolução de setembro 1893 a 1894.* Rio de Janeiro: (printed by author), 1894.

Souza e Silva, Augusto Carlos de. *O almirante Saldanha. Commandante em chefe na revolta da armada. Reminiscencias de um revoltoso.* Rio de Janeiro: Editôra A Noite, 1940.

———. *O almirante Saldanha e a revolta da armada. Reminiscencias de um revoltoso.* Rio de Janeiro: José Olympio, [1936].

Souza Soares, José de. *O militarismo na república.* São Paulo: Companhia Gráfica Editôra Monteiro Lobato, 1925.

Stein, Stanley J. *Vassouras: A Brazilian Coffee County, 1850–1900.* Cambridge, Mass.: Harvard University Press, 1957.

Stokes, William S. "Violence as a Power Factor in Latin American Politics," *Western Political Quarterly,* V (September, 1952), 445–82.

Taunay, Visconde de. Alfredo d' Escragnolle. *Algumas verdades, a propósito de um opusculo. (Estudos sociais).* Rio de Janeiro: Leuzinger, 1891.

———. *Império e república.* São Paulo: Cia. Melhoramentos de São Paulo, [1933?].

———. *Memórias do Visconde de Taunay.* São Paulo: Instituto Progresso, 1948.

Teixeira, José Candido. *A república brazileira. A última propaganda. Apontamentos para a história, datas gloriosas, factos memoraveis.* Rio de Janeiro: Imprensa Nacional, 1890.

Teixeira, Múcio. *A revolução do Rio Grande do Sul. Suas causas e seus effeitos.* Pôrto Alegre: Typ. Jornal do Comércio, 1893.

Teixeira Mendes, Raymundo. *A bandeira nacional. Representação enviada ao Congresso Nacional propondo modificações.* Rio de Janeiro: Na sede Central do Apostolado Pozitivista do Brasil, 1890.

———. *Benjamin Constant. Esbôço de uma apreciação sintetica da vida e da obra do fundador da república brazileira.* Rio de Janeiro: Imprensa Nacional, 1936.

———. *A commemoração civica de Benjamin Constant e a liberdade religiosa.* Rio de Janeiro: Na Sede Central do Apostolado Pozitivista do Brasil, September, 1892.

———. *Exame do projecto de constituição apresentado pelo governo provisório e indicação das correcções indispensaveis para harmonisar sufficientemente tal projecto com as exigencias capitães da situação brazileira.* Rio de Janeiro, 1890.

———. *A política pozitiva i o regulamento das escolas do exército.* Rio de Janeiro, April, 1890.

Thompson, Arthur. *Guerra civil do Brasil. Subsídios para a história. 1893–1895. Vida e morte do almirante Saldanha da Gama.* Rio de Janeiro: Emprêsa Editôra Carioca Ltda., 1959.

Tinoco, Brígido. *A vida de Nilo Peçanha.* Rio de Janeiro: José Olympio, 1962.

Torres, João Camillo de Oliveira. *A democracia coronada. Teoria política do império do Brasil.* 2d ed. Petrópolis: Editôra Vozes, Ltda., 1964.

———. *Estratificação social no Brasil. Suas origens históricas e suas relações com a organização política do país.* São Paulo: Difusão Européia do Livro, 1965.

———. *O positivismo no Brasil.* 2d ed. Petrópolis: Editôra Vozes, Ltda., 1957.

Tourinho, João Gonçalves. *História da sedição na Bahia em 24 de novembro de 1891, organisada pelo bacharel João Gonçalves Tourinho.* Bahia: João Gonçalves Tourinho, 1893.

Tribuna. 1890.

Tribuna Liberal. 1889.

Vagts, Alfred. *A History of Militarism, Civilian and Military.* Rev. ed. London: Hollis & Carter, 1959.

———. *A History of Militarism: Romance and Realities of a Profession.* New York: W. W. Norton & Co., 1937.

Venancio (Filho), Francisco, ed. *Euclydes da Cunha à seus amigos.*

São Paulo: Companhia Editôra Nacional, 1938.

———. *A glória de Euclydes da Cunha.* São Paulo: Companhia Editôra Nacional, 1940.

Viana, Hélio. "Rui Barbosa e Eduardo Prado. História de uma amizade," *Revista Brasileira,* III (June, 1943), 68–83.

Viana Filho, Luis. *A vida do Barão do Rio Branco.* Rio de Janeiro: José Olympio, 1959.

———. *A vida de Rui Barbosa.* 6th ed. São Paulo: Companhia Editôra Nacional, 1941.

Vilar, Frederico. "As revoluções que eu vi: a intervenção estrangeira em 1893," *Cultura Política,* IV (October, 1944), 73–90.

Villa-Lobos, Raul. *A república brasileira em 1890.* 2d ed. Rio de Janeiro: Typ. Universal de Laemmert & Cia., 1890.

———. (pseud. Epaminondas Villalba). *A revolta da armada de 6 de setembro de 1893.* Rio de Janeiro: Laemmert & C., 1897.

———. (pseud. Epaminondas Villalba). *A revolução federalista no Rio Grande do Sul. (Documentos e commentários).* Rio de Janeiro: Laemmert & C., 1897.

Villeroy, Augusto Ximeno de. *Benjamin Constant e a política republicana.* Rio de Janeiro: n.p., 1928.

Vincent, Franck. *Around and About South America: Twenty Months of Quest and Query.* 5th ed. New York: D. Appleton & Co., 1895.

Vita, Luís Washington. *Alberto Sales. Ideólogo da república.* São Paulo: Companhia Editôra Nacional, 1965.

Werneck, Américo. *O Brazil. Seu presente e seu futuro.* Petrópolis: Typ. da Gazeta de Petrópolis, 1892.

———. "A dictadura militar republicana," *A Revolução* (Campanha, Minas Gerais), I, No. 13 (March 31, 1889), pp. 1–2.

———. *Erros e vicios da organisação republicana.* Petrópolis: Typ. do Correio de Petrópolis, 1893.

Wheeler, George W. *Captain Wheeler's Narrative of His Wanderings in Brazil.* Philadelphia: n.p., 1899.

Wickizer, V. D. *The World Coffee Economy, with Special Reference to Control Schemes.* Stanford: Food Research Institute, Stanford University, 1943.

Williams, Mary Wilhelmine. *Dom Pedro the Magnanimous: Second Emperor of Brazil.* Chapel Hill: University of North Carolina Press, 1937.

Winter, Nevin O. *Brazil and Her People of Today.* Boston: L. C. Page & Company, 1910.

Wright, Marie Robinson. *The New Brazil.* Philadelphia: George Barrie & Son, 1901.

Wyckoff, Theodore. "The Role of the Military in Latin American Politics," *Western Political Quarterly,* XIII (September, 1960), 745–63.

Zea, Leopoldo. *The Latin-American Mind.* Translated by James H. Abbott and Lowell Dunham. Norman, Okla.: University of Oklahoma Press, 1963.

Index